Consumption and Market Society in Israel

Consumption and Market Society in Israel

Edited by
Yoram S. Carmeli and Kalman Applbaum

BERG

Oxford • New York

First published in 2004 by
Berg
Editorial offices:
1st Floor, Angel Court, 81 St Clements Street, Oxford OX4 1AW UK
838 Broadway, Third Floor, New York, NY 10003-4812, USA

Berg is an imprint of Oxford International Publishers Ltd.

Library of Congress Cataloging-in-Publication Data
A catalogue record for this book is available from the Library of Congress.

British Library Cataloguing-in-Publication Data
A catalogue record for this book is available from the British Library.

ISBN 1 85973 684 X (Cloth)
1 85973 689 0 (Paper)

Typeset by JS Typesetting Ltd, Wellingborough, Northants.
Printed in the United Kingdom by Biddles Ltd, Guildford and King's Lynn.

www.bergpublishers.com

Contents

Notes on Contributors

Kalman Applbaum teaches anthropology at the University of Wisconsin-Milwaukee. From 1995 to 1999, he lectured at Tel-Aviv University and at the University of Haifa. He is the author of *The Marketing Era: From Professional Practice to Global Provisioning* (2003). His current research concerns the adoption of new antidepressants in Japan and its effect on the practice of psychiatry and mental health care.

Julia Bernstein is a PhD student at the University of Haifa. Her main field of interest is material culture. She is currently researching food-related practices among Jewish immigrants from the former Soviet Union.

Daphna Birenbaum-Carmeli is a sociologist at the University of Haifa. Her main interests are middle-class culture and medical sociology, especially new reproductive technologies.

Yoram S. Carmeli is with the Department of Sociology and Anthropology, University of Haifa. His main interest is the crisis of modernity. In this context, he has published extensively on the British circus. He has also researched and co-authored on social and cultural aspects of new reproductive technologies.

Tania Forte received her doctorate from the University of Chicago in 2000. She is a lecturer in the Department of Behavioral Sciences at Ben Gurion University of the Negev. She is currently completing a manuscript on women's senses of selves in Galilee. Her current research is on the production of international network images of the Israeli-Palestinian conflict.

Tamar El-Or is a senior lecturer in the Department of Sociology and Anthropology at the Hebrew University, Jerusalem. Her field of research engages topics of gender religion and knowledge. Among her publications are the books: *Educated and Ignorant: On Ultra Orthodox Women and Their World.* Boulder CO: Lynne Reinner, 1994; *Next Year I will Know More: Literacy and Identity among Young Orthodox Women in Israel.* Detroit: Wayne State University Press, 2002.

Ronit Grossman (MA Haifa University, 2001) is a course coordinator in the Department of Sociology, Political Science and Communication at the Open University of Israel. Her academic fields of interest are: cultural studies, community studies, anthropology of tourism and the Kibbutz society.

Adriana Kemp is a lecturer in the Department of Sociology and Anthropology, Tel Aviv University. Her fields of research are labor migration, citizenship and identity; boundaries and nationalism. She has published several articles on non-Jewish and non-Palestinian labor migration in Israel.

Fran Markowitz teaches anthropology in the Department of Behavioral Sciences at Ben-Gurion University of the Negev in Beersheva. Expressing long-term interests in identity, community and diaspora, her current projects include an ethnographic analysis of the Black Hebrews' homecoming to Israel and the discursive and practical manifestations of Sarajevans' multiple cultural legacies.

Daniel Miller is Professor of Anthropology at University College London. His recent books include *The Sari* (with Mukulika Banerjee, Oxford: Berg, 2003), *The Dialectics of Shopping* (Chicago, 2001); Ed. *Car Cultures* (Berg 2001), and Ed. *Home Possessions* (Berg, 2001). Next will be Ed. *Materiality* (Duke, forthcoming)

Eran Neria is a lawyer, completing his graduate studies in anthropology. He is also interested in education and Israeli geography.

Rebeca Raijman is senior lecturer in the Department of Sociology and Anthropology at the University of Haifa. She received her PhD in sociology from the University of Chicago. She is currently conducting a comprehensive research regarding the emergence on new (migrant) ethnic minorities in Israel, the socio-political organization of undocumented migrant communities and the politics and policy of labor migration in Israel.

Amalia Sa'ar, PhD, is a cultural anthropologist. Amalia does research among Israeli Palestinians, focusing on gender politics and urban conditions. Her latest research project is on micro-enterprise among disempowered Israeli women, of diverse ethnic and religious backgrounds. She teaches at the University of Haifa.

Natan Uriely earned his PhD in sociology from the University of Illinois at Chicago. He is currently a senior lecturer and the chairperson of the Department of Hotel and Tourism Management at Ben-Gurion University of the Negev. Dr Uriely's main fields of interest are the sociology of tourism and leisure.

–1–

Introduction

Yoram S. Carmeli and *Kalman Applbaum*

An account of consumption and market orientation in Israel can be indexed in two dimensions, political-economic and sociocultural. In the first, the phased evolution of the Israeli economy in its first fifty years (1948–1998; we will return below to account for the years since Israel's jubilee), is roughly characterized by the transition from state developmentalism to economic liberalization and finally to globalization. In this respect, Israel, in spite of its particular history, is virtually a model economic citizen of the second half of the twentieth century, having traversed the several characteristic stages posited by the optimistic theories underlying neoliberalism.

From the perspective of what Joseph Stiglitz and others have referred to as the Washington Consensus on global economy (Stiglitz 1998), Israel's market liberalization, privatization, and the transition to consumerism and global marketism seem to offer few unique characteristics. A closer look yields the presence of numerous extenuating factors, however: the reliance on foreign aid; a socialist legacy embedded in state economic apparatuses; assimilation of vast immigrant populations; the outbreaks of existentially threatening wars resulting in both disruption of economic programming and a massive drain on budgetary and human resources; extreme but dubious capitalization on foreign labor; paltry levels of foreign direct investment due to political instability; and the Arab boycott.

It is in this dual context – conformity and divergence from international models – that we wish to introduce the question of consumption and consumerism in Israel. One may begin by pointing to two oft-cited statistics in Israeli economic scholarship. First, between 1975 and 1995 Israel's GDP grew by a factor of seven. Israeli per capita income in 1996 was US $16,690, which placed Israel squarely as a comparator to the Asian and other "tigers" (Shafir and Peled 2002: 1). This graduation to economic affluence has enabled Israelis to participate in the global consumerist movement that has grown most conspicuously during the past three decades. Accordingly, between 1950 and 1996 private consumption per capita in Israel rose an average of four percent per year, meaning that by the later date Israeli consumption was five and a half times what it had been at mid-century. The substance of items consumed begins to depict a scenario common to virtually all other industrialized countries: an increased reliance on branded commodities and a rise in the prominence of luxury, personal use, private sphere items. In the 1950s elementary articles (clothes, foodstuffs, etc.) made up 51 percent of the consumer basket; in 1996 this number had shrunk to 29 percent (Ram 2000: 223). Travel abroad (from 154,000 exits in 1970 to 2.5 million in 1995), private cars (from 33 per 1000 in 1966 to 204 per 1000 persons in 1996), personal computers, mobile telephones, Internet subscriptions and of course credit cards and personal debt have typified the new consumption (Ram 2000: 224).

The productivity and economies of scale of Israeli manufacturing and agribusiness as well as macroeconomic factors help account for the improved purchasing power of Israelis over this period. But of greater interest to us here is the mounting spending orientation of Israelis. Until the 1970s, production in Israel rose faster than did consumption; thereafter the trend reversed, seemingly irrefragably. What had before been classified as luxury items (and therefore subject to steep taxation) – appliances, automobiles, travel abroad, capacious housing, and various forms of leisure activity – came to represent the very nucleus of the new Israeli consumption.

It is fair to conclude that consumption, a constituent in a broader social economic political regime, very much pervades most sectors of Israeli society. Israeli trade has moreover taken after the fashion of North America and Western Europe. The landscape is dappled with the evidence of globally standardized models for shopping: McDonald's, Home Depot, Toys R Us, and the myriad local and international imitations thereof. Advertising and market research have become primary vehicles for communication, persuasion, competition, and cultural expression, allegedly traversing class and ethnic boundaries (more on this below). Growing crowds are drawn to central sites of consumption, to a general pool of "mythologies" (Barthes 1972) and desired lifestyles.

In this new condition, the language and symbolic significances sedimented upon the will to own reflects a new sphere of self-fashioning. Emergent are patterns of personal distinction and related hegemonies (Bourdieu 1984), as well as the shaping of collective identities and associated outcomes for resources and life chances. Lifestyle in accordance with class hierarchies (Katz-Gerro and Shavit 1998), and consumption in the idiom of ethnic positionings (for example Regev 2000) reflect these two levels of negotiation. The state, which in Israel continues to be highly involved in redistribution of resources, is furthermore an agent in the cultural and social hierarchization suggested by these processes (Shavit 2000; Katz and Sella 1999).

As a set of practices and aspirations relevant to one degree or another to most Israelis, consumerism has become a constitutive element of the Israeli economy, polity, and state, much as production had in the past. The consumer world – its rules, its images, its repressions – is constantly reproduced by the myriad objects and practices that fill it. As a matter of habit and consciousness, Israelis spend much of their time dealing with banks and the stock exchange. They pursue leisure by consuming commodities and images in shopping malls, pubs, and restaurants, and of course watching television (Katz et al. 2000; Greitzer 1988). Within this shared world of consumption, there evolves a conjoint language of market metaphors – satisfaction of needs, lifestyles, commodities, sellers, and customers – which applies to a growing number of spheres of life (for example Liberman 1999). It is an omnipresent, largely taken-for-granted culture scape. As much as it is a "world of dreams" it is also a pragmatic world of habits and routines, organizing people's everyday lives (Kosik 1976). It is a world in which Jewish Israeli middle classes make plans, possess, accumulate, and forget.

The political ideology and the power structure naturalized and normalized through this consumer world are not unique to Israel. Referring to the capacity of consumption to mask class stratification, Baudrillard labelled this the "democratic ideology" of consumption, which is built upon the assumption of the "myth of Equality." The egalitarian myth, according to Baudrillard, states that in regard to needs, happiness and well-being all humans are taken to be equal. The equivalence of needs is projected on to homogenizing objects (TV, cars, deodorants). But it is less the continued inequity of access to consumer objects that worries Baudrillard than the compulsory (but nevertheless seen as natural) obedience to consumerism itself.

> There is a double mystification. On the one hand, there is the illusion of a "dynamic" of consumption, of an ascending spiral of satisfactions and distinctions toward a paradoxical summit where all would enjoy the same prestigious standing . . . On the other hand, there is an illusion of a "democracy" of consumption . . . [O]ne can formally gather together widely separated social categories: the real discrimination is made at the level of selective practices (choice, taste, etc.) and above all, of more or less strong adherence to the very values of consumption (1994 [1981]: 60).

What this might mean in the Israeli context is illuminated for us with the observation that the pervasive privatization in the business domain in the late 1980s and 1990s spelt the decline of the state's involvement in the welfare of citizens both through the selling off of public corporations and its withdrawal of subsidies protecting the poor, the uninsured, and the laboring (Grinberg 1993). The counterpart to the political ideological stance of neoliberalism that accepts consumption as a means to democratic needs satisfaction (even while amid consumer plenty poverty levels soared) is the domestic adoption, the internalization of the intelligence system, and theories of human satisfactions behind the permeation and dispersion of commodity culture as embodied by marketing and advertising (Applbaum 2003).

Privatization in Israel, suggests Uri Ram, signals the decline of collectivist tendencies on political, monetary, ideological, and emotional levels. "Selling public corporations is just the spearhead of a sweeping societal privatization, and of the simultaneous crumbling of the collectivist-nationalist (once called socialist-Zionist) world, with its institutions and beliefs" (Ram 2000: 109). From this critical theory standpoint, the total privatization-as-collectivism-busting trend seems to have left in its wake two familiar artifacts. One is a this-worldly individualism, which Dumont (1986: 5) categorically associated with the reversal of traditional social relations, such that the "relations between men are subordinated to relations between men and things." The second artifact of total privatization, so closely associated with modern consumerism, is a replacement ideology that justifies and adapts the new "possessive individualist" ethic, in C. B. Macpherson's (1970) expression, to prior mores. This is the formula that Baudrillard (reviewing Western consumerism) cynically refers to as the "democratic alibi." We can again quote Ram, who echoes Baudrillard's theory of simulacra and simulation (1994 [1981]) when he says: "The [American-style] malls have emptied city centers and have become the preferred pastime of middle class families. They offer sterile zones, isolated from the humid and belligerent Middle Eastern environment. They create the illusion of being 'here' and feeling 'there' – as any proper globalist simulation should" (Ram 2000: 114).

And yet, consumerism itself is a target of popular criticism in Israel, which we believe inhibits its capacity to remake society in its image – the market as "social structure in reserve" (Dilley 1992). Ubiquitous are condemnations of the income disparity that has accompanied Israel's abandonment of state-administered welfare in favor of the free market mechanism. Previously renowned for its comparatively egalitarian structure, Israel is now one of the industrialized world's most economically polarized countries. Consumption patterns exacerbate the growing gap between rich and poor. Internal political objections to military operations (such as the unpopular Lebanon War, ended in 2000), or the unwillingness some have expressed towards serving in the occupied territories, has on occasion been interpreted as a softness associated with a stereotypic bourgeois fear of death.

Pundits have seized upon this reflexive understanding of consumerism, taken to be a cause and expression of moral decay. It has been held to represent a dangerous softness implanted in and now creeping through the nerve centers of the traditional Israeli character – those which, in their absence, threaten the country's survival. Threatened most are the collectivist sentiment from which emanate several crucial characteristics: the positive will to self-sacrifice; austerity (implying the sacrifice of resources for purposes of national redistribution); fertility (demographic reproduction and even expansion is necessary to survival of the Jewish state; children being regarded as consumers rather than producers is held to have led to a decline in the birth rate in industrialized nations); and finally physical prowess (necessary to turning out pioneers and soldiers) (Almog 1994; Weiss 2002). Thus Yossi Melman, an Israeli commentator, writing in the early 1990s, objects:

> Israel has become a consumer society, a quintessential leisure-time nation . . . But for some, waking up and realizing that they are not living in the comfort of America leaves

> them frustrated and empty . . . many young Israelis are emigrating: escaping Israel . . . Israel's social fabric has frayed . . . The idealism of the past has made way for a materialism of such proportions that it borders on sheer greed and extreme hedonism (1993: 207–23).

This tendency to blame myriad social ills on consumerism is one reason why we prefer to take the self-reflection of critics such as Melman as itself being primary data to be analyzed. It is not just a matter of sloppy social science. The critique of consumerism tends to issue from a formerly unquestioned mainstream of Israeli society, the facticity and legitimacy of which is itself under intellectual revision. More strikingly, the idea of a mainstream Israeli is put at question by new divisions that are expressed and visible through the consumption habits of a variety of groups (for example Ultra-Orthodox, Israeli Arabs, new immigrants). Through consumption, these groups make explicit their divergence from the idealized mainstream, at the same time that they derive at least part of their model for consumption behavior from that of middle classes. Our attention to cases from these groups provides both an alternative to and echo of the familiar master narratives that had historically issued mainly from Jewish, largely Ashkenazi, Zionist perspectives.

It is germane at this point to introduce how we shall use consumption as an analytical category. Anthropological inquiry into consumption has grown unwieldy; even the few chapters of this volume do not all agree with each other on a single characterization. However, one feature is common to all the chapters, namely, an understanding of consumption that differs both from the economists' and pundits' versions. In all cases consumption emerges as an embedded domain, a total social phenomenon, to paraphrase Mauss (1990 [1950]) as well as a window to modernity in general and Israeli modernity in particular. Such understanding of consumption is implied in any of the foundational anthropological approaches to the subject – Sahlins's (1972) idea that in their consumption objects help constitute the "meaningful calculus" of social life, and hence a symbolic-system-cum-cognitive order; Douglas and Isherwood's (1979) view of consumption as a system of communication; Bourdieu's (1984) theory that consumption is an unwitting group strategy to social differentiation and domination; or Miller's view of consumption as a vehicle in the reckoning of identity construction (Miller 1987). (For a review of the relationship held to exist between modernity and consumption, see Slater 1997.) It is along this sociocultural limning of consumption, which by its nature affirms consumption's centrality to the individual and collective geists of our time, that we seek to decipher its dimensions and import for present-day Israel.

We regard consumption as both a fulcrum within contemporary Israeli society and an analyst's window into the society. More microcosmically, we endorse Daniel Miller's notion: "To be a consumer is to possess consciousness that one is living through objects and images not of one's own creation" (Miller 1995: 1). We do not engage Miller here in the full extent of his formulation, but borrow this fragment in a more restricted sense. We contend that in contemporary Israel consumption can with distinctive pertinence be characterized as a secondary relationship ("possessing the consciousness that one is living through . . .") because in its novelty it has emerged as a subject for both public debate and private self-reflection. It has done so both within and between the ethnic, religious, class, and institutional divisions that in overlapping patchwork fashion make up Israeli society. This also applies, though in a modified manner, to those who cannot afford to participate or who exclude themselves from the consumer arena.

Plenty, Normalcy, and Diversity

The rise of the Israeli-Jewish middle class has been traced to community-building in the pre-state era, and later to economic and political policies and ideologies of the 1950s–1970s (Carmi and Rosenfeld 1976; Ben-Porat 1999). More recently, in the mid-1990s, middle-class aspiration has found expression in the developing perception of the peace process as a stepping-stone to prosperity. The logic of this association became especially compelling with the dissolution of Cold War politics in the Middle East. Conflict that had started a century earlier under the divide-and-rule of British colonialism was perceived as reaching its conclusion under the incipient aegis of global capitalist enlightenment. This understanding had external confirmation. Many foreign companies that had been wary of establishing even franchises in Israel would now target it as a new frontier.

A second bond between peace and economic prosperity drew its strength from the self-conscious desire middle-class Israelis expressed to be part of a modernized, globalized world, participating in the company of "enlightened" democratic nations. By the 1990s, consumerism and free marketeerism had become perhaps the most visible features of global unity, and for better or worse, free-choice consumerism has become the predominant global proxy for peace and prosperity (a former *New York Times* correspondent for the Middle East, Thomas Friedman, declaimed that no two countries with a McDonald's in it have ever been at war).

Consumerism in short, promised to be a conveyance to normalcy, inclusion, and affluence as well as a demonstration to self and others that Israel had arrived at this state of modern grace. Moreover, having borne – by themselves or through their parents and grandparents – central responsibility for collective pursuits, what they took as the future of the Jewish people, many middle-class Israelis in the 1990s were relieved to place increasing emphasis on the private spheres of their lives. Indeed, in many circles consumption has come to the fore as a pivotal symbol of the private sphere, coinciding to various degrees with a break away from collective demands and commitments.

Liberation in this context means relative freedom from the burden of state-induced, self-imposed ascetic pioneering as framed within the Zionist ethos (Feige and Roniger 1992; Ben-Eliezer 1998), including departure from the Zionist-Socialist civil religion (Liebman 1988), from the "big [sacred] place" to the "little [mundane] place" (Gurewitch and Aran 1991), and from a mythological/historical past to a more prosaic present. If normalization and emancipation from the exile (*galut*) of the Jewish people was a goal of early Zionists, particularly those with a socialist-secular conviction, liberation in the present circumstances means away from these very collective pursuits – on the wings of private consumption. Moreover, the wish to emulate the West suggests that the characterological ambivalence Israeli Jews have established between ordinary nationhood on the one hand and the claim to being a Light to the Gentiles, per the biblical elocution, on the other (Yehoshua 1981: 144–7), was inclining, in middle-class circles, toward the former. This preference, symbolized in the advent of opulent shopping centers and international franchises, were taken as visual affirmations of the mundaneness of the country's living situation in the 1990s.

Despite Israel's apparent conformity to global criteria for a society and economy driven by consumption and market orientation, what Israel is predominantly known for to the outside world – its unremitting military conflict – deters one from making the ordinarily facile association between affluence and bourgeois consumerism. The calm of post-World War, post-deprivation, post-subjugation-to-the-vagaries-of-nature sort of outlook implied by the handing over of human needs to the market and to forces of consumption, which is the ideological trademark of neoliberalism, is a calm that must be far more vigorously imagined in Israel than in North America or Western Europe, even while these are the civilizations of abundance many Israelis, as consumers, seek to emulate. In contrast, therefore, with circumstances in the West, consumption in Israel grows amid and despite the chaos of war and smoldering domestic conflict. It is this departure from the Euro-American norm that perhaps calls out to be theorized first in Israel's case.

Fixing one's gaze upon the internal moral debates triggered and, for the social observer, evoked by the implicit ethic of modern consumerism – themes that come up in several of the mini-ethnographies in this volume – is as yet uncharted in the Israeli context. The reasons for this neglect are themselves implicated in the presentation of context for Israeli consumption.

Mainstream middle-class Israel's voluntary submersion in the general pattern of global consumption is marked by the aspiration to global chic and modern lifestyles alongside a reflexive disposition. In Chapter 2 of the present volume Markowitz and Uriely show how "mainstream" consumption community dweller's habits are qualified by the specter of disparities of access and local/global distinctions. The shoppers they study in a Beer-Sheba mall reflect on both their peripherality and sharing in the global modernity. Comparably, Birnbaum-Carmeli describes in Chapter 3 how residents of an upwardly mobile neighborhood of Tel-Aviv grapple with their national image as upstart consumerist, with all the enviable and execrable connotations this implies. A kind of nostalgic guilt over the loss of the ideal of collective austerity and national purpose is also there. Beyond these middle-class examples, an alternating suspicion toward or exaggerated enthusiasm for consumerism is also embedded within other groups' discourses – Orthodox Jews, Israeli Palestinians, Russian immigrants. These internal debates betoken the fact that, for both established and divergent sectors, modern consumption is recognized as an alien import, and that its adoption is consequently accompanied by internal misgivings characteristic to their concerns.

The discourses of the various groups need, however, to be traced not only to sectorial concerns, but to a more general complexity that underlies Israeli society. Though emulating Western countries' extensive privatization, and though broadly engaged in the aforementioned quest for freedom from the yoke of collective burdens, Israel's ethos has historically had only limited commitment to the classical tenets of Western consumerism: individualism, liberalism, the legal rational legitimacy of the state and of state laws. A comprehensive treatment of this subject is beyond the scope of the present introduction. We would like, however, to bring out some suggestive elements vis-à-vis consumption in Israel as divergent from the idealized affluent-society model. For example, Sprinzak (1993) analyzes what he terms the Israeli political and economic "illegalism," meaning the non-primacy of the legal order. The roots of illegalism in Israel have been largely attributed to the origin of the founding fathers in East European countries who lacked a tradition of civil and individual rights, and were informed instead by a deeply rooted *shtetl* (small Jewish community of Eastern Europe) view of state law as a feature of the oppressive Gentile society (Sprinzak 1993: 177). With the establishment of the state and capitalist market, the spirit of illegalism endures in issues such as forgery of state-dictated standards, impaired payment morality, and disregard for intellectual property rights (VCR cassettes, CDs, and computer software are copied and sold for reduced prices; Koren 2002), which pervade Israel's marketplace. The emanating distrust between salespersons and consumers, which intensifies in times of economic distress, undermines the pre-contractual infrastructure of consumer normalcy.

The insight derived from looking into the background of Jews' exile life, primordial communities, migratory society, and its relevance to individual–collective relations and to consumer abnormalcy may be expanded beyond the question of illegalism. Ezrahi describes the long seclusion of Jews within their families and communities as a key to understanding Israel's public culture. The "bustling" of Israelis in the new public spaces (Ezrahi 1997, ch. 2) remains unmediated or underregulated. For our concern in consumerism we can raise examples of untamed, anomic behaviour in public spaces ranging from the overtly loud use of cellular phones to the extravaganza of residential architecture. The same interpretive framework can possibly be applied to account for Israelis' acute environmental abuse and, possibly, to Israelis' lethal use of their cars and roads.

In considering the effects upon consumption of the unique communal and migratory background of Israelis and in light of the relative weakness of the ideological bases for Western consumerism in Israel, we may reconsider Baudrillard's West-centered critique for the case of Israel: How relevant are the ethics of "possessive individualism" and the "democratic alibi" in a largely immigrant society that has no solid liberal-rational or class tradition; in which the majority – i.e., the Jewish citizenry – perceive themselves as "primordially" equal (Kimmerling 1985), even while economic gaps are constantly growing and becoming ever more visible and conspicuous?

The question is heightened further in view of the ongoing war situation. The chronic military challenge to the country's borders carries important symbolic reverberations even for consumption. The expulsion of Arab populations during the 1948 war and the occupation of the West Bank and Gaza after 1967 have created both a complex refugee problem (of which Israeli Palestinians are constant "reminders") and an endemic crisis of political legitimacy. For Jewish Israelis, the world of consumption, playful and placeless, helps distract attention from the problematics of and challenges to Israeli existence. The presumably deterritorialized malls that have popped up like gigantic toadstools on the outskirts of densely populated landscapes (see again Markowitz and Uriely's Chapter 2 and Birenbaum-Carmeli's Chapter 3 in this volume) are a good place to examine the paradoxical constitution of consumer oblivion and emulation of the West. At one level, this is generically true in the sense with which Sharon Zukin avers, "As markets have been globalized, place has been diminished" (1991). In a more particular regard, in Israel many malls are also built on formerly Arab lands (see Berger's illuminating book on the history of Dizengoff Center [1998]). Thus Israeli malls not only insulate shoppers from the weather and the environment, they also insulate mainly Jewish shoppers from the placement of the malls and from the preponderance of Arab workers (mostly from the West Bank and Gaza) who have built and continued to maintain in the 1990s the spaces while making up only a tiny minority of their visitors. The absence of reference to the spoken language of its own Palestinian million-strong minority (roughly 20 percent of Israel's population) symbolizes in one more respect how Israeli aspirations to "normalcy," in this case through consumption, is itself an assertion of a primarily Jewish community and, therefore, a pervasive conservatism and not evolution or enlightenment towards some global standards.

The disposition toward and patterns of consumption among the various sectors as described in the present volume disclose both specific sectorial reservations toward consumerism as well as each sector's positioning vis-à-vis the foundational parameters of primordiality, immigration, and the war situation. Grossman's Chapter 4 ethnography of a kibbutz in the wake of consumerism encapsulates contemporary social and political marginalization and economic impoverishment of this once-elite group. For Kibbutz Gvanim's members, the collapse of egalitarianism amplifies the widening gap between their economy, which is deteriorating in the age of privatization, and the rise of private consumption. It also foretells a growing visible internal inequality. In their difficult economic condition the members of Kibbutz Gvanim turned the kibbutz and their own lives into a commodity, an object for tourist gaze. While for tourists a sheltered gaze on the kibbutz may encapsulate a nostalgic, esoteric image of Israeliness, the community of the kibbutz collapses under this new gaze and the economic reality which underpins it.

The Jewish immigrants from the Former Soviet Union (FSU) are characterized by high education and strong affiliation to Euro-Russian culture. They therefore tend to refrain from social integration and keep to themselves, as described by Bernstein and Carmeli in Chapter 6. This partial reservation is reproduced in the consumption arena, where FSU immigrants retain a link to community-based services, mainly for symbolic purposes. In the eyes of many immigrants, capitalist consumerism is both to be despised (as "American") yet craved for, perceived as a source of alienation and joy at the same time. However this ambivalence toward the consumer society also echoes the basic attitude of many FSU immigrants toward the state of Israel itself to which they emigrated following the collapse of the USSR rather than out of Zionist commitment. Through a discourse of festive food consumption they locate themselves vis-à-vis old and new contexts, challenging the traditional language of *aliya* (immigration to Israel, literally "going up") and the canonical religion-anchored definition of the Jewish state.

Within communities with compactly defined boundaries, the awareness that consumption may be experienced by its individual members as an elevation of personal freedom can lead to feelings that "traditional" arrangements are at threat, much as Miller's reference to the "consciousness" of consumption would imply. As in other non-Western and industrializing nations, the social and political backlash to consumerism, to its culture and fallacies, can be detected in Israel. Alongside or perhaps in response to privatization and growing sumptuary cleavages, parochial trends are rising which stand opposed to globalism, universalism, and individualism. The ultra-Orthodox community is a case in point. In the present volume, El-Or and Neria's Chapter 5 refers to the relatively secluded sectors of ultra-Orthodox (*haredi*) Jews. The ultra-Orthodox are restricted in their participation in the consumer market by religious dictates (kosher rules, for example) and by economic limitations, which derive primarily from the choice of many to attend institutions of religious learning rather than participate in the labor market. El-Or and Neria observe that some of the ultra-Orthodox in Jerusalem regard consumption as the fourth trial presented to the Jews in history (the first three being Enlightenment, the Holocaust, and Zionism). Economic limitations coincide with ideological-religious ambivalence toward the State, which extreme ultra-Orthodox sections view as sacrilegious because it implicitly claims to replace the Messianic redemption. Less extreme Orthodox Israeli Jews condemn middle-class consumerism as a symbol of a hollow secular lifestyle, a seduction to be continually resisted. During the 1990s, however, with the expansion of the ultra-Orthodox sector and a growing political participation, ultra-Orthodox Jews also started to participate in mainstream consumption processes. Marketing professionals in turn have "discovered" the religious consumer (Nevo 1996; Gorfein 2000). However, given their religious creed and economic limitations, these people do not fully share the consumer conformity. Many confine their participation to touring and peeping into the spectacle of the "others." As much as it creates a common space and shared meanings, consumerism touches upon sectorial boundaries and societal defining parameters.

Alongside the middle classes' reflection, the discourses of the Kibbutzniks, the Russian immigrants, and the ultra-Orthodox are all vehicles through which their Israeliness is negotiated or recast; the collective entities of state, society, and each group's location vis-à-vis others are given new meanings through consumption dialectics. These meanings, again, are made possible only if the consumer experience mimics, encapsulates, and reproduces the realness of that which preceded it in terms of a familiar everyday environment. Consumption writ large is possible only in tandem with a quotidian consumption that functions in pragmatic, mundane, taken-for-granted regularity. This applies to excluded non-Jewish groups as well.

The conflict between two national movements and the ambivalence between Jewish-primordialism vs. liberal-civic statehood places Israel's Palestinian citizens at the margins of the Israeli middle-class world. In addition to being indigenous natives and syntagms for the enemy, Israeli Arabs have also been a mirror for the primordial dilemma of the relations between the Jewish people and their land (Rosenzweig 1971 [1930]; Gurevitch and Aran 1991; Ben-Ari and Bilu 1997). In the present volume, Palestinian citizens of Israel appear on the margins of Jewish economy. For these second-class citizens in a Jewish state, mainstream consumer normalcy can be seen as oppressive insofar as it is directed toward the nurturance of Jewish oblivion to their predicament. For many years their exclusion from mainstream Israeli life was balanced by relative prosperity and partial embourgeoisement (Beshara 1993). The Jewish middle-class consumer world remained unthreatened. In the 1990s, two trends within Arab circles might be noted. On the one hand, as described in Sa'ar's Chapter 7 in this volume, high mobility consumerism has taken root, stirring internal transformations that draw Israeli Palestinians simultaneously closer to the two separate systems: the non-Israeli Palestinian marketplace in the occupied territories, and the high capitalist Israeli world. Internal tensions have been generated while identities are being redefined within a multiplicity of contexts.

On the other hand, being subject to the political and economic limitations which result in discouragement from participation in the middle-class consumer world, some Israeli Palestinians have developed a collectivist mode of provision defining a separation and/or opposition to the state. Political and symbolic exclusion, as well as alternative and marginal systems, can always provide a vantage point for anthropological inquiry. In their effort to attain a home, families in an Arab village optimize the production and consumption of familial and communal resources. Rather than relating to housing as a consumer commodity, as has occurred elsewhere in Israel, in Forte's Chapter 8 case study a family home is being gradually built by members and relatives, to be "organically" extended and modified with the gradual transformations of the family and its changing needs. However, this is not, at least not only, a sign of traditional economy. As described by Forte, in the context of the state's political limitations this mode of providing and consuming is also a politics of resistance, emerging against the dominant Jewish-state, including its market society and its everyday middle-class tenets.

Finally, as elsewhere, foreign workers arrived in Israel as a result of globalization and economic growth. In Western consumer society these workers and (trans)-migrants often constitute a marginal type sector. In Israel they have been admitted in great numbers to replace Palestinian workers from the West Bank and Gaza during the years of the first intifada (1987–1990). Foreign labor is concentrated in particular fields of production (agriculture, construction) as well as in consumption-related sectors such as personal services, restaurants, and the tourism industry. As such the foreign workers contribute to the production of Israel's middle-class consumer normalcy, even while their own needs (education, health, schooling, religious services) are placed outside Israel's baseline welfare system. Raijman and Kemp's Chapter 9 goes beyond the confines of material consumption to show how, being outside the world which they help produce, foreign workers provide for their own needs by creating an infrastructure for communal life. The exclusion and the particular consumption patterns of the foreign workers epitomize the understructure of globalization, the national vs. civic dilemma of the state of Israel, and the oblivion to the marginalized supported through its aspiration to consumer normalcy. Interestingly, in the case discussed by Raijman and Kemp – the rise of the Evangelical Church among the foreign workers – the exclusive embeddedness of Zionism and Jewish nationality is symbolically destabilized by the foreign workers' own claim to a particular Evangelical-Zionist conviction.

The Fragility of Israel's Consumerism

The 1990s saw the destabilization of consumption-based everyday normalcy by social, economic, and political upheavals. Concerns regarding the intensification of ethnic and economic cleavages stemmed from the peace prospects and economic prosperity (Smooha 1998). These have later given rise to economic recession and war-related anxieties. The everyday "America-like" reality that was tied together through consumption processes and through the exclusion of particular sectors was further disclosed in its fragility. While it is reasonable to predict continued adherence to global consumer trends, two general preconditions for consumer normalcy in Israel have surfaced. The first is along the internal dimension, namely, the growing economic and social cleavages wrought by a market orientation. The second is the ongoing war situation that threatens the texture of consumerist everyday life from the outside. These elements, which have always been present to some extent in the Israeli condition, have come to the fore since the beginning of the 2000s with the outbreak of the *Al-Aqsa* Intifada and a global financial crisis. Though they can be traced also in the ensuing chapters, the peripherality of these elements to the chapters' central theses is due to the relative affluence and peacefulness that characterized the period of data collection.

The fragility of this one-sided consumer normalcy in regional terms becomes evident in the periodic eruptions of the struggle between the two national movements centered upon the single territory. The 1996 bombing of the Dizengoff Center mall in Tel-Aviv signaled the start of a new era in the Israeli–Palestinian conflict in which the symbolism of consumption as normalcy was raised to the fore. The targeting of the mall specifically on a children's holiday (*Purim*) was pernicious and provoking. However, it is possible to also read into the Jewish public's response a strong note of outrage over desecration of the symbol of a mall as hallowed locus of Jewish middle-class leisure pursuit. An extension of this logic, the propagation of outdoor cafés throughout the 1990s, which were often given Euro-American-sounding names, can be interpreted as an emulation of those lifestyles enjoyed by peaceful, prosperous nations. Shopping centers, discos, and cafés are targets for terrorism not only because they contain high concentrations of civilians, but also because they characteristically represent profligacy and material privilege. The epitomized expression of normalcy, consumption in Israel is in practice a most fragile zone; a sphere where normalcy is disclosed in its impossibility.

Indeed, the atmosphere of threat and violence accompanying the *El-Aqsa* intifada has battered the Israeli economy. Soaring unemployment and the threat of terrorist attacks in public spaces has shaken consumer confidence and with it also the ethos of consumerism. As the government report states, "The Israel 'consumption celebration' ended in 2001. The quality of life of 'Mr. Israeli' (per capita consumption) rose 4% in 2000. It crawled 0.6% in 2001. Altogether, in 2001–2002, the GDP/Person growth annual percent declined by an unprecedented 6%. Tourist numbers declined 60% as compared to early 2000" (http://www.mof.gov.il/research/dec02.pdf, Ministry of the Treasury, Government of Israel). Purchases of new cars dropped 10.5 percent. Purchases of electrical appliances dropped

10 percent (after a sharp 17 percent rise in 2000). Shopping malls and markets are not packed as in the past. The moving pleas of the Finance Minister – 'Go out to the malls and buy blue and white' – were also not particularly effective.

Consumerism is not only a source of normalcy or "dream worlds" in the Israeli realm. Writ large consumerism and consumer attitudes touch upon the symbolic infrastructure of the Jewish state – the country as the "holy land," or the secular territorial dream of having ("all") Jews settled in Israel (Melman 1993; Gurevitch and Aran 1991). Against this spiritual "ascent" (*aliyah*) stands its contrast of emigration – the crossing of the system's boundaries to leave for safer and wealthier countries. For years emigration has been an object of denial and denunciation. *Yeridah*, or "descent," which always appears more attractive to Israelis in times of economic and political unrest, has become easier precisely under the combined aegis of globalization and consumerism. Paradoxically, the more consumerist and globalized Israel is perceived to be, the more emigration may be perceived as of smaller significance. *Yordim* (descenders) are less apologetic at present than once (Sobel 1986: 193; Rebhun and Waxman 2000). Emigration touches upon the liquidation of commitments. The country itself becomes a commodity in the global market – a "brand state," in Peter van Ham's locution (2001). To win some of the citizenry's tenuous commitment to staying, the country needs to be attractive and a "good deal."

The theme of emigration is a good place to conclude. For it is precisely when participation in the state project itself (including the Zionist dream-destiny) becomes not a primordial commitment but a choice comparable to so many other purchase decisions that we can see consumer culture reach its logical endpoint. When disappointed by an internally impaired infrastructure and by external conflict, consumerism, a source and epitome of normalcy, not only collapses. It foregrounds an uncertain future driven by political discord. Israeli consumers must time and again confront the "value" of their endeavor on primordial grounds.

References

Almog, O. (1994), *The "Sabras": A Sociological Profile*, Tel-Aviv: Am Oved (Hebrew).

Applbaum, K. (2003), *The Marketing Era: From Professional Practice to Global Provisioning*, New York: Routledge.

Barthes, R. (1972), *Mythologies*, trans. A. Lavers, London: Jonathan Cape.

Baudrillard, J. (1994 [1981]), *Simulacra and Simulation*, trans. F. S. Glaser, Ann Arbor: University of Michigan Press.

Ben Ari, E. and Bilu, Y. (eds) (1997), *Grasping Land: Space and Place in Contemporary Israeli Discourse and Experience*, Albany: State University of New York Press.

Ben-Eliezer, U. (1998), "State versus Civil Society? A Non-Binary Model of Domination Through the Example of Israel," *Journal of Historical Sociology*, 11: 370–96.

Ben-Porat, A. (1999), *Where They Are, This Bourgeois? The History of Israeli Bourgeoisie*, Jerusalem: Hebrew University (Hebrew).

Berger, T. (1998), *Dionysus at Dizengof Centre*, Tel-Aviv: Hakibbutz Hame'uhad (Hebrew).

Beshara, A. (1993), "About the Question of The Palestinian Minority in Israel," *Theory and Critique*, 3: 7–20 (Hebrew).

Bourdieu, P. (1984), *Distinction: A Social Critique of the Judgement of Taste*, Cambridge, MA: Harvard University Press.

Carmi, S. and Rosenfeld, H. (1976), "The Privatization of Public Means, the State-made Middle Class, and the Realization of Family Value in Israel," J. G. in Peristiany (ed.), *Kinship and Modernization in Mediterranean Society*, Rome: Center for Mediterranean Studies.

Dilley, R. (1992), "Contesting Markets: A General Introduction to Market Ideology, Imagery and Discourse," in R. Dilley (ed.), *Contesting Markets: Analyses of Ideology, Discourse and Practice*, Edinburgh: Edinburgh University Press.

Douglas, M. and Isherwood, B. (1979), *The World of Goods: Towards an Anthropology of Consumption*, New York: W. W. Norton.

Dumont, L. (1986), *Essays on Individualism: Modern Ideology in Anthropological Perspective*, Chicago: University of Chicago Press.

Ezrahi, Y. (1997), *Rubber Bullets*, New York: Farrar, Straus and Giroux.

Feige, M. and Roniger, L. (1992), "From Pioneer To Frier: The Changing Models of Generalized Exchange in Israel," *European Journal of Sociology*, 32: 280–307.

Gorfein, J. (2000), "Forgotten at Home (Sha'hehoo oti babayeet)," *Ottot*, 233: 30–2 [Hebrew].

Greitzer, N. (1988), "Ayalon Mall – Geographical Aspects of a New Phenomenon in the Commercial Urban Landscape of Israel," *City and Region*, (EeR Ve'ezor) 8: 87–97 (Hebrew).

Grinberg, L. (1993), *Histadrut Above All*, Jerusalem: Nevo (Hebrew).

Gurevitch, Z. and Aran, G. (1991), "About The Place: Israeli Anthropology," *Alpayim*, 4: 9–44 (Hebrew).

Katz, E. and Sella, H. (1999), *The Bracha Report: Culture Policy in Israel*, Jerusalem: Van Leer Jerusalem Institute (Hebrew).

Katz, E., Haas, H., Weitz, S., Adoni, H., Gurevitch, M., Sciff, M. and Goldberg-Anabi, D. (2000), *Leisure Patterns in Israel: Changes in Cultural Activity 1970–1990*, Tel-Aviv: The Open University (Hebrew).

Katz-Gerro, T. and Shavit, Y. (1998), "The Stratification of Leisure and Taste: Classes and Lifestyles in Israel," *European Sociological Review*, 14(4): 369–86.

Kimmeling, B. (1985), "Between Primordial and the Civil Definition of the Collective Identity: Erez Israel of the State of Israel?," in E. Cohen, M. Lissak, and U. Almagor (eds), *Comparative Social Dynamics*, Boulder: Westview.

Koren, O. (2002), "Worsening in the morality of payment", *Ha'aretz*, 1.8.2002 (Hebrew).

Kosik, K. (1976), Dialectics *of the Concrete: A Study on Problems of Man and World*, Dordrecht: D. Reidel.

Liberman, J. (1999), "Economic Metaphors in the Educational System," *Mifne*, 19–22 (Hebrew).

Liebman, C. S. (1988), "Conceptions of 'State of Israel'," *Israeli Society: The Jerusalem Quarterly*, 47: 95–107.

Macpherson, C. B. (1970 [1962]), *The Political Theory of Possessive Individualism: Hobbes to Locke*, London: Oxford University Press.

Mauss, M. (1990 [1950]) *The Gift: The Form and Reason for Exchange in Archaic Societies*, trans. W. D. Halls , London: Routledge.

Melman, Y. (1993), *The New Israelis: Personal Accounts of Changing Society*, Jerusalem: Shoken (Hebrew).

Miller, D. (1987), *Material Culture and Mass Consumption*, Oxford: Basil Blackwell.

—— (1995), *Acknowledging Consumption*, London: Routledge.

Nevo, R. (1996), "Close but Distant", *Ottot*, 189: 13–14, 46 (Hebrew).

Plattner, Stuart (1985), "Equilibrating Market Relationships," in S. Plattner (ed.), *Market and Marketing: Monographs in Economic Anthropology*, No. 4, Lanham: University Press of America.

Ram, U. (2000), "Between Nation and Corporations: Liberal Post-Zionism in the Global Age," *Israeli Sociology*, 2(1): 99–147 (Hebrew).

Rebhun, U. and Waxman, H. I. (2000), "The 'Americanization' of Israel: A Demographic, Cultural and Political Evaluation," *Israel Studies*, 5: 65–91.

Regev, M. (2000), "To Have a Culture of Our Own: On Israeliness and its Variants," *Ethnic and Racial Studies*, 23(2): 223–47.

Rosenzweig, F. (1971 [1930]), *The Star of Redemption*, London: Routledge & Kegan Paul.

Sahlins, M. (1972), *Stone Age Economics*, Chicago: Aldine-Atherton.

Shafir, G. and Peled, Y. (2002), *Being Israeli: The Dynamics of Multiple Citizenship*, Cambridge: Cambridge University Press.

Shavit Z. (2000), *Teudat Tarboot Hazon 2000*, Jerusalem: Ministry of Science, Culture, and Sport (Hebrew).

Slater, D. (1997), *Consumer Culture and Modernity*, Cambridge: Polity.

Smooha, S. (1998), "Transformation in the Israeli Society after Fifty Years," *Alpayim*, 17: 239–61 (Hebrew).

Sobel, Z. (1986), *Migrants from the Promised Land*, New Brunswick, NJ: Transaction.

Sprinzak, E. (1993), "Elite Illegalism in Israel and the Question of Democracy," in L. Diamond and E. Sprinzak (eds), *Israeli Democracy Under Stress*, Boulder, CO: Lynne Rienner Publishers.

Stiglitz, J. E. (1998), *More Instruments and Broader Goals: Moving toward the Post-Washington Consensus*, Helsinki: United Nations University, World Institute for Development Economics Research.

van Ham, P. (2001), "The Rise of the Brand State," *Foreign Affairs*, September/October): 2–6.

Weiss, M. (2002), *The Chosen Body: The Politics of the Body in Israeli Society*, Stanford: Stanford University Press.

Yehoshua, A. B. (1981), *Between Right and Right*, New York: Doubleday.

Zukin, S. (1991), *Landscapes of Power: From Detroit to Disney World*, Berkeley: University of California Press.

–2–

Of Thorns and Flowers: Consuming Identities in the Negev

Fran Markowitz and *Natan Uriely*

> La ville est plurielle, à la fois parce qu'elle est composée de multiples quartiers et parce qu'elle existe singulièrement dans l'imagination et les souvenirs de chacun de ceux qui l'habitent ou la fréquentent.
>
> Marc Augé, Pour une Anthropolgie des mondes contemporains

Set in Israel's northern Negev, Beersheva's concrete and glass cityscape arises unexpectedly from a monotonous vista of yellowish land, sporadically dotted by black goat-hair tents. Yet despite this seemingly specific setting, Beersheva is quite similar to many mid-sized regional centers throughout the world. Rather than a homogeneous, coherently planned metropolis, the gateway to the Negev appears to be and often functions as a multiplicity of contrasting urban sites. Its population is multi-ethnic and multi-lingual. Its architecture spans many periods and modes. Its residential centers range from dilapidated tenements to posh suburban living, and its commercial enterprises, once concentrated in the city hub, have been scattered unevenly from that site to a variety of surrounding shopping malls.

Apart from Ben-Gurion University's surrealistic, hypermodern campus bordering on a crumbling neighborhood, Beersheva's most glaring dichotomy lies in the contrast between its major commercial-leisure zones, the Old City and BIG. At first glance, the Old City, which until the end of the 1980s was *the city* (or the downtown), seems to express a local specificity. Its architecture is characterized by Arabesque arches and stones excavated from nearby quarries. Like the preindustrial city described by Sjoberg (1960), much of Beersheva's Old City is functionally specialized with certain streets each dedicated to one kind of product or service. Shops lining these streets are small and personalized, squashed together side by side, often without signs or shop names (see Carrier 1994: 362–8). Contents sometimes spill onto the adjacent sidewalk while inside the store they are parsimoniously displayed and often out of the customer's reach. Shopping in the Old City is usually tantamount to visiting a specific *someone*'s shop. Customers come to consult with a particular specialist for the product or service they require, and in the bargain they engage in conversation about mutual kin and acquaintances. Marked in their interactions as members of particular families, ethnic groups, social classes, and linguistic communities, customers and shopkeepers share news and gossip as goods and money change hands (see Markowitz 1993: 85–6).

By contrast BIG, an outdoor shopping mall located on the Beersheva by-pass road that links the city to the suburbs and to the Tel-Aviv highway, evokes spaciousness and anonymity. BIG's shops border a huge square parking lot that reflects the shopping center's name. Characterized by transparent glass fronts and colorful signs, these big stores, franchises of international and national chains, invitingly lure any and all customers inside to revel in their worlds of goods. Items in prodigious amounts speak to the possibility of ease and abundance for everyone. Blind to the constraints of ethnicity, family connections, or even the ability to pay, an anonymous "everyone" is bidden to look at, touch, and fondle the goods; they are urged to play with them, try them on, and experience the happiness that they (symbolically) promise (Baudrillard 1998 [1970]: 49).

The BIG stores speak to modernity and plenty. Their crisp spaciousness, bright colors, and abundance of goods link regionally and ethnically marked Israelis in the peripheral, dusty south of the country to the center of Israel and to the wide Western world. Contrarily, shopping in the Old City overrides such anonymity and transcendence. Yet despite these differences, both sites of consumption represent and manifest forms of globalization, pragmatic shopping, linkages between goods and identity, and ways of imagining the self and the other. Our goal for the remainder of this chapter is to show, through narratives and practices of shopping, that while both sites are imbricated in processes of globalization, these processes are multiple and yield different results (Kearney 1995; Tsing 2000). Moreover, the semiotic system of identity and consumption that animates their use is locally based, constituted through ongoing negotiations between historical narratives and changing political and economic events. Whereas Beershevites and other Israelis often point to the Old City as uniquely local, closer examination reveals it to be a manifestation of the global as well. Conversely, although BIG, which seems to typify the nowhere yet everywhere "non-place" (Augé 1994; 1998), it too is steeped in the local as people give it history and meaning through their uses of and narratives about it.

This chapter is informed by and reacts against the already clichéd dichotomy of global and local (for example Barber 1995) and its equally glib, albeit uneasy hybrid, the "glocal" (Ram 2000; Watson 1997).[1] Rather than accepting the ontology of any of these terms, we prefer to follow Appadurai's (1988: 13) analysis of "commodities as things in a certain situation" as we explore the *shopping for things* in certain sites in Beersheva. We have, therefore, opted to investigate the Old City and BIG as two shopping and leisure environments of everyday life, which may also provide a symbolic removal from the "here and now." Specifically, we examine the ways that both sites enable people to oscillate between the pragmatic tasks of provisioning shopping and what they may experience as alternative distant "dream worlds provided by the surrounding goods" as they shop (Lehtonen and Mäenpää 1997: 148, *pace* Baudrillard 1998 [1970]). Like Miller et al. (1998), Shields (1992) and Slater (1997), our goal is to reveal and explicate how the activities of shopping relate to and interact with shopping sites to construct dynamic processes of identity that interact with and define both the sites and the shoppers. We ask: What do people mean when they say that they shop at one place or another because it is convenient? Are people shopping to escape the constraints of the present, to enact them, or both? How do the venues at which they shop expand or constrict their identity possibilities and notions of goods availability? What are the sorts of choice that shopping sites present to shoppers for trying on, experimenting, playing with, discarding, or importing both goods and identities? Does shopping at particular locales produce "exotics at home" (Di Leonardo 1998), articulators of complex distinctions (Miller et al. 1998: 79, after Bourdieu 1984), or transformers of identity involving the self and possible selves (Lehtonen and Mäenpää 1997: 164)? "Global" and "local" become flexible, contextualized terms when informed by such consuming questions.

Along with our interest in the interrelation between place and identity via shopping, this chapter with others in the volume, aims to fill deep lacunae in the anthropology of Israel. Most cultural analyses of Israel's built environment have focused on how Zionism inscribes itself in the landscape (Ben-Ari and Bilu 1997b; Zerubavel 1995) through archeological sites that demonstrate a continuous Jewish presence in Israel-Palestine (Abu El-Haj 1998) and the sacrifices made on its behalf by the Jewish people (Ben-Yehuda 1995; Handelman and Shamgar-Handelman 1997). Contemporary edifices, such as the Museum of the Diaspora on the campus of Tel Aviv University and shrines to saintly leaders of formerly diasporic Jewish groups, attest to Israel as the originary homeland and to the rectitude of return from exile (Ben-Ari and Bilu 1997a; Weingrod 1993).

Yet at the same time as the sacred past-as-present has been memorialized in the landscape, bigger, more blatant monuments to modernity have been built in the land of Israel. Beersheva's early twentieth-century downtown was commissioned by the Ottomans to accord with the Euro-modern grid plan of a German architect; Tel-Aviv's ultramodern coastline and downtown towers portray life in a fast-paced, high-tech globalized world. So too do the brightly-lit shops in enclosed, air-conditioned malls where the latest brand names, musical groups, fast food, movies, and clothing link Israel to the major production and consumption zones of Europe and North America. Alongside the shrines that connect present-day Israel to its biblical past, these malls of modernity attest to the vitality of Israel's future. But what kind of future is this to be? By examining how and why Israelis in Beersheva go shopping in BIG and in the Old City we ask if and if so how, these sites coalesce or clash with the Zionist project of "making the desert bloom." How do different Israeli identities encourage patronage at different shopping sites? How do the different shopping sites attract their particular clientele? Our goal in this chapter is to begin to show how the quotidian practices of shopping intertwine with specific sites, specific shoppers, and the national project in varying ways. Our hope is that these examples of how, in Beersheva's Old City and BIG, local narratives of identity and desire confront, utilize, and sometimes overlap with globally produced products, trademarks, and imaginations will contribute to a larger, nation-wide understanding of consumption in Israel.

Methods

This chapter is based on research conducted by a team consisting of the authors and three student assistants from Ben-Gurion University. Data were obtained through eighteen ethnographic observations in the Old City and BIG conducted over a twelve-month period during the 2000/2001 academic year. During each of these field visits, the researchers augmented their observations by conversing with consumers and shopkeepers. Shop clerks often discussed their clientele, or lack of it, while the shoppers focused on why they were at that particular locale and what they were doing .

Supplementing these informal interviews, formal meetings were held with key actors in city government to shed light on the history and administration of the Old City and BIG. In-depth interviews were conducted with members of the Beersheva Old City Commission and from the Chamber of Commerce, Beersheva's municipal geographer, and officials in the Ministry of Housing. The entrepreneurs, planners, architects of BIG, and its current administrators were interviewed as well. All phases of fieldwork were supplemented by consulting historical documents and published articles from local newspapers and academic journals.

In addition to formal field research, the authors frequently visited each site, often to shop. One of us (Uriely) resides in the Old City, while the other (Markowitz) lives in suburban Meitar. Both closely follow the ebb and flow of construction and population movements in our respective communities. Fieldwork-as-consumption continues until this day, informing our own shopping and identity practices as well as illuminating those of our near and distant neighbors.

Consuming (in) the Old City

Beersheva's Old City is mainly comprised of hundred-year-old houses and buildings of Arabesque architecture that, unlike most other cities in the Middle East, were built on a grid with a pedestrian strip at its center. These days, its dusty, under-watered parks, littered streets and boarded-up buildings – including what was once a beautiful mosque – make the Old City feel like an underdeveloped, if not neglected, urban zone.

During the daytime, parts of the Old City come alive as the hub for service-oriented shops and offices. Department stores, franchises of national and international chains, and designer boutiques are noticeably absent in this urban zone where certain streets are devoted to furniture, clothing, gifts, electrical appliances, toys and sundries. The merchandise in these Old City shops is often of low quality and low price. Supplementing and often competing with these stores are itinerant peddlers who set up temporary stalls on the pedestrian strip and surrounding streets. Some offer handmade jewelry and ornaments, others vend cheap decorative goods brought from the Far East and Russia, while still others sell stolen foreign cigarettes, copied videocassettes, and scorched discs.

A large variety of professional offices surrounds the profusion of shops and stalls. One long dingy street is home to dozens of real-estate brokerages packed together side by side. Bank branches, insurance agencies, lawyers' and accountants' offices, many of which are located in the old Arab houses, attract a wide clientele from throughout the Beersheva area. The few doctors, dentists, and pharmacists who have established themselves in the Old City specialize in particular populations; their shingles are often written in Russian, Arabic, or Romanian along with the ubiquitous Hebrew.

Dotting the commercial hub are several coffee shops and small, cheap restaurants, some along the main streets, others on narrow lanes. They serve standard Middle Eastern specialty snacks – such as falafel, shwarma, hummus, and kebabs – to pedestrian shoppers while also functioning as meeting places for local storeowners and other "regulars." These customers include prostitutes, junkies, foreign workers, un- or underemployed Beershevites, and black-market money-changers who might sit all day over a glass of muddy coffee conducting their business. At night, the Old City becomes the shady site of Beersheva's ostensible nightlife. Neon signs flash outside several bars, pubs, and a growing number of illegal sex and gambling institutions.

The Old City's current state of neglect might stem from a Zionist reading of local history. Beersheva's early history, if we can rely on the Bible as a historical document, is long but broken. Beersheva first appears in the book of Genesis as an important stopping place for Abraham during his journeys in the Promised Land. The second patriarch, Isaac, also dwelled in Beersheva for some time, and Jacob later stopped there with his sons on their way to Egypt. Beersheva reappears in the Bible only after the Israelites resettled in the Land of Israel, where it is mentioned as the southernmost boundary of that land.

The city's modern history began when the nineteenth century turned to the twentieth and the Turks of the Ottoman Empire decided to constitute a separate district between those of Jerusalem and Gaza. To do this, they re-built Beersheva from an empty desert (El-Areff 2000 [1937]). Differentiating it from the narrow, winding alleys that typify many Middle Eastern cities, the Ottomans hired a German architect to build Beersheva as a rationally planned, modern metropolis. Their goal was to control the nomadic Bedouins and ultimately sedentarize them by luring their most promising sons to school where they would learn trades and professions. However, twentieth-century wars disrupted the flow of daily life in Beersheva. The first Battle of Beersheva drove the Ottomans out of Palestine and put it squarely within the British Mandate, while the second confirmed Beersheva's placement in the new State of Israel. Though the city was built, its original plans never came to fruition.

After the constitution of the State of Israel in 1948, many new residential neighborhoods were constructed throughout the growing city of Beersheva. Most residents of the Old City moved out, and this area was relegated to be the northern Negev's major shopping and entertainment zone. The commercial centrality of the Old City, which was not very old, continued until the late 1980s when the indoor mall, Kenyon ha-Negev [Negev Mall] opened for business just a kilometer away.

Prior to the 1980s, local residents referred to the Old City area as *the* city, reflecting its importance as the only urban place in the Negev region. The central post office, all banks, and virtually every shop, restaurant, and professional office had been located there. But when the Kenyon opened its doors to reveal that many stores had moved out of their original locations into gleaming new quarters, *the city* was transformed into the Old City. This linguistic shift signaled the area's anachronism as an entertainment and commercial center as well indexing the relatively old age of its buildings. Curiously, however, although they physically disappeared from the site, even today when directions are sought from Beershevites to specific places in the Old City these are often phrased in terms of what used to be: "Go to where the Mashbir once was, and then turn left;" or "Go to the Old Post Office, and continue down the street." Such practices suggest that "What can be seen designates what is no longer there" (De Certeau 1984: 108). In becoming the Old City, Ottoman-built Beersheva endures not so much as a site of memory but as an intangibly glimmering ghost town overlaid on the shabby reality of contemporary space.

Not surprisingly, the major theme pervading our conversations with shopkeepers in the Old City and with members of the Chamber of Commerce was their frustration with the slow-down of business in the area. While some mentioned the new shopping malls that opened for business during the 1990s as the main reason for the deterioration of business, others had complaints that were aimed more directly at municipal authorities. These referred to various problems such as the dirty streets, the lack of parking spaces, and the growing amount of illegal activities in the area. For example, the owner of a small gift shop proclaimed:

> I've had this store for already fifteen years. When I opened the store, this area was the town's commercial center, and I had a lot of business. For some time, the area also attracted artists and quality people who noticed the beauty of the area and opened galleries on Smilansky Street. Nowadays, however, there is no business here and even worse, no hope for this place. All the mistakes that one can imagine were made here. OK, the main road became a pedestrian strip, but parking lots are small and expensive. Kenyon ha-Negev was built too close to this area, and even the fountain built to decorate the pedestrian strip looks like a sewer. Look at the junkies, the prostitutes and all the miserable people that hang around this area . . . I would not come in here if I didn't have to.

Some remarked that this deterioration is a shame because the Old City, with its lovely Arab houses and uniquely tiled courtyards, holds great potential to become a sophisticated entertainment zone or artist colony. They, like the gift-shop owner, shook their heads while talking about previous plans to revitalize the area that came to naught. Why had this been the case?

Many people from throughout Israel, especially those of the middle-class Jewish sector, view Beersheva as an underdeveloped Bedouin city. Archival documents indicate that this perception has been historically rooted for decades. Discounting the fact that Ottoman Beersheva was built to be a modern city, post-1948 municipal planners designated the Old City as a "primitive urban area' (Gradus 1979). Rather than being appreciated the site's Arabesque architecture and its European grid plan were demeaned as uncivilized and backward. Non-Jewish space, despite the facts of its composition, is incompatible with the progress-modernization narrative of Zionism and incongruent with Israeli architects' schemes for building a modern city. The urban underdevelopment that has characterized the Old City should thus be understood as a local manifestation of the Zionist national project and decades of Israeli–Palestinian conflicts. In this context the local Arabic esthetics of Beersheva's Ottoman-era buildings have come to represent a potentially threatening "dissonant heritage" (Turnbridge 1994) rather than a pleasing architectural motif, and instead of being highlighted or maintained the Old City has been left to deteriorate. Since the late 1980s, newer, bigger, and brighter commercial zones have been erected in its stead.

Having described how the current condition of the Old City is related to the tides of Beersheva's local history, we must now note the impact of global forces as well. Far from being a homogeneously Bedouin city, the Old City's demographic composition reveals a startlingly diverse urbanity. In addition to the gray marketeers waiting along the pedestrian strip to change shekels into dollars or to deceive the gullible through the sleight of hand of a shell game, this area is filled with the sights, sounds and persons of many ethnic minorities and immigrant groups. Signs written in Cyrillic letters over shops selling Russian videocassettes, books and records, second-hand goods, smoked sausages and dried fish, as well as seasonal

Christmas trees and Easter eggs coexist with Judaica shops and the white headdresses of Bedouin men. Romanian, Turkish, Thai, and Chinese food products are increasingly evident in the Old City, accompanying the foreign workers who speak these languages as they congregate in makeshift cafés along side-streets. These "others," who are not quite within yet certainly not outside of Israeli society, move comfortably off the beaten path in the Old City. They sit over coffee, beer, kolbasa, or felafel conversing loudly in their own languages as music from their home countries enlivens the atmosphere. Yet because forces of the global economy played a significant role in the arrival of many of these "others" to the lower levels of Israel's globalized labor market, they might be seen as unwilling agents of these very globalization processes (Kearney 1995).

Middle-class Jewish Israelis, who come to the Old City to shop for particular products or to obtain professional services, often feel uncomfortable. Suddenly it is they who become marked in this multi-ethnic, globalized world. The languages, the dialects, the smells and sounds combine with a locally familiar but ideologically foreign architecture to estrange the natives in their own land. This feeling of estrangement is heightened by the presence of so many male foreign workers. Middle-class Israeli men often turn their discomfort into disdain by distancing themselves from the Old City, which they describe as "third world" to reflect the foreign workers' origins as well as the geopolitical placement of the Middle East. For women, shopping in the Old City is not only strange, but also risky and dangerous. Creeping danger was mentioned by many women interviewed on the site and was quite evident in the field notes of one of our female research assistants who wrote, "A man in a black T-shirt is gazing at me in a scary way. I look down at my notebook and act as if I am busy with writing. After he passes I look behind me and notice that he is gesturing at me in a derisive way while laughing." This passage succinctly describes what we have heard from many female shoppers; to avoid the threatening, negatively exotic atmosphere of the Old City, they concentrate wholeheartedly on the pursuit that brought them there in the first place. They purchase their washing machine or consult with their accountant, and then leave as quickly as possible.

As much as middle-class Jewish Israelis interviewed at the site stressed that most of the people in the Old City are "not like me" and that they shop there in discomfort, the same place functions as a phenomenological zone in which marginalized "other Israelis" engage with people like themselves in familiar surroundings. For them, the Old City is the comfortable multi-cultural, albeit locally accessible alternative to the Western, progress-oriented homogenizing BIG world. Shopping in the Old City allows temporary workers, new immigrants, the peripheralized unemployed and underemployed to reinforce connections to places, people and things – to demonstrate who they are and that they matter. Russian Jewish immigrants who once gained respect from jobs in technological institutes but now work as cashiers, clerks or cleaners, might feel a bolstered sense of self when they enter a Russian delicatessen or bookstore and exchange broken or accented Hebrew for their flawless mother tongue. Romanian foreign workers, who at all other times are virtually invisible as they work long hours in the building trades, make the Old City their own at the weekend. They play Romanian and Gypsy music full blast in the deserted streets, while consuming beer and exchanging news about their fellow guestworkers in other parts of the country, as well as from the faraway place they call home.

Following Michel de Certeau (1984: 108), several recent analyses of shopping milieus conclude that people elect to purchase things in particular locations because they feel good there (Falk and Campbell 1997; Lehtonen and Mäenpää 1997; Miller et al. 1998). "Feeling-good', however, is a spatial practice that means different things for different folks as it encapsulates expressions of identity, including the warmth of familiarity and the desire for something new. Middle-class Jewish Israelis are ill at ease in Beersheva's Old City, not because it is unfamiliar territory but because its local manifestation of the global estranges them in their own land. They shop there for specific products or services that can be found in no other locale. By contrast, Bedouins, Russian immigrants, working-class Mizrahi men, and foreign workers from Europe and Asia move with ease in the Old City provisioning themselves with the smells and tastes that represent home in a milieu that combines the familiar and the foreign.

Although middle-class Israelis are wont to dismiss the Old City of Beersheva as a quintessentially local expression of a dissonant Arab heritage, we have shown that this commercial zone is much more globally influenced and multi-cultural than their impressions bring to bear. Yet the Old City's globalism is barely visible for it fails to correspond with "progress" – the glossy images, brand names, the concrete and glass materials that constitute ultra-modern buildings, and the fast pace of a computerized world. When middle-class shoppers happen to acknowledge the global diversity of the Old City they do so negatively by conjuring up shabby images of the Third World.

A sign on one of the pedestrian strip's shops boldly proclaims, "Foreign money exchanged without the commission of the Bank of Israel." This sign symbolically sums up our notion of shopping in the Old City. It is a bundle of often contradictory practices that derives from the global condition as well as representing a multicultural alternative to the mainstream of contemporary Israel.

BIG in the Negev

The BIG outdoor shopping mall was built in the late 1990s on a repaved and widened section of the Hebron Road that bypasses central Beersheva while linking the Old

City to the suburbs and to the Tel-Aviv highway. We remember marveling as BIG epynomously emerged in bright, phosphorescent colors and sharp rectilinearity from the monochromatic rolling hills of the Negev. Rather than present itself as a "shopping oasis" in the desert, this commercial center, with its long rows of glass-fronted shops abutting a huge but orderly parking lot, was designed to evoke America. And if anyone should fail to make the connection between Beersheva's BIG and the USA, the bright red, white, and blue marquee highlighting the letters B-I-G alerts one and all that this is the case.

BIG's name and landscape speak to the colorful world of limitless opportunities that America represents to many Israelis. But for Markowitz, who was born and raised, and lived most of her life, in the United States, BIG appears as a cartoon-like simulacrum of the already passé suburban shopping plazas that were built early in the 1960s. This impression of BIG is disturbing because it is comprised more of parodic media images – such as from the popular TV series, *That 70s Show*, or the 1990 feature film, *Edward Scissorhands* – than of contemporary American shopping centers. Yet conversations about BIG with Israeli friends, neighbors, and colleagues since it opened for business in 1998, as well as more recent interviews with shoppers at the site, revealed that no one else shared these jolting impressions. Quite the contrary. Beershevites invariably described shopping at BIG as a delight because far from viewing it as a hyperreal parody, they experience it as part of the big, bright, clean, and efficient USA without having to leave the little State of Israel. Shopping week after week or day after day for life's small necessities may serve to remind people that they themselves and their country are trivial and small. Shopping at BIG, however, tells them that Israel and Israelis are very much part of the success story of the big, Western world.

These two overlapping views of BIG – a disturbing caricature of America versus a pleasurable conception of it – complement the ideas that motivated its construction. Beersheva's BIG was the first to open in a chain of outdoor shopping malls of that name located on highways outside a number of mid-sized Israeli cities, including Ashdod, Bet-Shemesh, Kiryat Ata, and Netanya. BIG's founder informed us that he modeled these centers not on the strip malls of 1960s suburbia, but on a more recent American phenomenon, the outlet mall. Outlet malls are typically built along major thoroughfares on large parcels of land beyond the borders of urban centers and suburbia. Like fast-food restaurants, these shopping plazas often lure weary travelers away from the road to rest and relax for a while, but they are also destinations in and of themselves. By averting the mark-up of retail sales in high-rent specialty or department stores, outlet malls promise low prices for high-quality, brand-name "direct from the factory" merchandise. BIG's founder, however, combined the spread-out, open-air design of American outlet malls with the retail stores that Israelis expect to see in a shopping center, mainly franchises of readily recognized, national and international (primarily American) chains. Notably absent are designer boutiques, art galleries, and exclusive cafés whose prices and reputation would place them beyond the reach of most middle-class consumers (cf. Guano 2002). Beersheva's BIG includes a huge Super-Pharm drugstore, a Tsomet Sepharim bookstore, Sakal Electronics, Baitli Furniture, and a Burger Ranch fast-food restaurant, all representing successful Israeli corporations. Its largest and most crowded shops are franchises of Ace Hardware, Home Center, Toys R Us, McDonald's, and Office Depot, all readily recognized from their names and logos as American.

The penetration of international businesses into Israeli consumer markets occurred full-force in the 1990s as the State of Israel responded to economic processes of globalization by reducing what were once astronomical taxes on private businesses and on foreign goods. Prior to the 1990s, it was difficult to find large American-style self-service stores staffed by uniformed, polite, and informed sales personnel in Israel, especially outside of Tel Aviv or Jerusalem. But by 2001 many sorts of enclosed indoor and spread-out outdoor shopping malls had sprung up throughout Israel. Entrepreneurs and urban planners tend to give names like BIG and Mega to these open-air sites and generally refer to them as "power centers" since they represent large national and international businesses and big money.

Most shoppers at BIG are native-speakers of Hebrew and seem to be comfortably ensconced in Israel's middle classes. But along with them we have heard and observed several Russian-speakers, immigrants from Ethiopia, and Arabic-speaking men and women. While the Old City might offer individuals from these demarcated groups an opportunity to exercise ethnic identity in the public sphere, BIG's message of worldliness via consumption for comfort offers a "way out" of their marked and marginal status. At BIG, where money or credit cards, not family connections, ethnic background, or recency of arrival counts, they are Israeli consumers in Israel, just like anyone else. Two women from the Bedouin town of Tel Sheva told our researchers that they come to BIG because of "the sense of freedom that we feel here. BIG is wide and open. We come in our own car and park near the stores. We don't run into all the people we know." What they were stressing is that shopping at BIG frees them from the constraints of their daily life in a town where, because everyone knows everyone else, behavior is highly regulated. Just a few miles down the road they can let their hair down, wander into clothing and toy stores and test out the freedom of being an anonymous customer browsing among oodles of goods with no one's watchful eye upon them.[2]

The idea of being an unmarked person at BIG extends way beyond ethnic or gender boundaries. All shoppers easily stroll up and down the wide store aisles selecting merchandise to look at, touch, and try on. Unlike the personalized shopping practices in the Old City where familiarity in customer-shopkeeper relationships demands some level of verbal interaction and a certain amount of money changing hands, browsing the store shelves at BIG demands nothing of the sort. BIG's patrons interact mainly with the profusion of objects presented on store shelves, and may not have to talk with a soul, even when sales clerks ask, "May I help you?" Shoppers can spray themselves with perfume, try on outrageous outfits, leaf through books, and play with toys without fear that they are being watched and judged by people they know. Just as important, these stores' open invitation to participate in their worlds of goods comes without the obligation to make a purchase. Far from producing alienation, this focus on commodities is often experienced as liberating and fun (Augé 1998; Baudrillard 1998 [1970]; Falk and Campbell 1997).

Indeed, just about everyone with whom we spoke at BIG replied that they shop there because it is easy and comfortable. They note that unlike the Old City and Kenyon ha-Negev there is no parking problem at BIG and that it is simple to go from one shop to another. They mention driving to one store, parking, shopping, putting parcels in the car, then driving to another store and repeating the process. These men and women are affluent Israelis; not only do they own private automobiles but they think nothing of the cost of gasoline as they drive the relatively short distances between stores.

BIG's enormous parking lot invites shoppers to drive there at the same time as it minimizes accessibility via public transportation. A bus does stop at BIG, but its service is slow and undependable. One woman told us that although she does not own a car she comes to shop at BIG because she likes the stores there. Along with her positive comments about the good lighting, pleasant air-conditioning, and inviting merchandise displays in the stores, she expressed frustration with the unreliable bus service that links BIG to residential Beersheva. In addition to the fact that buses arrive only once an hour, she noted that the drivers are often disdainful to their passengers, sending them the distinct message that BIG is for consumers with cars. While waiting for the bus to arrive she noted:

> The main problem with BIG is the lack of proper public transportation services. There are not enough buses to and from BIG, and they do not even follow the official timetable. The price of a bus ride is high, and information about the BIG route is hard to get. I think that the BIG shops lose a lot of money because of the public transportation problem. Many people prefer to shop at Kenyon ha-Negev because they do not own cars.

Potentially lost money notwithstanding, BIG, which was designed to attract car-owning customers, was built beyond the orbit of Beersheva's major bus routes. "Car-owing customers" designates a particular kind of shopper: middle-class, family people, successful Israelis with enough money or credit for the purchase and maintenance of an automobile.[3] These family-oriented Israelis come to BIG to be with others like themselves as they shop with their children at Toys R Us, bring them to the Bowling Center and Super Kef (*kef* is Hebrew for "fun') for sports and video games, or to McDonald's and Burger Ranch for a "Happy Meal." These sites are popular attractions, part of BIG's benign global character which, unlike the heavily male and unpredictable globalism of the Old City, is of the homogenizing "It's a Small World" variety.

Parents and children feel warmly secure at BIG, despite its size. It is regularly patrolled by a brightly colored security vehicle, and the guards at each shop entrance are inconspicuously dressed and courteous. Their function is more to reassure shoppers that they are safe and, along with the sporadic and unreliable bus service, to keep out undesirables than to police the behavior of patrons who already know how to act at the site.

The playground in the middle of BIG's parking lot is another reminder to each consumer that this is a family-oriented place where children are welcome and provided for. Adults bring their toddlers and young children to the playground where they swing, slide, and run around. During early evening hours most of the adults are fathers who watch over the youngsters while their wives shop for food, clothing, and housewares (see also Miller et al. 1998). A father of two told us:

> I come here with the children two or three times a week. The children love BIG. They hope I'll buy them presents or at least take them to eat at McDonald's where they get surprise presents with their Happy Meals . . . I also feel comfortable and safe to be with my children here in a nice environment where everyone you see are families, people of good quality. You won't find junkies here, alcoholics or all those spooky types that sit over a glass of beer all day long in the Old City.

BIG's colorful and secure space provides a multi-purpose, low-cost alternative to one's own home. Filled with mothers, fathers, and their children, it attracts more of the same who patronize BIG because along with the surprises and variety of its merchandise are all the other people who are "just like me."

What's BIG in the Negev is shopping at a place that provides the freedom of anonymous consumption along with the comforts of tidiness, safety, and ease of access. BIG's message to its shoppers is that they can experience the best of America while resting assured that their fellow consumers are middle-class, family-oriented Israelis wedded to the Zionist message of progress, Westernization, and homogeneity. Yet along with all of the positive remarks we heard about BIG, some Beershevites expressed the same cynicism that accompanied their comments about the Old City. Many answered our query about why they come to BIG by ironically posing another question, "Where can you go in Beersheva *except* BIG?" A more poetic and geographically suitable version of the same idea was offered by a salesman in one of the stores who explained BIG's popularity by quoting the popular saying, "Every thorn in the desert is a flower." The gist of these remarks is that Beersheva and the surrounding region is ugly, peripheral, forgotten, and neglected. Anything that even begins to approach beauty, centrality, and modernity is heartily embraced and appreciated. Negev-dwellers thereby place BIG in perspective. They harbor no illusion that their brightest shopping center replicates America or links Beersheva to it, but they seize the opportunity of consuming (at) a site that offers at least a taste of it.

Conclusions

The glimpses we have offered of Israelis *shopping for things* in Beersheva's Old City and at BIG have begun to reveal some of the complexities involved in the interrelationship between people and goods, people's identities and the Zionist nation-state, and the possible alternatives that merchandising and merchandise pose to them. Although on the surface, the Old City and BIG appear to be opposite sorts of site – the first a local place steeped in the history and geography of the region, while the second represents the hyperreal "non-place" described by Augé (1994; 1998) – the words and practices of Negev-dwellers demand quite a different interpretation.

In light of our ethnography, we argue that whereas both the Old City and BIG reflect processes of globalization, they are both also rooted in local contexts. The Old City, built by the Ottomans to be a modern urban center, served as the Negev's commercial hub until the late 1980s. All residents of the Beersheva area were drawn there for shopping and leisure activities. Nowadays, however, it functions more as the publicly demarcated home away from home for "others" than for veteran locals. Although it remains a distinct possibility that restoration of the Old City's Arabesque architecture could have resulted in an attractive site of local exotica, government officials and urban planners chose instead to leave it to deteriorate. As a result, the Old City today has become a sadly perverted version of what the Ottomans had aspired to. Instead of representing rationality and modernity, in the mind's eye of Israel's middle and professional classes it is an embarrassing and ominous marker of "Third World" Middle Eastern underdevelopment.

Our forays into BIG suggest that the impersonal global and the intimate local are intertwined at this site as well. While BIG's external facade, which appears as a hyperreal, homogenized non-place designed for unmarked consumers, reflects the late modern global condition, its actual and symbolic usages are well embedded in the multiply constituted local context of Israeli society. That BIG is perceived as a positive representation of modernity and "the West" derives from the same progress-oriented, Zionist ideology as the Old City's designation as "primitive." BIG's overwhelming popularity as a leisure zone beyond its status as a consumption center is directly connected with the fact that the Old City has been left to crumble, demonstrating the incompatibility of a Turkish-Arab site with Western-oriented, upwardly mobile Jewish Israeli families. BIG and the Old City should therefore be seen as two sides of the same Israeli coin.

Zionism, as Gover (1994) argues, is a fundamentally Western ideology which has been adopted as a uniquely Israeli identity. Its key slogans emphasize progress, democracy, secular nationalism, and modernity, which, in contrast to an Orientalist view of Islam and Arab cultures (Said 1979), make many Israelis see themselves as more similar to their Western counterparts than to their Middle Eastern neighbors. This tendency has characterized Israel's earliest social elite (Elon 1981) and remains strong among contemporary members of the educated, established middle classes (Ram 1998; Shamir 1996). Thus, it is certainly not surprising that places like BIG, manifestations of what appear to be the "global" and Euro-American modernity, are willingly consumed as part of the mainstream local identity.

We note as we conclude that Beersheva differs from larger, more prosperous global cities (like Tel Aviv and Jerusalem, not to mention Buenos Aires, London, New York or Tokyo) where the middle and upper classes are presented with ever-expanding opportunities for exploring and addressing desired identities at the expense of working-class and poor individuals (Guano 2002; Sassen 1991). Situated in the geopolitical-economic periphery of Israel, Beersheva has no upper class, and holders of university degrees and pursuers of careers in the liberal professions or big businesses are in a distinct minority. Urban planners and private entrepreneurs have forgone creating spectacular luxury malls whose shops and services would be prohibitive to all but a tiny minority enticed by fantasies of emulating the super-rich. Instead, Beersheva's public consumption zones offer a wider range of alternatives to its working class and marginal populations than to the bourgeoisie. As a result, it seems that middle-class Beershevites who hyper-invest in the few sanitized models of the global that stress the good life are joined by a wide range of working-class and ethnicized individuals to escape from the dangers that seem to increase every day in the Middle East.

Which leads to our final point: our findings indicate that, state hegemony notwithstanding, members of different social groups often attach different meanings to the same site and utilize it in different ways. Middle-class Israelis avoid the Old City when they can because they perceive its Middle Eastern structures as foreign, unpleasant, and threatening. Members of ethnic minorities, foreign workers, and un- or under-employed Israelis, however, may find in the Old City a comfortable public place that validates, even values, who they are. BIG, built far from the madding crowds of the central city, overwhelmingly attracts "consumers with cars," middle-class, family-oriented Jewish Israeli men and women and their children. But members of ethnic minorities shop there as well. Both groups come to BIG to avoid the intimacy of the Old City and the populations that give that site its particular flavor, but they do so for different reasons. BIG provides middle-class

Israelis a sense of familiarity by surrounding their aspirations for the global with "people like me" while at the same time it offers a sense of freedom to marked ethnic minorities who wish to celebrate anonymity in the public sphere.

Just as Foucault (1980) has taught that gender and sex are ideologically immersed social constructs constituted so "that we can never know in advance what will 'count' as sexual in another culture" (Kulick 1995: 7), our ethnography of shopping in the Negev has demonstrated that despite the look of a place or the slogans that surround it, we can never know in advance what will "count" as global or local in any particular context. This chapter has demonstrated that the spatial practices of and narratives about Beersheva's Old City and BIG are both contingent on local contexts and processes of globalization. They provide a window for understanding the complexities of material cultural and its often contradictory usage in the context of urban consumption and market society in Israel.

Acknowledgments

This chapter is a revised version of "Shopping in the Negev: Global Flows and Local Contingencies," *City and Society*, 14(2), 2002. Its research was funded by a grant from the State of Israel's Ministry of Science, Culture and Sport for the interdisciplinary project, "Globalization in Israel: Implications in the Negev," administered by Uri Ram and Yehuda Gradus, Ben-Gurion University of the Negev. Yishai Shklanovsky, Hadas Dreiher, and Sharon Rotman were industrious, perceptive, and enthusiastic research assistants. We thank them for a job well done.

References

Abu El-Haj, N. (1998), "Translating Truths: The Practice of Archeology and the Remaking of Past and Present in Contemporary Jerusalem," *American Ethnologist*, 25: 166–88.

Appadurai, A. (1988), "Introduction: Commodities and the Politics of Value," in A. Appadurai (ed.), *The Social Life of Things: Commodities in Cultural Perspective*, Cambridge: Cambridge University Press.

Augé, M. (1994), *Pour une Anthropologie des mondes contemporains*, Paris: Aubier.

—— (1998), *Non-Places: Introduction to an Anthropology of Supermodernity*, London: Verso.

Barber, B. (1995), *Jihad vs. McWorld: How Globalism and Tribalism are Shaping the World*, New York: Times Books.

Baudrillard, J. (1998 [1970]), *The Consumer Society: Myths and Structures*, London: Sage.

Ben-Ari, E. and Bilu, Y. (1997a), "Saints' Sanctuaries in Israeli Development Towns," in E. Ben-Ari and Y. Bilu (eds), *Grasping Land: Space and Place in Contemporary Israeli Discourse and Experience*, Albany: State University of New York Press.

—— (eds) (1997b), *Grasping Land: Space and Place in Contemporary Israeli Discourse and Experience*, Albany: State University of New York Press.

Ben-Yehuda, N. (1995), *The Masada Myth: Collective Memory and Mythmaking in Israel*, Madison: University of Wisconsin Press.

Bourdieu, P. (1984), *Distinction: A Social Critique of the Judgement of Taste*, Cambridge, MA: Harvard University Press.

Carrier, J. (1994), "Alienating Objects: The Emergence of Alienation in Retail Trade", *Man*, 29: 359–80.

De Certeau, M. (1984), "Walking in the City," In M. de Certeau, *The Practice of Everyday Life*, Berkeley: University of California Press.

Di Leonardo, M. (1998), *Exotics at Home: Anthropologies, Others, American Modernity*, Chicago: University of Chicago Press.

El-Areff, (2000 [1937]), *Annals of Beersheva and its Tribes*, Tel Aviv: Shoshani Press (in Hebrew).

Elon, A. (1981), *The Israelis: Founders and Sons*, Jerusalem: Adam Publishers (in Hebrew).

Falk, P. and Campbell, C. (1997), "Introduction," in P. Falk and C. Campbell (eds), *The Shopping Experience*, London: Sage.

Foucault, M. (1980), *The History of Human Sexuality: An Introduction*, Vol. 1, New York: Vintage.

Gover, Y. (1994), *Zionism*, London and Minneapolis: University of Minnesota Press.

Gradus, Y. (1979), "Urban Planning Development in Beersheva," in Y. Gradus and A. Stern (eds), *The Book of Beersheva*, Jerusalem: Keter (in Hebrew).

Guano, E. (2002), "Spectacles of Modernity: Transnational Imagination and Local Hegemonies in Neoliberal Buenos Aires," *Cultural Anthropology*, 17(2): 181–209.

Handelman, D. and Shamgar-Handelman, L. (1997), "The Presence of Absence: The Memorialism of National Death in Israel," in E. Ben-Ari and Y. Bilu (eds), *Grasping Land: Space and Place in Contemporary Israeli Discourse and Experience*, Albany: State University of New York Press.

Kearney, M. (1995), "The Local and the Global: The Anthropology of Globalization and Transnationalism," *Annual Review of Anthropology*, 24: 547–65.

Kulick, D. (1995), "Introduction. The Sexual Life of Anthropologists: Erotic Subjectivity and Ethnographic Work," in D. Kulick and M. Willson (eds), *Taboo: Sex, Identity, and Erotic Subjectivity in Anthropological Fieldwork*, London: Routledge.

Lehtonen, T., and Mäenpää, P. (1997), "Shopping in the East Centre Mall," in P. Falk and C. Campbell (eds), *The Shopping Experience*, London: Sage.

Markowitz, F. (1993), *A Community in Spite of Itself: Soviet Jewish Émigrés in New York*, Washington, DC: Smithsonian Institution Press.

Miller, D., Jackson, P., Thrift, N, Holbrook, B. and Rowlands, M. (1998), *Shopping, Place and Identity*, London: Routledge.

Ram, U. (1998), "Citizens, Consumers and Believers: The Israeli Public Sphere between Fundamentalism and Capitalism," *Israeli Studies*, 3: 24–44.

Ram, U. (2000), "'Promised Land of Business Opportunities:' Liberal Post-Zionism in the Glocal Age," in G. Shafir and Y. Peled, *The New Israel: Peacemaking and Liberalization*, Boulder, CO: Westview.

Said, E. D. (1979), *Orientalism*, New York: Vintage.

Sassen, S. (1991), *The Global City: New York, London, Tokyo*, Princeton: Princeton University Press.

Shamir, R. (1996), "Society, Judaism and Democratic Fundamentalism," in D. Barak-Erez, *The Jewish State and Democratic Society*, Tel Aviv: Ramot (in Hebrew).

Shields, R. (1992), *Lifestyle Shopping*. London: Routledge.

Sjoberg, G. (1960), *The Pre-Industrial City: Past and Present*, New York: The Free Press.

Slater, D. (1997), *Consumer Culture and Modernity*, Cambridge: Polity.

Tsing, A. (2000), "The Global Situation," *Cultural Anthropology* 15(3): 327–60.

Turnbridge, J. (1994), "Whose Heritage? Global Problem: European Nightmare," in G. Ashworth and P. Larkham (eds), *Building a New Heritage: Tourism, Culture, and Identity in the New Europe*, London: Routledge.

Watson, J. (ed.) (1997), *Golden Arches East: McDonald's in East Asia*, Stanford: Stanford University Press.

Weingrod, A. (1993), "The Changing Israeli Landscape: Buildings and the Uses of the Past," *Cultural Anthropology* 8: 370–87.

Zerubavel, Y. (1995), *Recovered Roots: Collective Memory and the Making of Israeli National Tradition*, Chicago: University of Chicago Press.

–3–

Consumption and the Making of Neighborliness: A Tel-Aviv Case Study

Daphna Birenbaum-Carmeli

The signifying capacity of goods has been established by sociologists throughout the past century. While early theoreticians (for example Veblen 1953 [1899] and later Reisman 1952) emphasized the very import of commodities as vehicles of signification, more contemporary scholars (such as Douglas and Isherwood 1979; Baudrillard 1975, 1983; and Bourdieu 1984) have tended to focus on the politics of the production and reproduction of these meanings. Implied in the latter analyses is the view that the sphere of consumption is becoming increasingly prominent.

One feature of consumption is the transgression/bridging of traditional boundaries between the private and the public. Being a private experience conducted in a public space, consumption imbues individuals' lives with the social meanings that permeate the goods and services of their choice. In this respect, the proliferation of consumption both allows and requires inividuals to locate themselves – by means of consumer choices – within particular groups and outside others. Consumption, which constitutes an element in reproducing, sustaining, defending, contesting, and rejecting of culturally specific, meaningful ways of life (Slater 1997: 4), is thus immanent to both small-scale dynamics of group identity and subjectivity formation and macro-social processes of cultural reproduction.

These processes gain particular significance in tight geographical settings, especially in contexts of pervasive visibility. It is owing to this intensification that in some communities residents have made consumption a central sphere of social action. In the realm of the community – the prototype arena for "Keeping up with the Joneses" – consumer choices may come to the fore as vehicles for self-positioning vis-à-vis other community members as well as the broader social context. As such, consumption offers a rich vantage point for the study of community dynamics.

In this chapter I look through a consumption lens at Ramat Aviv Gimmel (RAG), a Tel-Aviv neighborhood I studied between 1988 and 1991 and revisited in 2000. On the basis of an analysis of the local discourse of consumption, I argue that in RAG of the late 1980s/early 1990s, residents were interested in glossing over economic and cultural differences and in assuming a seemingly monolithic social appearance. This situation appears to have changed in the following decade, when

RAG became a more homogeneous upper-middle-class neighborhood that befitted its social image. The chapter's focus is on the earlier period. I start with a brief presentation of the neighborhood's history and sociodemographic make-up and then progress to an ethnography of consumption as manifested around one's home, in the neighborhood's shopping centers, and in the working of the neighborhood committee. The chapter ends with some comparative comments, based on my 2000 revisit to the neighborhood.

Research was carried out mainly by fieldwork. In the years 1988–1991, I lived in RAG and conducted observations, participant observations, and in-depth interviews. Observations were conducted in houses and yards, schools, clinics, bus stops, commercial centers and amusement parks, and in local public events. I also interviewed residents and functionaries such as teachers, nurses, shopkeepers, bank managers, municipality officials, and architects. Letters, official documents, and press articles were collected and analyzed. Additionally, I was a member of the Neighborhood Committee and founded the local archive, the material of which I later analyzed. Toward the end of my fieldwork (late 1990) I conducted a neighborhood survey of 10 percent of the local households (350/3,500 at that time), which I replicated a decade later.

My fieldwork has taken place when Shamir's Likkud government was in power and the first *Intifada* was being waged.[1] Neither the peace prospects nor the high-tech prosperity of the 1990s were yet in sight, let alone the *Al-Aqsa Intifada* of the 2000s. In some circles, however, consumption was already playing an important role. RAG was one such place. In the late 1980s, the place was considered the epitome of capitalist prosperity. A closer look revealed, however, that the neighborhood's residents comprised a mosaic of various economic and social sub-populations. Few rich residents lived in the midst of a mixed middle-class population that included a significant number of families of modest economic resources. Given the status sensitivity of RAG residents (Birenbaum-Carmeli 1997) and the pervasive local visibility (Birenbaum-Carmeli 1998), consumption harbored a threatening potential of unveiling internal differences. Yet, according to my observations, this capacity was outweighed by its opposite, namely social leveling, through which residents constructed consumption as a sphere of local inclusion. This discourse and the cohesive image it conveyed, which echoed traditional Israeli collectivism, were still – in the early 1990s – an effective vehicle for obtaining officials' and media sympathy, as well as material advantages which benefited every resident.

Ramat Aviv Gimmel: Background and Context

Construction of RAG began in the early 1970s and intensified in the following decade. The neighborhood, which was fully planned by the municipality, included some 5,000 residential units, most of which were apartment buildings. As part of the government policy of social integration, a quarter of the apartments were two-bedroom public housing, offered for sale at subsidized prices to young couples who qualified for the Ministry of Welfare criteria. Alongside the public-housing buildings, more spacious apartment buildings, containing a range of novelties of the time (central air-conditioning, porter position, marble-walled lobby) were constructed. These three-, four-, and five-bedroom apartments were offered to the general public for full prices. A few exceptionally expensive units (such as combined apartments, penthouses) were sold in the 1990s for US$1–2 million. (Average home price in Israel in 1990 was $90,000; average Tel Aviv price was $120,000: Central Bureau of Statistics 1990.) Several dozen semi-detached houses were built at the neighborhood's perimeter. This somewhat exceptional blend was reflective of RAG's location at the most prestigious end of Tel Aviv as well as the city's interest in attracting younger couples to its area, and the state's policy of social integration by means of residential proximity.

As in many other Tel Aviv residential areas,[2] RAG's population was wholly Jewish. Palestinians were present only as builders and delivery workers. In the early 1990s, the Oriental/Ashkenazi[3] ratio was 2:5.[4] Compared to other affluent urban neighborhoods in Israel – where the respective figure was about 1:6 at the time – this proportion represented relative ethnic heterogeneity. Most of the residents defined themselves as "secular" and a 20 percent minority viewed themselves as "traditional" Jews.[5] Household composition was fairly monolithic, with over 80 percent consisting of married parents with young children. The remaining households were composed of older couples or single persons and students from the nearby Tel Aviv University. The local population was wealthier than the national average. By their self-reported income the residents divided into three almost equal groups – of up to average income; above average; and well above average income. While the distribution conjures up general prosperity, economic diversity within the local population was significant. Residents who struggled to cover fairly modest life expenditure, lived almost next door to people whose lives were free from financial constraint. The variability was reproduced in apartment sizes that ranged from 75 m^2 in the public-housing apartments to penthouses and houses of 300–450 m^2. With 93.5 percent of the residents with at least secondary education and 67 percent with post-secondary education, RAG residents were more educated that the average country population.[6] Politically, in 1990, the residents divided rather equally between left- and right-wing[7] supporters. For this part of town, whose residents were generally left-wing in their preferences, the ratio of right-wing supporters was high. This exceptionality reflected the neighborhood's economic-ethnic mix, which reproduced the prevalent association of political worldview with socio-economic parameters in Israeli politics.[8] In the media RAG was consistently celebrated as a symbol of affluence and stylized consumerism.

The following ethnography illustrates the significance of consumption as a sphere of interaction and self-positioning in RAG of the early 1990s. It traces three main spheres of local life, which the residents considered pivotal yet distinct: neighbors' casual meetings in their buildings' yards, regular encounters in local public spaces, primarily local commercial centers, and neighborhood-related instrumental engagements. The residents used all these encounters for mutual exploration, looking for guidance and reassurance regarding one's consumer choices. Consumer choices thus fluctuated between the private and the public, to be made, presented, approved, challenged, and reproduced. I start my presentation with the smaller scale sphere, of neighbors' interactions in private homes and in their buildings' yards.

The Discourse of Consumption

In neighbors' talks around one's home

As elsewhere, so in RAG, local socializing was primarily a women's affair. Whereas men participated in such encounters only rarely and briefly, many local women spent long hours in the company of neighbors. This happened mainly when they looked after their young children, who were playing in the building's common yard for 2–4 hours, every afternoon. The women participated in these interactions very casually and seemed to consider them as a halfway arena between their private apartments and the local public space. Being the main shoppers, the women often discussed consumption-related issues. The following ethnography depicts these encounters in and around their buildings.

Consumption-related issues were prominent in the daily talks of RAG women. In the politically-charged Israeli claimate, local women consistently avoided any topic of a political nature or connotation. Also shunned were occupation-related issues that could have unveiled the differences between the participants (Birenbaum-Carmeli 1997). Consumption, in contradistinction, was often dwelled upon. In accordance with general bourgeois morality (Ossowska 1986), the neighbors praised rational, sophisticated consumerism, mainly under the banner of "good value." When presenting in public exceptional bargains they obtained, RAG women usually emphasized abstract principles, rather than particular preferences, thus bestowing a generalized relevance on their private consumer accomplishments. In a daily afternoon gathering in a public-housing's yard, a woman responded to a neighbor's compliment on her new pullover by saying: "It was such a bargain that I said to myself: 'you don't leave such a pullover in the store for this price'." On a different occasion a resident referred to a piece of furniture which her affluent friends had bought. "I don't know the price, but I know they bought it for half the price. Whatever it had to cost, they paid a half." Yet another neighbor, from a luxury building, explained how subscribing to a swimming pool would help her lose weight:

> If I subscribe, I'll go swimming at least twice a week, otherwise, I will feel like a sucker (*freierit*). So I'll have to diet because I'll be too embarrassed to put on a swimsuit if I don't.

In the yard of a newly built luxury house a resident told her neighbors about a dinner at an elegant restaurant, which was offered at a fixed price to her partner's company. In her account, she, too, emphasized the excellent deal they managed to obtain: "Obviously, we selected the courses by the price column. We hardly glanced at the dishes at all, because anyway we ordered the most expensive courses."

The logic of "best value" was also applied to justify one's readiness to pay high prices. In these contexts, residents emphasized the extended durability, which presumably rendered the expenditure economically rational. One well-to-do resident thus reasoned:

> Indeed, [the carpet] cost us a fortune. But we realized that since it's of such a high quality, it will never wear out. So at the end of the day, it will be less expensive than getting a cheap rug that we'll have to replace in several years.

Searching for approval and acclamation, the speakers presented matters that belonged in their private lives to local spectators who measured their own consumer choices vis-à-vis the celebrated performances. While the protagonists differed greatly in their economic abilities, all seemed equally receptive of the consumer principles implied in these stories.

Nevertheless, the realization of these principles – accommodative as they were – was still beyond the reach of some residents. Public-housing inhabitants, as well as financially constrained newcomers to the more luxurious buildings, were all keen to partake in the local discourse. I suggest that it was to this end that the residents devised a set of practices and rhetorical "escape ways," which were modes of rationalizing and legitimizing economic restraint without resorting to financial grounds.

Moratorium on house decoration. Residents' private spaces were highly visible in RAG. Children's arrivals and departures often resulted in open doors; parents came to fetch their children from casual visits to local friends; neighbors frequented one another without previous notice. Residents were, therefore, familiar with the looks of each other's homes, which they considered of great importance. While some local apartments were conspicuously decorated, others were modest to the point of poverty. By an apparently prominent local code, residents in the modest apartments, always and with no exception, felt they needed to provide an explanation for this situation. Shared by all was an account for the meager appearance in terms of an educational worldview, which prioritized the children's freedom to the house's looks. These residents claimed that they preferred plain furniture that could be used freely rather than restricting their children because of costly decoration. It was therefore quite common for people of relatively modest financial resources to say that they had decided to postpone the decoration of the living room until the children grew up. In the filicentered Israeli context, where children are placed center stage and where a tradition of relatively free child education predates the state, this reasoning was broadly acceptable. It provided a legitimate moratorium on a considerable expenditure, without calling forward financial limitations or small apartments that resulted in heavy use of the living room. At the same time, some speakers indeed seemed to hold such educational ideology. In fact, it was owing to the considerable authenticity of this educational outlook among Israeli middle-class parents, still in the early 1990s, that it could "pass" as an accepted and hence effective explanation. Thus, when one resident explained to a new neighbor that she and her partner decided to buy new living room furniture only after their children have matured, the latter burst into laughter, saying: "Everyone does the same. Everybody is waiting for the children to grow before they change the upholstery or buy a new carpet. Funny, how similar it is amongst all." Another resident, who was highly impressed with her neighbor's new flooring, commented: "It's breathtaking. The moment you walk in, it's 'Wow.' But we will have to wait until the twins grow. It's not fair to take away their freedom to play and have fun. After all, it's their home, too." Such statements were deemed not only acceptable but even evidence of parental devotion, of a readiness to suspend one's own gratification for the less materialist goal of providing one's children with a development-enhancing surrounding. In the context of RAG's physical proximity and visibility of one's apartment, such rationalizations were crucial to some residents' sense of integrity and local inclusion. This was evident in the few cases of residents who were stigmatized as neglecting the appearance of their dwellings (for example not keeping it clean enough by the local standards). Interestingly, the repudiation, too, was on educational grounds, with the local critics claiming that such surroundings were harmful to the children's well-being.

Teenagers' clothes. Another contested sphere of consumption was that of teenagers' clothing. RAG youths insisted on wearing costly brand-named items, which many parents condemned. This issue, which was – so the parents stated – a source of ongoing familial disputes, was also discussed among the neighbors. Throughout my fieldwork, local parents kept raising this issue as the most troubling aspect of residing in RAG. They unanimously attributed the children's desire to obtain brand-name items to peer influence, which they associated with the lavish character of the neighborhood. (An influence of children's neighborhoods of origin on their responses to goods was confirmed by Page and Ridgway 2001.)

While all local parents, beyond economic differences, shared the condemnation of the teenagers' craving, not a single resident mentioned financial limitations as the source of objection. Rather, many residents emphasized that principles rather than money were at stake: "It's not the money," "even if I were a millionaire, I wouldn't want him to spend so much on a pair of jeans." This line of criticism was often framed within an ideological preference of the functional equivalent. Some residents traced this preference to socialist persuasions, which they retained from their childhood experiences in left-wing youth movements that preached for asceticism and modesty.[9] (Some adult residents seemed quite gratified by presenting themselves as persons of ideological convictions or what they referred to as "principles.") Others repudiated the unconditional yearning for fashion as a symptom of deficient personal stance. This presumably anti-capitalist "enclave" also echoed a nostalgic language of socialism that some residents embraced when locating themselves within a wider national context. Again, without exploring its validity, in the neighborhood context, this local reading of bourgeois consumption was acceptable as it reverberated established – if somewhat nostalgic – views of Israel's socialist era. As such, it allowed less affluent residents to avoid some expenses without disclosing financial hardships. In a similar fashion to the postponement of home decoration, so the ideological objection to brand-name items meant continued social inclusion for residents who could not afford the local standard of consumption. It is worth noting, however, that whenever these resisting residents could obtain the desired items for lower prices (for example on sale or abroad), they made use of any such opportunity. This did not refute, however, their ideological claim as the reduced cost presumably moderated the problem.

Meticulousness. As mentioned, the appearance of one's home was a major issue in RAG and women in particular, as the persons in charge of this area, were scrutinized for their performances. Women thus invested many resources in this sphere. Bearing in mind the local ecology, the challenge of cleanliness is somewhat harder to sustain than it is in other settings, such as Western Europe. In the late 1980s and early 1990s, most RAG homes had no air conditioning at all, or very partial systems that usually covered a single room. Windows were therefore kept open nearly all year round. Dust, which always abounds in Israel, was particularly ample because of the construction work that took place around. It infiltrated each and every home in the neighborhood. Many local women therefore performed cleaning chores on a daily basis. In many families of limited financial means, women devised by-passes through which they could trade some of the pecuniary costs of cleaning for time, and do so in a locally acceptable way. The issue at stake was home cleaning, known to be of great significance, especially for lower-middle- and working-class women (see Skeggs 1995). In RAG, due to the high visibility of one's home, residents could not conceal the presumably private matter of the cleaner's identity. Cleaning thus became a morally charged, publicly discussed issue. Many RAG women had no paid domestic help and performed all housework on their own. In order to justify this practice without revealing economic stress, some of these women claimed that their standards of cleanliness were too high to be accomplished by a paid worker. In one neighbor gathering in a yard of a public-housing project, the participants realized that none of them was using paid domestic help. While they did not appear quite embarrassed, the neighbors seemed relieved to learn that they were all in a similar situation. Soon, a consensus developed around the claim that "No one cleans as I do," or "it's not the way I like things to be done." One resident elaborated: "I can't bear the idea of having someone invade my privacy. Besides, there is no chance that the work will satisfy me, so I'll have to do everything over by myself." On a different occasion another neighbor declared: "I am crazy. I know I am, but I can't help it. I have to clean the bathroom for at least an hour before I consider it clean." Notably, as soon as the speaker resumed her paid work (as a lawyer), she hired a domestic worker and gave up all household work right away. Once again, then, in the context of cleanliness, economic considerations were not mentioned. Rather, the residents flaunted high standards that could only be met by themselves. Once again, it was the authenticity of this approach that rendered it acceptable, thus sustaining the "beholder's" respectability in the neighborhood world.

In the Commercial Center

Beyond the semi-private space of one's apartment building, residents also wrestled with consumption at a more public level. The main sites of this endeavor were the conspicuous shopping malls that dominated the local landscape in the early 1990s, stretching wide open along the neighborhood's main streets. This facade was, to a large extent, a product of residents' politics of space, and as such represented their spatial vision (Purcell 2001), as enacted throughout two decades of local activism.

When RAG was first inhabited in the mid-1970s, it housed primarily public-housing residents. Commercial services were not yet operating and consumption was a necessity to be resolved. In the early 1990s, sitting in the luxurious apartments they had acquired, veteran residents used a nostalgic language of pioneering, commonly associated with pre-state Zionism, to describe that period. They depicted the very lack of facilities as the basis for their past tightly knitted "Urban Kibbutz," where women shared taxis to the shops, helped one another prepare festive meals, and babysat for a neighbor's children when she ran to the pharmacy in the nearby neighborhood.

Several years later, in the late 1970s, two small shopping strips opened in RAG. These elementary shops catered to basic needs (supermarket, pharmacy, stationery supplies) but did not become sites of social gathering. In 1983, when RAG's image as a prestigious neighborhood was consolidating, a larger commercial center opened, followed by yet another, more conspicuous one, inaugurated in 1989. The two new centers were located at the heart of RAG, widely open to the street, with a large plaza connecting the pavements to the window cases. The local street thus became a stage for humans and objects, parading and carnivalizing the neighborhood space. The new center was maintained by a commercial company, which took great care to secure its uniform meticulous appearance and indeed accomplished an unprecedented standard. The retailers supported this image by sophisticated window designs and high prices. The media enhanced it by depicting the new center as the most exclusive in the city or indeed the most luxurious countrywide.[10] The presence of chain stores in the heart of the neighborhood space was interpreted as a further evidence of RAG's exceptional social standing and generalized prestige, which was appreciated by national and international corporations as well. The residents took great pride in the new center and even in the high prices. It was at that point that they placed consumption – physically and discursively – at the center of local public life, as a major sphere of local action and interaction.

As elsewhere (see for example Fiske 1990; Lehtonen and Maenpaa 1997), many RAG residents used the new commercial center for various ends other than shopping. Judging by the way they dressed and walked, by the rarity of some residents' acquisitions and by the frequency of extended social interaction, it appeared that for many the center's plaza became the neighborhood's main public space. Unlike their casual yard meetings, "going to the center" was a more bounded event, for which many residents prepared and dressed up. While pedestrian zones are generally known to facilitate local interaction (Lund 2002), the immense appeal of the RAG center seemed also related to the upward mobility that quite a few residents were experiencing. As RAG was transforming into a prestigious neighborhood, some upwardly mobile residents shunned their parental and childhood models. Many viewed the consumer preferences and lifestyles of their parents – many of whom were immigrant from East Europe and North Africa – as unacceptable. Alongside the significance of rejecting these particular patterns, the need for alternative models was a pressing source of anxiety. (For the wider prevalence of these phenomena see Douglas and Isherwood 1979 and Miller 1987.) Consumption thus became a fragile public ground that residents treaded with great caution, trying to identify and consume these objects and styles, which they perceived as a basis for a more distinguished location among their neighbors. The conspicuous commercial center, its affluent facade, the national and international chain stores, sophisticated displays, and high prices, seemed to provide the required reassurance. The residents thus explored the merchandise in the window cases as guidelines for appropriate consumption.

Of equal importance were one's neighbors, encountered in this public space. Together with the neighborhood's prestige and its increasingly affluent populations, the significance of local counterparts as sources of approval and guidance was on a constant rise. Shoppers watched one another, ready to measure and be measured (Falk and Campbell 1997). Rather than a detached space for daydreaming and strolling aloof, RAG commercial center was a public arena of self-formation through the consumption of "commodities of distinction" (Bauman 1988). This process assumed additional significance in the context of local familiarity (Miller 1987: 40). In the bounded, aspiring community of RAG, shoppers encountered one another not as generalized models but as particular individuals, many of whom they knew in person. Appearances on this local stage thus became formative of one's local position, rendering access to the commercial centers a crucial matter.

Once again, the residents developed ways that rendered the centers accessible to all. First, much public activity in the commercial centers was free. Presenting oneself and inspecting one's counterparts in the passageways and entertaining one's children in the plaza were free of charge and abundantly used by the majority of RAG residents. In the long summer evenings, young families and teenage residents herded through the center's alleys and in the cafés. Also free were the public events, which shop owners organized as promotion campaigns. These events, which offered free child entertainment, were conducted in an opulent style that implied the sophisticated connoisseur nature of its audience. At the same time, it required no financial resources thus leveling richer and poorer under a collective banner of local prestige.

Equally accessible was the ability to assess service providers (such as pediatricians, the bank manager, the neighborhood officer[11]). Some residents publicized their right and ability to assess in the form of praise letters to senior officials or to the national press. While they conjured up a privileged social location, these letters did not require any formal qualifications or financial investment. As such, they comprised yet another discursive practice that tied together the more and the less affluent residents, constituting RAG as a bounded social entity of eminence and privilege.

More prevalent was the filing of amenities-related complaints. This channel of self-formation was met by the retailers' servility – a marked statewide exception for its time – which RAG retailers endorsed in order to survive the harsh local competition. Residents could thus afford to complain about a clerk who was chewing gum, to bargain over bank fees, to demand that a blood test be performed after the laboratory working hours, to ask to replace presumably stale almonds which the customer had chewed and spitted. A supermarket manager depicted the local clientele as "using their rights beyond reason. They think they deserve everything," and a bank manager summed up her description saying that: "Any derivative of the word 'spoil' would fit." The owner of an underwear shop bitterly summarized: "Every woman in this neighborhood demands to be treated like Princess Diana, but we learned to 'swallow' it, because we have no choice." Aware of this local exceptionality one resident concluded her account of a local dispute stating: "Nowhere else would they even consider a replacement, but here, they compensated us very generously."

The significance of self-positioning through exertion of consumer rights surfaced most clearly when the problem at stake affected other communities as well. According to local service providers, RAG customers were more demanding than any of their counterparts anywhere. A RAG's clerk was the only one to be officially reported to the bank's headquarters, on grounds of smoking shortly after a new anti-smoking law became effective. RAG's residents were the most active complainants over shortage of bread in the local supermarkets on Passover evening.[12] In the field of education, school-related complaints were just as record-breaking, so the head-teacher observed (Birenbaum-Carmeli 1999). In several cases residents carried the disputes to legal instances. Here again, the claim to authority did not entail financial investment and as such was accessible to every resident. It may be said that some RAG residents carried to an extreme a more general trait that has been attributed to Israeli middle classes in general. According to Herzog (1992), in the absence of liberal tradition, Israelis often understand individualism essentially in terms of realizing their own rights, while compromising the rights of others, to a point of egoism.

The assessment of service providers augmented a sense of distinct, coherent local code of consumption. The following account of the closing-down of a local Delicatessen shop was typical. Highly content, the resident explained that:

> at first, [the deli owners] were really great and everybody went there. The place was always packed. But then, both the products and the service deteriorated and people stopped going in, until they had to close down. I was so proud of the neighborhood, that we all understood what was going on and just stopped entering the shop.

Again, such public assertion of consumer privilege was accessible to every resident irrespective of economic or cultural capital. Any RAG resident who was attentive enough to the local talk-of-the-day could claim to deserve high-quality service, thus locating oneself within the desirable company.

Gradually, the center itself has become a commodity to be consumed. Importing its prestige from the neighborhood public sphere into their private lives, many residents saw the local center as an anchor of belonging. Residents of all financial standing celebrated it as their personal property, i.e., symbolically belonging to themselves, thus comprising a sign of relative inalienation (Miller 1987: 121). Residents looked at the commercial center as a mirror of their own selves, reflecting and constituting the social image they craved for. Such blurring of the private and the public reverberated in a resident's response to a friend's admiration of the center: "Well, little wonder it's so magnificent. After all, **I** live here. They built it for **me**, so they couldn't have possibly build anything less beautiful than this."

Using the center for shopping was, however, not as equally accessible. The high prices, which the residents cherished as a symbol of affluence, were unaffordable for many. When elegant boutiques first opened in the new center, their commercial failure was quickly evident. The closing-down of quite a few of these stores was, however, reconciled with the image of wealth by the claim that "people here all shop abroad." This incongruous situation was soon addressed by retailers who opened new stores of a different style. Among the exclusive boutiques, plain shops that offered functional daily items started to operate. However, the growing diversity, which corresponded to the demographic heterogeneity of the neighborhood, left the monolithic image of affluence intact. Owners of the simpler stores, who compromised the quality of their products, were nevertheless cautious to offer only strictly fashionable items (mostly clothing but also houseware and food) and maintained immaculate showcases, which matched the center's facade. The extreme success of these shops was soon emulated by many boutique owners who added to their exclusive collections some moderately priced items in order to draw more customers into the store.

Like the spatial integration of public housing and multi-million residences, so the shops were mashed. The center had no more and less exclusive sections as the shops were mixed throughout. A sophisticated clothes boutique neighbored a shop that offered marketplace clothing, and an exclusive childwear store bordered on a fruit and vegetable shop. The total mix allowed all local residents to use the conspicuous center without disclosing or generating a local hierarchy. Rather, the residents overlooked the diversity and generalized the image of affluence as the epitome of the neighborhood and of their own prestigious social standing.[13]

The marginalization of differences was also manifested at the stated level. In the local survey, three-quarters of the respondents agreed that "When you receive very good service, you should remain loyal to the provider." Over 80 percent agreed that "before any purchase is carried out, one should compare qualities and prices" and that "when purchasing a durable commodity, one should pay more in order to obtain a better-quality product." Not less than the emphasis on rational consumerism, the extent of the local consensus is of significance. Again, given their diverse socio-economic origin and current position, the similarity in residents' views seems to be – at least in part – a locally produced discourse of consumption.

In the Neighborhood Committee

The more established that RAG's image became, the more its individual residents viewed "the neighborhood" as a commodity to be consumed. Working within a clear vision of the local space, they attempted to reshape their surroundings so as to match the vision (Purcell 2001). In ways similar to those played out at the interpersonal and local public spheres, residents invoked through their spatial politics a bounded entity of distinction. The main vehicle of their operation was the neighborhood committee, which is the third sphere of neighborhood life I am looking at.

In the early 1990s, the neighborhood committee consisted of self-nominated RAG residents. Only a few members were involved regularly, while most activists participated on an ad hoc basis, mostly in order to tackle an issue that was a private concern of theirs. (For a similar focus on concerns of immediate space/time consequences, see Eliasoph 1998). The affected resident/s would approach one of the more active committee members and, after having their initiative informally approved,[14] would start operating as a neighborhood representative. This included using the committee's letterhead and presenting oneself as a member of the neighborhood committee. In some periods, activists operated in issue-specific subcommittees and conducted plenary meetings only seldom, as rituals of collective consumption of their class position.

The issues attended to by the committee varied. Some residents summoned the local affluence to demand comparatively luxurious services like additional gardening around their homes. Other activists demanded that "In one of the country's most exclusive neighborhoods, two parking spaces per apartment should be mandatory." Still others generalized the local aesthetic sensitivity through claiming that "Placing the waste bins at the entrance is probably convenient for the municipality workers but disagrees with the residents' aesthetic standards." Expressing their collective refinement and prestige through such demands, RAG residents were thereby also provided with an opportunity to boast political understanding and sophistication. Comments such as "Residents felt that the meetings were conducted for the sole purpose of distracting their minds and in order to gain time" allowed committee members to present themselves and their neighbors as politically savvy and non-manipulable. A similar claim was implied in the professional advice they offered to the authorities. The following excerpt from a letter to the Mayor of Tel Aviv and the Minister of Energy is but one illustration. Warning against a potential disaster lurking in the nearby oil terminal, three local lawyers indicated:

> We think that the following tests should be carried out and reported to the residents: a. does the terminal present a threat in case of leaking, explosion or terrorists' attack. b. To what extent are the security guidelines observed. c. To what extent is the municipality involved in the subject. We think that the retired General H., who headed the Haifa Gas Inspection Committee, should be consulted. It is crucial that the residents know that the municipality is taking care of this subject.

The personal interest that committee members had in the particular issues that they addressed may suggest that the neighborhood committee was not only a vehicle of effective campaigning but also a channel of legitimization. Activists seemed to rely on the neighborhood committee particularly when presenting themselves to officials as neighborhood delegates while tackling an essentially private problem. Thus, one member acted to divert air traffic from its route above his home. Another one campaigned against waste disposal in a lot that bordered on his own building. At another edge of the neighborhood, some residents wrestled with city and state authorities, aiming to obliterate an urban plan to build a cemetery at the neighborhood's boundaries.[15] A different case was that of a resident who owned a ticket agency in RAG. This private owner found out that his field was increasingly controlled by an evolving cartel. Using the committee's letterhead and his title as a member, the owner sent out formal letters to senior officials, claiming that given the high taxes they were paying, RAG residents were entitled to quality services within their community. He did not mention, however, his private financial interest.

A compelling illustration of the role of the neighborhood committee in the reshaping of private consumer interests as collective community pursuits was provided by a local activist. Explaining why she had signed a petition demanding that an acoustic barrier be erected between the neighborhood and the planned motorway, she said:

> To be honest, I couldn't care less. On the contrary – I definitely want a motorway nearby so I can get to work faster. What do I care if they suffer some noise? Let them suffocate on it! Yet, tomorrow I will have a problem and I, too, will want the whole neighborhood to back me up, so today I am signing their petition.

Contrary to older Israeli myths of mutual care and loyalty, the indifference that imbued the activist's statement suggests that rather than a sense of community, of sharing neighbors' concerns, some residents collaborated with their neighbors in order to secure future support of their own forthcoming causes.

In the light of ample such evidence, the neighborhood committee emerges as a legitimizatory "umbrella" through which residents reconfigured consumer activities – mostly aimed at promoting one's private interests – as community volunteer work. As in other spheres of the neighborhood's life, so in the context of its very consumption, participation was within the reach of all local residents. Any resident could volunteer, members were not required to make monetary investments, and each member equally carried the authority of a community representative. Indeed, the most prominent members in the neighborhood committee during the fieldwork years were a woman and a man (not related) of moderate economic standing who lived in public housing apartments. (Interestingly, both managed to convert their local public activism into employment. One obtained a new job as a state-representative community worker in the USA. The other translated contacts she had acquired though local activism into membership in the Tel Aviv city council.) The majority of the neighborhood activists were, however, relatively wealthy people whose cultural and economic capital matched the class position that they claimed for in their activism. Yet, their claims were for a collective class position, which was presumably applicable to the local population as a whole. Thus, when they acted on behalf of the neighborhood in meetings with officials, when they appeared on the national television and press, when they organized wide scale campaigning events (Birenbaum-Carmeli 2000), committee members constituted themselves as representing the whole neighborhood, which they portrayed as a cohesive social entity, operating consensually for the benefit of all its members.

The ethnography of the neighborhood committee needs to be complemented by considering those topics which its members chose to avoid. Owing to space limitations I will briefly consider two main absences: the Russian immigration and local security. These topics, both of which went beyond the local realm, differed greatly in their presence on the neighborhood agenda. The fieldwork period (1988–1991) covered the most intensive years of immigration from the Former Soviet Union, during which roughly 500,000 Jewish newcomers arrived in Israel. Weighed against a total population of some 5 million persons, the influx of immigrants was extremely intensive. In RAG, committee members repeatedly raised the subject, claiming that they were eager to support Russian immigrants. Time and again activists discussed various local public events that could be organized, such as a fundraising bazaar, a donation campaign of used clothing and toys, or concerted invitations of immigrants to the Passover *Seder*. Yet, none of these plans was materialized, during the entire fieldwork period, when the immigration was at its peak. The unrealized plans stood in sharp contrast to the members' activism and effectiveness when handling matters that were of private interest for them.

In contradistinction to the repeated reference to FSU immigrants, local security was never mentioned in committee meetings. Although the *Intifada* was at its height and although residents suffered some consequences in their own lives within RAG, no member has ever raised the subject. Activists referred to such issues only in personal exchanges, occasionally, when walking out of a meeting. One committee member revealed that he and his wife always accompanied their children, even within the neighborhood boundaries, for fear of the "Arab workers who fill the construction sites." A female member said she stopped using the supermarket delivery services because she was afraid to admit carriers to her home. Another member recounted rumors that workers intentionally blocked pipes in the luxury buildings they were constructing and wondered whether there was any truth to the story. On one occasion a member mentioned that the local civil guard planned to look for and expel Arab workers who stayed on site illegally overnight. The term he used (*Be'ur Kinim'*) carried the double meaning of removing nests as well as removing head lice. A discussion of the local attitude to national politics and to the Palestinian issue is beyond the scope of this chapter. I will therefore only suggest that the avoidance may be attributed to both the conflictive potential of the issue as well as to the members' readiness to compromise other people's rights. In any event, the constitution of the Palestinian issue as a non-issue, to be circumvented in local talk, is instructive.

Discussion

RAG's discourse of consumption needs to be located within its broader Israeli context. During the early 1990s, the collectivist elements that have historically imbued the Israeli ethos[16] have become largely nostalgic. Still, the language of collectivism has remained familiar and effective. The view of people as primarily parts of a larger whole, and the primacy of the group over the individual (Ezrahi 1998), though not as prominent, still echoed in kindergarten parties (Shamgar-Handelman and Handelman 1991), in schools (Katriel 1991), and in army units (Aran 1974; Lieblich 1989). In the early 1990s, many Israelis still exhibited high devotion to the national quest and sought closeness and community in interpersonal affiliations (Katriel 1991; Handelman and Katz 1990). At the same time, the sense of "social solidarity" has been greatly eroded, giving rise to present-orientated, self-centered individualism (Ram 1998; Herzog 1992).

Within this context, RAG's consumer discourse raises several questions. Why did the residents used a collectivist language of inclusion? Why were the less affluent residents ready to make the effort required in order to fit the local consumer standards? Why were the wealthier residents ready to marginalize/suspend intra-neighborhood differences? I suggest that at that time collectivist claims were an advantageous strategy, which benefited both local groups in terms of social and economic standing.

The use of a collective language in order to obtain public resources prevailed in the neighborhood since its inception. In the 1970s, the residents collectively demanded services equal to these of their affluent counterparts from nearby neighborhoods. In the 1980s, they flaunted the local socioeconomic diversity as exemplary residential integration and required such services that befitted a national showcase. When refused by the authorities, activists dwelled on the lurking internal gaps that would surface and destroy the neighborhood's life in the absence of the demanded public services (Birenbaum-Carmeli 2000: 32, 1999). Later on, when RAG became a symbol of affluence, activists used a collectivist language primarily in order to reinforce their demands. The road petition mentioned above was typical. At that point, collective appeals proved effective for drawing political and media support, which eventually advanced their consumer interests by improving services and raising property prices, from which all RAG residents benefited.

Within this quasi-collectivist system each group had its own consumer interests. Less affluent residents wished to be included in the neighborhood world. By devising "escape ways," by making extensive use of the local facilities and public spaces, and by accepting the consumer initiatives that more affluent residents put forward, less powerful residents tried to emulate the relatively monolithic lifestyle and agenda which their more powerful counterparts prescribed. This interest was apparently fairly consistent, as throughout my fieldwork I have never come across a local dispute that ran along class lines.[17] An understanding of this interest of less affluent residents to be included alongside – even co-opted or regulated by – their wealthier neighbors, may be suggested in terms of the benefits that a monolithic local image conferred onto them. Such an image meant that to external audiences any RAG resident, including less affluent ones, belonged to the undifferentiated prosperous entity which the name of RAG has come to designate. The generalized image soon translated into social prestige and property value, which soared throughout the neighborhood and included public-housing apartments as well. The steep rise in real-estate prices was the main reason for which many residents of modest means entitled their RAG apartment[18] "The lottery of my life." For some of these residents, who traded their state-subsidized apartments for spacious accommodations in other – less expensive yet "decent" – middle class neighborhoods, RAG's collective image of prestige represented an opportunity to class mobility. Those who remained in their small RAG apartments benefited from the public services and improvements that their affluent neighbors, as neighborhood representatives, managed to obtain from the authorities. Less material though of great importance was their neighborhood-based social image, which was more distinguished than that which they would have acquired on account of their own capital. In a long-run perspective, many less affluent residents viewed their residence in RAG as offering their children a chance for intergenerational class mobility.

As for the more affluent residents, when they arrived in RAG, in the early 1980s, their less affluent neighbors had already been living in the neighborhood for some five to seven years. Indeed, the predominance of public-housing projects was a main factor that shaped the relatively moderate prices in RAG during these years. The demographic heterogeneity was therefore beyond negotiation. Quite soon, however, since their proportion in the local population had increased, the wealthier residents took the lead on the neighborhood stage. With few exceptions, they were the ones who named problems and initiated local campaigns, who approached city and state officials and represented the neighborhood in the media. This transformation embodied the politics of hierarchy in RAG, where

> The authorized speech of status-generated competence, a powerful speech, which helps create what it says, is answered by the silence of an equally status-linked incompetence, which . . . leaves no choice but delegation – a misrecognized dispossession of the less competent by the more competent, of women by men, of the less educated by the more educated, of those "who do not know to speak" by those who "speak well." (Bourdieu 1984: 413–14)

Well aware that particular individuals rather than others consistently represented the neighborhood, the residents attributed this fact to the activists' caring and energetic temperament. No evidence suggested that the less powerful felt dispossessed. This "generosity" on the part of the wealthier population may be read as serving several purposes. First, it regulated the less affluent residents who had predated their wealthier neighbors in RAG. Taking on board their weaker counterparts served to curb that degree of heterogeneity that existed in the neighborhood when they arrived and helped accomplishing their own spatial vision of RAG. Secondly, wealthy activists occasionally summoned the local diversity as to frame their consumer pursuits as the collective "struggles"[19] of a socially mixed community. Obtaining their demands by means of this rhetoric also served to protect/raise their own quality of life and property value. Owing to the positive historical repercussions that collectivist claims still invoked among political and media functionaries in 1990 Israel, RAG "representatives" were more likely to gain sympathy and support. Indeed, officials who accepted the demands made by RAG's activists – some of whom were personal acquaintances of theirs – often justified their decisions by claiming that the neighborhood was a flagship of social integration. In some of these cases, the mixed-population argument seemed to serve both activists and officials as a fig leaf for privileging an established neighborhood.

The heterogeneity argument prevailed, however, during the mid-1980s, when RAG demographic composition was shifting and this rhetoric strategy could no longer obscure the consumer interests of the affluent claimants. From then on, residents based their entitlement to services on the high taxes they were paying. It may thus be seen as a transitory stage that residents eventually traded for a certain displacement of their less affluent neighbors. While certainly related to factors other than the wishes of their wealthy neighbors, the local presence of less affluent residents receded along the years. Some residents established themselves and moved to larger RAG apartments, while others left the neighborhood. Subsequent residents, who could afford the high local prices, were generally better-off. The wealthier residents thus gradually realized their spatial vision of RAG as a higher-middle-class neighborhood, housing affluent habitants.

The eventual displacement of less affluent residents may suggest the non-pluralist nature of the presumably inclusive discourse of consumption in RAG. The more numerous and powerful the wealthy residents became, the less they "admitted" their less affluent neighbors into their world. In the 1990s, all parties practically denied local diversity by assuming a language of affluent sameness (Birenbaum-Carmeli 1997) that conjured up similarity in lifestyle, consumption, and social location. RAG consumer discourse may therefore by seen as non-integrative at the symbolic level. Rather than recognizing diversity, residents made an effort to conceal internal variability. Rather than legitimizing social-economic differences between neighbors, they denied their very existence, thus symbolically refuting the feasibility of residential heterogeneity.

Epilogue: Ten Years Later

In the subsequent decade, RAG's prestige has augmented. Its public space has been upgraded by a retailers-initiated project that integrated the two main local malls (that opened during the 1980s) into a single complex. As it stands now, a large, lavish strip mall dominates the heart of the neighborhood, materializing the centrality of consumption for its residents. The collective consumption of the neighborhood is still orchestrated by the neighborhood committee, whose members now have to win their positions in local elections. Committee members and residents kept working for issues such as stopping freight trains' travel during the night or petitioning to remove cellular antennas from the roof of the commercial center.

RAGs image of affluence has also augmented during the decade. Israel's first soap opera series, launched in 1993, was entitled *RAG*. The series drew much public and media attention (and professionals' deprecation) and continued to be aired for years. The series depicted RAG as a home of the rich, an arena of financial and power intrigues. Although it bore but little resemblance to actual life in the neighborhood, many residents found the extravagant image flattering. For many Israelis, who have never been there, RAG became a symbol of wealth, if somewhat spoiled or corrupt. The choice of RAG as the presumed location and as the series' title is interesting, as RAG is clearly not the wealthiest neighborhood in Israel. In fact, several more opulent areas might have better adhered to the images invoked in the soap opera. The producers' preference of RAG may thus possibly suggest that unlike the richest areas, which were probably perceived as remote and beyond the reach of ordinary Israelis, RAG was viewed by many as the top of that which is high but still obtainable.

A similar position was conveyed by more recent media allusions to RAG. New residential projects were advertised in statewide newspapers as "Modi'in's [a new town] RAG" (March 14, 2000, Ma'ariv) or "RAG now has a young pretty sister" (June 23, 2000, Ha'aretz). Later on, with the outbreak of the *Al-Aqtsa Intifada*, hardline Minister Uzi Landau publicly condemned RAG as the home of "complacent elite groups whose only interest is in their coffee and croissant or wine with cheese" (May 29, 2001).[20]

My own follow-up neighborhood survey, conducted in early 2000,[21] also supports the congealment of local wealth. The residents, who grew older and parented more children, reported higher levels of education and earnings as well as larger apartments (see Table 3.1).[22] The changes may reflect the economic betterment of some residents as well as the departure of more public-housing dwellers who left RAG for larger accommodations outside. New residents were relatively well to do.

Table 3.1 Socio-demographic changes in RAG

	1990	*2000*
35–44 year olds (%)	39.32	24.38
45–54 year olds (%)	12.07	30.63
Average no. of children	2.12	2.34
Academically qualified residents (%)	44.75	53.31
Average apartment area (self-reported in sq. meters)	121.66	130.64
Average income or less (%)	35.2	23.2
Above average income (%)	34.2	35.2
Well above average income (%)	30.6	41.6

**Source*: Birenbaum-Carmeli, Neighborhood surveys, 1990; 2000.

Private consumption has also expanded. While the rise was part of the countrywide prosperity – or widening gaps – of the 1990s, RAG figures still exceeded the national equivalents (see Table 3.2 for illustrations).

Table 3.2 Ownership of durable goods and services (in percentages)

	1990	*2000*	*National average**
PC	81.11	91.44	38
Microwave oven	86.76	92.35	51
Tumble dryer	88.10	78.90	25
Television	100.00	100.00	90
2+ sets	45.60	73.70	
3+ sets	7.23	37.60	
Video camera	41.41	47.40	
Car	99.00	93.27	54
2+ car	36.45	51.68	
2+ Telephone lines	19.03	52.90	
Mobile phone	38.04	93.58	45 (1998)
2+ lines		59.94	
Paid domestic work	46.88	80.00	

* CBS and Center of Social and Economic Research, Tel Aviv municipality, July 2000; 1998 data.

Of particular interest is the drastic increase in employment of paid domestic workers. In the light of women's standpoints ten years earlier, the hiring of paid help in later years seems to support the understanding of previous presentations as "escape ways," aimed primarily at saving one's face in the neighborhood arena.

Local consumer services remained a main source of resident satisfaction. Among the last survey respondents, satisfaction of the local commercial facilities approached levels of 70–80 percent (Table 3.3).

Table 3.3 Residents who agreed with the following statements (percent)

	1990	*2000*
The local facilities are very convenient	69.91	77.16
The local facilities are of very high standard	61.32	69.38

Source: Birenbaum-Carmeli neighborhood survey.

These figures accord with the finding that the higher a neighborhood's prestige in Israel, the more positive the residents' responses (Schnell and Goldhaber 2001). As such the figures are also reflective of RAG's position as the third topmost neighborhood citywide (out of 60 neighborhoods: Tel Aviv Municipality 1999).

While retaining a prestigious image, RAG has nevertheless been "normalized" during the prosperous 1990s, when affluent areas mushroomed throughout Israel. Now part and parcel of a wider scene of comfort, the neighborhood lost some of the uniqueness it had claimed to possess. In the 2002 listing of the "country's best" in several consumer categories, published by Israel's popular newspaper (*Yedioth Aharonoth*, March 26, 2002), RAG was not mentioned. Newer shopping centers and sport clubs have apparently taken the lead. Yet, with houses selling for over a million US dollars (in April 2000, prior to the *Intifada*), RAG may be viewed as having blended into the established North Tel-Aviv area surrounding it. The neighborhood's new position and "mindset" can be illustrated by the opening of a second-hand clothes store in 2001. Sophisticatedly set and offering "top international designers'" clothes, the store became a success, sugggesting that some local women were now confident enough to purchase such items.[23] Having said that, the store is still located in the mall's parking lot.

References

Aran, G. (1974), "Parashooting," *American Journal of Sociology*, 80(1).

Baudrillard, J. (1975), *The Mirror of Production*, St. Louis, MO: Telos.

—— (1983), *Simulations*, New York: Semiotext(e).

Bauman, Z. (1988), "Sociology and post modernity," *Sociological Review*, 36: 790–813.

Ben-Rafael, E. and Sharot, S. (1991), *Ethnicity, Religion and Class in Israeli Society,* Cambridge: Cambridge University Press.

Birenbaum-Carmeli, D. (1997), "Sound Silence: Non-Issues and marginalization of differences in an Integrative Neighborhood in Israel," *Urban Anthropology*, 26: 133–63.

—— (1998), "Residential Integration and Its Constructed Reflection: An Israeli Case Study," *Visual Anthropology*, 11: 33–46.

—— (1999), "Parents Who Get What They Want: On the Empowerment of the Powerful," *Sociological Review,* 47(1): 62–90.

—— (2000), *Tel Aviv North: The making of a New Israeli Middle Class*, Jerusalem: Hebrew University Press (Hebrew).

Bourdieu, P. (1984), *Distintion: A Social Critique of the Judgement of Taste*, London: Routledge & Kegan Paul.

Central Bureau of Statistics (1990), *Monthly Price Review*, October.

Central Bureau of Statistics and Center of Social and Economic Research, Tel Aviv-Jaffa Municipality (2000), *Tel Aviv-Jaffa, Statistical*, no. 8 (Hebrew).

Douglas, M. and Isherwood, B. (1979), *The World of Goods: Towards an Anthropology of Consumption,* Harmondsworth: Penguin.

Eliasoph, N. (1998), *Avoiding Politics: How Americans Produce Apathy in Everyday Life*, Cambridge: Cambridge University Press.

Ezrahi, Y. (1998), *Rubber Bullets: Power and Conscience in Modern Israel*, New York: Farrar, Straus and Giroux.

Falk, P. and Campbell, C. (1997), "Introduction," in P. Falk and C. Campbell (eds), *The Shopping Experience*, London: Sage.

Fiske, J. (1990), *Reading the Popular*, Boston: Unwin Hyman.

Handelman, D. and Katz, E. (1990), *Models and Mirrors: Towards an Anthropology of Public Events*, Cambridge: Cambridge University Press.

Herzog, H. (1992), "The Individualist's Split Personality," *Politika*, 42–46: 48–9 (Hebrew).

Katriel, T. (1991), *Communal Webs: Communication and Culture in Contemporary Israel*, Albany: State University of New York Press.

Lehtonen, T. and Mäenpää, P. (1997), "Shopping in the East Centre Mall," in P. Falk and C. Campbell (eds), *The Shopping Experience*, London: Sage.

Levi, S., Levinson, H. and Katz, E. (1993), *Beliefs, Religious Observance and Social Relations among Jews in Israel*, Jerusalem: Guttman Institute (Hebrew).

Lieblich, A. (1989), *Transition to Adulthood during Military Service: The Israeli Case*, New York: State University of New York Press.

Lund, H. (2002), "Pedestrian Environments and Sense of Community," *Journal of Planning Education and Research*, 21(3): 301–12.

Miller, D. (1987), *Material Culture and Mass Consumption*, Oxford: Basil Blackwell.

Ossowska, M. (1986), *Bourgeois Morality*, London: Routledge & Kegan Paul.

Page, C. and Ridgway, N. (2001), "The Impact of Consumer Environments on Consumption Patterns of Children from Disparate Socioeconomic Backgrounds," *Journal of Consumer Marketing*, 18(1): 21–40.

Purcell, M. (2001), "Neighborhood Activism among Homeowners as a Politics of Space," *Professional Geographer*, 53(2): 178–94.

Ram, U. (1998), "Citizens, Consumers and Believers: The Israeli Public Sphere between Fundamentalism and Capitalism," *Israeli Studies* 3: 24–44.

Reisman, D. (1952), *The Lonely Crowd: A Study of the Changing American Character*, New Haven: Yale University Press.

Schnell, I. and Goldhaber, R. (2001), "The Social Structure of Tel-Aviv-Jaffa Neighborhoods," *Environment and Behavior*, 33(6): 765–95.

Shamgar-Handelman, L. and Handelman, D. (1991), "Celebrations of Bureaucracy: Birthday Parties in Israeli Kindergartens," *Ethnology*, 30(4): 293–312.

Shapira, Y. (1977), *Democracy in Israel*, Masada: Ramat-Gan (Hebrew).

Skeggs, B. (1995), "Women's Studies in Britain in the 1990s: Entitlement Cultures and Institutional Constraints," *Women's Studies International Forum*, 18(4): 475–85.

Slater, D. (1997), *Consumer Culture and Modernity*, Cambridge: Polity.

Tel Aviv Municipality, Center for Social and Economic Research (1999).

Veblen, T. (1953 [1899]), *The Theory of the Leisure Class*, New York: Mentor.

Yiftachel, O. (1997), "Israeli Society and Israeli-Palestinian Reconciliation: Ethnocracy and its Territorial Contradictions," *Middle East Journal*, 51: 1–16.

–4–

Tourism and Change in a Galilee Kibbutz: An Ethnography

Ronit Grossman

Kibbutz, Tourism Industry, Tourist Gaze

The late 1970s and 1980s were considered difficult periods for the Kibbutzim in Israel, pushing further an ongoing decline that had started years before. The rise of right-wing governments diminished governmental support and accelerated the deterioration of the Kibbutz's prestige. From the inside, second- and third-generation Kibbutz members were urging the lessening of collective constraints. Several scandalous intrigues and leadership failures had harmed the Kibbutz economy. The final stroke was the national financial crisis, the result of the government's deflationary policy, which crashed the Israeli stock exchange and, thus, the Kibbutzim's investment attempts. Many Kibbutzim now found themselves in deep financial trouble. With the loss of its national appeal and mounting debts, the Kibbutz as a way of life seemed to be waging a battle of little hope. Privatization, which had already swept the country, started to penetrate the Kibbutz, as well.

The appeal of Kibbutz tourism – i.e., of hosting and displaying itself to the world – became for the Kibbutz a strategy for facing both its economic and image crises. Kibbutzim developed a heritage industry that included pioneer settlement museums and archives. In some Kibbutzim, tourism developed further, to become a major source of employment. In Kibbutz Gvanim, tourism-related revenues yielded over 60 percent of the community's income in the late 1990s.

The discussion here deals with the relationship between tourism and the community from the perspective of the community's members. It describes members' efforts to institute Kibbutz tourism in such a manner that both its organization and its style of hospitality would reflect the main values of Kibbutz society. The ethnography looks at the first tourism workers – i.e., Kibbutz members, most of them women – who had to invent strategies to enhance their prestige, given their low status compared to that of production workers in general and agricultural workers in particular. The transformation that occurred in the Kibbutz's perceptions of work, largely shaped by Gvanim's tourist industry itself, as well as broaden labor-market transformations, ultimately made tourism an attractive branch of employment in comparison with other Kibbutz options. In Gvanim, the expansion of tourism during the 1990s went beyond "employment," as it led to a transformation of the entire Kibbutz space into a tourist arena. Tourism eventually became central to the construction of both a new Kibbutz identity and the communal organization in Gvanim. The Kibbutz members themselves invented an ironic nickname for it – "The Tourist Kibbutz."

My ethnography of Gvanim is based on local archive documents and fieldwork, conducted over a three-and-a-half-year period (1996–2000). As I was a member of the Kibbutz prior to and during the fieldwork period, this account is derived from my experience at different levels of participation.

"Kibbutz Hospitality": The Early Years

Unlike the Kibbutzim that turned to tourism only in the past decade, Kibbutz Gvanim has been engaged in tourism since the early 1960s. In the country at large, these were the years prior to the Six Day War, when Israel was struggling in terms of both its economy and security. The government, ruled by the Labor party, was at that time massively involved in the economy. Although no longer at its pre-State peak, the Kibbutz movement still enjoyed a high degree of governmental support, as well as high public prestige. Industry, which gradually became more important to the country's economy, was later adopted into the Kibbutz's economy, too.

Reading protocols of Gvanim's general assembly meetings in the 1960s reveals that Kibbutz Gvanim had difficulty establishing successful agricultural and manufacturing industries, such as those implemented at other Kibbutzim. Therefore, tourism – i.e. taking advantage of Gvanim's unique northern landscapes and introducing outsiders to a Kibbutz environment – seemed both reasonable and economically necessary.

In Kibbutz Gvanim, the entry into the tourism business tested the Kibbutz's underlying social principles and values and challenged those who upheld these values. The Kibbutz society considered productive work, especially agricultural work, sacred. Rhetorical efforts to adapt tourist-related tasks to Kibbutz life and ideology were notable in the early discussions of the tourism project. However, tourist-orientated employment was perceived as fundamentally opposed to Kibbutz values, which glorified "hard" work and physical labor, typical of the productive branches in those days. Members expressed their opposition to working in service branches and commercial areas, and tourist work was branded "easy work," therefore making it less status-worthy. Thus, for example, one Kibbutz member said: "Working in such a place isn't very hard. Someone who can't work in agriculture can work there; it's light work."[1]

In addition, members of the Kibbutz were concerned about the type of tourists they would attract. As long as tourism was going to be adopted as a branch of the Kibbutz industry, it should cater to the working-class tourist. As one member claimed: "We should develop the place as a hostel for tourist groups, summer-vacation camps, and hikers, and not for hosting rich tourists." Another member said, "We should establish a popular tourist enterprise for the working class." Another issue of concern was the location of the guesthouse, about 250 meters south of the Kibbutz residences. One of the members suggested planting a banana grove to separate the guest area from the Kibbutz.[2]

Finally the tourism idea was adopted. After a year of discussions at the general assembly meetings, the Kibbutz members decided to establish a guesthouse that would employ Kibbutz members only. At the cornerstone-laying ceremony, members buried a scroll containing the guesthouse's founding principles:

> *Founding Declaration for the Guesthouse*
>
> *Today, the 28th of November, 1962, we hereby intern this scroll in the cornerstone of the "Sea View" Guesthouse for tourists and hikers from near and far. The social and cultural atmosphere of this building shall be Israeli and appropriate to the Kibbutz movement. We strive to propagate a familiarity with and love of both the Galilee and the Kibbutz way of life among many, and thus create friends and supporters for our country. This project will broaden our economic base and serve as a place of employment and a source of livelihood for our members. The Galilee, an ancient name, famous among nations, reminds us of the prosperity of the distant past known to this region, and the recent blossoming of its barren lands brought about by the Kibbutz settlements. May this project grow and prosper!*
>
> *The undersigned,*
> *Members of Kibbutz Gvanim*[3]

The declaration by the Kibbutz members testifies to their efforts to combine the tourism business with Kibbutz life. The objectives characterized the project as a Zionist-educational enterprise. A nationalistic significance was added, as the Kibbutz-tourist encounter became a means of making friends and creating alliances "for our country." The guesthouse's possible economic contribution to the Kibbutz was mentioned only after presenting these national and educational objectives.

The guesthouse was opened in the summer of 1963, and its first guests were Kibbutz members. Impressions of the celebration dinner prepared by the guest-house employees for the members of the Kibbutz were summarized by one Kibbutz member in the following manner: ". . . And everyone thought to himself, if only we had such meals and such service in our dining room 365 days a year."[4] This comparison between the guesthouse services and those supplied to Kibbutz members accompanied the early manifestations of Kibbutz tourism. It occasionally also came up in other contexts at that time, and later it became more explicit.

Beginning in the 1960s, the Kibbutzim allocated many resources to raising their standard of living, partly to improve the Kibbutz image in the eyes of its own members and partly to present the Kibbutz as offering a quality of life and social relationships that surpassed those available outside. In Gvanim, the physical presence of the guesthouse alongside the Kibbutz sharpened aspirations for a higher standard of living. To the great regret of the tourism workers, some of the members perceived the guesthouse as an alternative site for spending leisure time. At the time, the Kibbutz lacked a clubhouse for its members. According to an account from that period given by an employee in the guesthouse's cafeteria, "The cafeteria has become the main attraction for Kibbutz members, which bothers the cafeteria workers, obliges them to serve Kibbutz members, and severely disturbs the guests."[5] The Kibbutz member in charge of maintenance complained that Kibbutz members repeatedly cut flowers from the guesthouse gardens to decorate their own homes.

The attraction of the guesthouse as a recreation center for some Kibbutz members did not transform it, however, into a preferred workplace. Most Kibbutz members refrained from working in the tourism branch. In the eyes of the general Kibbutz membership, certain aspects of working in tourism marred its appeal, making it difficult to recruit workers in that field. Kibbutz members who worked in the guesthouse indicated that its distance from the Kibbutz courtyard was a marked disadvantage. Apparently, their feelings did not stem only from the 250 meters that separated the guesthouse from the periphery of the Kibbutz residences. Working in shifts, which is typical in the tourist industry, was noted by these members as the central cause for their feelings of social isolation. Feelings of social isolation were also based on their impression that no matter how hard they worked or how much they contributed to the community, the tourism staff wouldn't be appreciated by the rest of the Kibbutz membership, because of the definition of tourism as "easy work."

Nevertheless, there were those who were passionate about the enterprise and enabled the establishment of a permanent Kibbutz staff to work at the guesthouse. The economic success of the guesthouse was a source of pride for the staff. The guests, unlike the early vision, were not "working-class" or Kibbutz members, but middle-class Israelis and many foreign visitors and tourists. However, staff members attested to their love of the tourism world and emphasized the efforts invested in their enterprise. Thus for example, one of the members wrote the following in the Kibbutz newsletter:

> Sometimes it seems that because I don't have the opportunity to see the world – the world comes to me. Tourists come from different countries, different types of people with different languages and dress. It's interesting. I don't mind staying on another hour or returning to work whenever necessary. There has always been voluntary service work

> at the Kibbutz. I remember, when I first began working at the guesthouse, I felt a resistance within me at the fact of having to serve guests. Today I think that the tourism awareness should be prevalent among all Kibbutz members and not just the tourism staff. We are a Kibbutz guesthouse and the guests should feel the uniqueness of the way we live.[6]

The difficulty in recruiting Kibbutz members, especially for the hotel's kitchen work and housekeeping, led to the permanent employment of hired workers. In this way, one of the central Kibbutz values was marred, as was the Kibbutz-like character of the guesthouse. Employing hired workers created a distinction between Kibbutz members, who staffed positions that involved direct contact with tourists – for instance at the reception desk, the souvenir store, and the dining room – and those who filled low-paying, low-status jobs, like room cleaning and maintenance. Most of the "behind the scene" jobs were filled by women from a nearby Arab village. Yet, from the tourists' viewpoint, the facade of the Kibbutz character remained intact.

"Monkeys in a Cage"

In the 1990s, the Gvanim tourist branch was expanded to increase existing business and develop new initiatives. In addition to the renovation, expansion, and upgrading of the guesthouse to hotel status, there were two highly significant undertakings that directly influenced the membership and Kibbutz life. The first was the conversion of empty children's houses, which were located in close proximity to Kibbutz residences, into rooms to let for bed-and-breakfast facilities. The second was the opening of the Kibbutz dining room to the public, enabling visitors to dine with Kibbutz members.

The Gvanim dining room, like dining halls in other Kibbutzim, was the center of social life, where the concept of Kibbutz togetherness was realized. Its central location was a concrete reflection of its role in the community. The dining hall was where the Kibbutz general assembly gathered and where holiday celebrations were held. In 1996, because of the Kibbutz's economic difficulties, as well as arguments about mismanagement and food waste in the dining hall, the general assembly made a decision to privatize the food budget. Rather than gathering for meals financed by the common budget, Kibbutz members were given magnetic cards. A cash register was placed in the dining room to register and bill each meal to the member's personal budget (to avoid the use of money within Kibbutz confines). In addition, it now became possible to purchase packaged meals to eat at home. Most members preferred this possibility, especially on Friday nights and holidays.

The manner in which members utilized the dining hall during a period of economic and social crisis reflected their relationship to the Kibbutz. The preference of many members to eat at home expressed a trend toward seclusion and a negation of the very essence of the dining room as a place for social encounters. With the increased development in tourism and the decreased significance of members' presence in the dining room, a decision was made to open the dining room to the bed-and-breakfast visitors.

At first, the presence of tourists in the dining room was sparse and random. Later, in 1998, the dining room and the tourist connection became more established. (I myself worked in the dining hall at that time.) The entrance of groups of tourists into the dining room disturbed the habits of the senior Kibbutz members. For example, an old-timer was left helpless for a moment when a party of tourists occupied "his table" of twenty years. The dining area reserved for the tourists faced the Sea of Galilee, a location that Kibbutz members also considered attractive. Moreover, different food was served to tourists, which required the differentiation of resources and much maneuvering on the part of the kitchen staff. In some instances, tourists would be fed after 2:00 p.m. when members had already left the dining hall. When dining hours overlapped because of the arrival of tourist groups, the "stations" serving Kibbutz members were abandoned or delegated to temporary workers (like myself), leaving the permanent staff to concentrate fully on serving the tourists. On days requiring the preparation of meals for both tourists and Kibbutz members, the quality of the members' meals suffered, and resources were largely designated for the preparation of the tourists' meal. In one instance, the manager of the kitchen told me: "The poor members, today we're serving chicken cutlets (*schnitzl*) to the tourists and the Kibbutz members get only hot dogs."

The tourists usually arrived in one group and sat in the area designated by the dining room staff. All interactions occurred between the tourists and the dining-room staff, and not directly with other Kibbutz members; however, it should not be concluded that life on the Kibbutz was not of interest to the visitors. One question frequently asked by tourists was if the food they were served was also served to the Kibbutz members. This question related to the "authenticity" of the hospitality. Some, not satisfied with just asking, paused to observe me serving food to Kibbutz members.

The division of the dining room into "tourist" and "Kibbutz member" sections was further materialized with the decision to put up a wooden fence between them. This demarcation of the "tourist section" was primarily a solution for the dining-room staff, which repeatedly had to deal with several Kibbutz members who persistently chose to sit in the tourist-designated section. The Kibbutz members didn't take this lightly. An older member, who always refused to work in the tourist branch, described to me her feelings regarding the presence of tourists in the Kibbutz thus: "I am really mean to tourists. When they walk by my house, I wait for them to pass before I go out. I am truly ashamed when groups of tourists arrive in the dining room. The food is terrible, and they stand on the side listening to the guide explaining to them about our meals – as if we were monkeys." When the fence was erected, this member said to me: "You see? Now we really are monkeys in a cage; we sit here and they look at us from the other side of the fence."

The division of space into "tourist section" and "Kibbutz section" facilitated the dining-room staff's work. It could not, however, entirely eliminate confrontations with the Kibbutz members. For example, one Friday night, no empty tables remained in the member area, so a woman Kibbutz member sat with her family in the tourist section. When the dining-room manager asked her to move to the membership area, she shouted at the manager: "There is no available space. If you continue this behavior, members will stop coming to the dining room entirely." In another instance, Kibbutz members waiting in line for their meal were told that "there were no more main courses." At the same time, they looked over at the meals being served to the tourists, and one member said: "Why do you say that there is no more food? I see that food is being served to the tourists." The dining room manager replied: "We have no choice. That is what was promised them, and we must fulfill our obligations. The tourists get preferential treatment because they support the place [Gvanim]." The exchange was followed by an open display of anger directed toward the staff. One member said angrily that he no longer intended to frequent the dining room.

While the behavior of the dining-room staff was accounted for, in this last incident, in terms of the continuity of the Kibbutz – clarifying that it was the tourists who subsidized the members' meals – the member's threats to boycott the dining room, in addition to displaying insult, implied a real change in perception. The dining room and members' relationship with the dining-room staff were redefined in terms of customers and service providers.

In all my observations, the dining-room confrontations transpired without tourist involvement. The confrontations were between the staff and a small number of members who used the dining room, mainly on Friday nights, apparently as a demonstrative expression of their right to do so, since they did not choose to have all their meals there. The use of the dining room changed so extensively during this period that members frequenting the dining room on a regular basis were perceived as "lacking alternatives."

The Tourism Kibbutz

In the early 1990s, the country was again under a Labor government. The peace process carried new promises. The economic situation, at least in the short run, was beginning to improve, as Gvanim's tourism-based income increased. The growth and an increase in its rational organization made the tourism branch separate in this respect from the rest of the Kibbutz economy. Managers of the tourism venture demanded administrative autonomy. Moreover, employees in the tourism branch often complained openly that their work was hard and that they were "supporting the Kibbutz." One of the more senior hotel workers told me: "I'm sick and tired of supporting members who don't work." The hotel manager, a Kibbutz member, said: "I feel that service work is so demanding; you give more and more hours, more than a member doing any other work."

Later on, from the mid-1990s, the Kibbutz's economic situation became more difficult. Not unlike many other Kibbutzim, Gvanim could not cope with its enormous debts, which constantly had to be renegotiated with the banks and the government. Gvanim's crisis was specifically aggravated by the significant decrease in the volume of international tourists to Israel that began to take place from 1996.

Members were forced to make decisions that brought on radical changes in their lifestyle. Following the pressures exerted by influential Kibbutz members, professional advice was sought from an outside organizational consultant (as was done at many other Kibbutzim) – at a high price. A revision plan, drawn up and dubbed the "Breadwinning Model" (*model hitparnessut*), was put forward – and bitterly resented by many. The plan included cutbacks in the parameters that defined Kibbutz partnership. Several domains of collective consumption were to be completely eliminated. Rather than *avoda* (labor), as a calling that had been the anchor in the Kibbutz's Zionist-Socialist ethos, the leading concept in the new plan was "breadwinning" (*parnassa)*, which measured Kibbutz work tasks in terms of wages and rentability. Redefining the mutual agreement between the individual and the community, the new plan determined that "the member is responsible for his/her breadwinning" and suggested "differential wages,"[7] thus constituting an extreme break from the Kibbutz's basic principle of Equality.

In the period of transition, when Kibbutz institutions had ceased to function and the "Breadwinning Model" had not yet been implemented, the emergent differentiation among members was based on an individual's earning abilities. The leaders of the revision plan decided that members' wages would be determined according to what was considered appropriate in the various sectors of the Israeli economy. It became clear that many of those working in the Kibbutz's service areas would receive minimum wages and that, owing to the trend toward cutting back on personnel in non-productive branches, these jobs were not secure.

Not so for workers in the tourism branch. Their workplace had a special status. As the spatial and social borders that separated the Kibbutz from the tourism areas became less evident, the realm of tourism became gradually more central and necessary to Kibbutz life. Whereas at the initial stages exposure to the outside world was considered unfavorable, ultimately it was the increased organizational and economic separation from the community that enabled the tourist branch in Gvanim to become an embodiment of the new, imported paradigm. During the formulation of the "Breadwinning Model," both members who favored the plan as well as external consultants easily demonstrated the direction of change necessary, by repeatedly referring to the tourist branch as an example. When one Kibbutz member, an agriculture worker, wondered how these changes would affect this branch, he was told: "Agriculture will be administered exactly like tourism, as a private, for-profit industry that is separate from the community."[8]

As for their personal lot, the tourist workers in Gvanim felt, during that time, very fortunate. Their workplace, important to the Kibbutz, was finally acknowledged as such and, at least for the time being, secure. The kitchen and dining-room staff had been able to anticipate the coming change (which explains their aforementioned adherence to the Kibbutz' interests when facing members' complaints). The managers of the tourism branch were expecting to be adequately remunerated for their senior positions. The distance from Kibbutz life, so troublesome in the early decades, turned into an advantage in face of the social crises that accompanied the economic one. A reception clerk told me: "I'm cut off from what is happening on the Kibbutz. Each morning I dress up nicely, ride my bicycle to the hotel, and in a matter of moments I'm in another world."

As the community tried to embrace the overall productive and cooperative reorganization of the "business" model, tourism workers, particularly the hotel workers and managers, became the target of the others' jealousy. One Kibbutz woman who had worked for many years in the Kibbutz kitchen, shared her feelings regarding the tourist workers and the revisions: "They were smart to remain working at the hotel all these years . . . Today they are managers without studying anything. And what are we? All these years we worked in a kitchen that is falling apart . . . and we hear only that there's no money – no money. We prepare meals for weddings that are as good as the hotel food, but I will never be paid a salary of a chef. I'll get nothing!"

In Kibbutz Gvanim, the " Breadwinning Model" (like similar plans in other Kibbutzim) seemed to portend another, greater threat to Kibbutz collectivity. This was the potential partition and selling of Kibbutz communal property. In this respect, the hotel was perceived during the transition process not only as an attractive and envied workplace but among the major assets that could be sold to outside parties, thus providing for members' future. The gradual separation of the hotel and its workers from the community was threatening and have been looked at with suspicion in this respect. Having invested a lifetime of Kibbutz work, some veterans were particularly upset. One of the older members said at a Kibbutz general assembly: "we created this asset through 60 years of work." (By "this asset" he meant the whole material capital of the Kibbutz – including the hotel – which was now painfully reduced to a mere commodity.) "This property," he continued, "should be ours to bequeath. It must remain ours." Opposite the old man were the hired consultants who were leading the revision plan. They represented a rational economic and pragmatic view, pressing for the general reorganization plan. They too referred to the hotel as a symbol of security, a life preserver. "If you don't change things now, it will be the end of it all. The banks will soon come and take your hotel from you!"[9]

Endnote

As initiators of the tourist development, the Kibbutz members showed marked confidence in their ability to create a "Kibbutz Tourism" that would be compatible with the Kibbutz character. Moreover, in planning to integrate tourism among their economic branches, the members pedantically separated the tourist area from the "real" Kibbutz, by dividing the physical space and creating a "tourist bubble" distinct from the Kibbutz area. With this bubble, members of Gvanim intended to protect their Kibbutz community life, to ensure the continuation of the "socialist bubble" in a country that was abandoning these values.

However, in the context of a transforming society that included the Kibbutz, the existence of the hotel alongside the Kibbutz became a basis of comparison from the day the "guesthouse" was founded. Physically close but initially socially distant, the distinctions between "Kibbutz" and "tourism" eroded, both in terms of the physical as well as the cultural and organizational aspects. Eventually, as this account has shown, the hotel and its world would overcome the Kibbutz. By the time I discontinued the collection of data, it was not clear what future the Kibbutz has in this different world.

–5–

The Ultraorthodox Flaneur: Toward the Pleasure Principle. Consuming Time and Space in the Contemporary *Haredi*[1] Population of Jerusalem

Tamar El-Or and *Eran Neria*

> Around 1840 it was briefly fashionable to take turtles for a walk in the arcades. The flaneurs liked to have the turtles set the pace for them. If they had had their way, progress would have been obliged to accommodate itself to this pace. (Benjamin 1970: 197)

It is little wonder this endnote by W. Benjamin from his essay "On some motifs in Baudelaire" is frequently cited. The image is one of turtles as pets, and elegant Parisians strolling behind the icon of slow movement under fashionable arcades. The symbolism captures a brief moment, a critical point in time: on one side the flaneur, the hero behind the turtle, and on the other side the heroine, "progress'. He is trying to hang onto an urban experience of pleasure, of "fun pour fun," while "progress' has other things on her mind – crowds to get through, carriages to take across town and time to be well managed. Benjamin closes his endnote by citing Taylor`s watchword, "Down with dawdling," which ultimately carried the day.

The privilege of flaneurism was not solely dependent on the era. Moving around the new metropolis, exploring the space with one's own moving body, was class- and gender-dependent as well (Wolff 1995). Benjamin's take on that brief moment sought to close the distance between him and Baudelaire, the subject of his essay, and to reconstruct the different experiences of the urban poet in mid-nineteenth-century Paris. Benjamin was actually trying to understand the same questions a century later, when "progress" had turned into "modernity" and the independent flaneur was lost in the crowd of consumers.

The bourgeois male flaneurs were not the only ones to be trampled by progress. This chapter tells about a community for which progress was the ultimate threat as well as the main driving force – ultraorthodox urban Jews.

The pre-progress moment allowed resistance to what modernity eventually did to the crowds and to the flaneur. Benjamin closes his essay with Beaudelaire's realization of the transient nature of that resistance: ". . . he envisaged the day on which even the lost women, the outcasts, would be ready to advocate a well ordered life, condemn libertinism and reject everything except money" (Benjamin 1970: 193).

The subjects of this chapter did not resist money in order to maintain libertinism. But, like the "lost women" and the "outcasts," they rejected the culture of luxury and abundance in order to differentiate themselves from the crowds – in this case the Jewish crowds who for the first time in history were experiencing life in an open cultural market. Consumerism, the ultraorthodox say, is the fourth in a series of trials visited upon the Jewish people in recent history. The first was the enlightenment, which was perceived as a spiritual disaster; it allowed the Jews to become citizens of European cultures and nations, offered different knowledges, and invited border crossing. Then came the Holocaust, a physical trial, unveiling, according to the ultraorthodox historiography, the falsehood of the enlightenment and brutally reducing the number of Jews even further. Zionism is the national disaster that offers yet another false dream of rescue and revival. The current disaster, the trial of luxury/consumerism, is, according to a leader of the community, "no less of a threat. It looks innocent, and it is aimed toward a much weaker generation than the previous ones" (Hertzman 1985: 22).

Let us begin with the end of the story, the fourth trial. It appears that one of the last urban communities to resist the culture of consumerism is about to give in. They were never really out of the game, they were just against turning it into a fetish and enjoying it, knowing that once they did it would be very difficult to remain on the threshold. The ethnography of this chapter follows ultraorthodox women, families, and men as they cross the line and join the crowds in the malls, the city center, the parks, the zoo, restaurants, and fast-food stands. It describes the ways in which they explore their own city of Jerusalem, which during the last 20 years has become increasingly orthodox. This trend invites examination of the options for flaneurism in its twentieth-twenty-first-century version, enabling us to reconsider the relations between urban/modern experiences, consumerism, movements of the transit body, and exploration of one's own city within a specific cultural context.

The analysis of these changes rearranges the city borders and thus the urban rhythm of Jerusalem 2000. Furthermore, it might offer new understandings of contemporary orthodox/secular experiences in mixed urban zones.

Before delving into these explorations, let us look at the city of Jerusalem in relation to its ultraorthodox inhabitants.

Exile at Home, or at Home in Jerusalem

> . . . the analysis of the metropolis as the focal point of the circulation of commodities and individuals also concentrates upon the sphere of circulation, exchange and consumption. (Frisby 1997: 21)

Jerusalem is Israel's largest city, in both population and size.[2] At the end of 1998 the non-Jewish population in greater Jerusalem was 180,900 (30 percent), and the Jewish population was 421,200 (70 percent), of which 126,100 (30 percent) were ultraorthodox (*haredi*). The total land area is 126,000 dunams.[3] Jerusalem has 85 percent more people than Tel Aviv (Israeli Central Bureau of Statistics), Israel's other metropolis, and 241 percent more area (Choshen 1998: 5).

During the 1990s the population of Jerusalem decreased by about 7.5 percent: most of the people who left the city were young (25–40 years old) and non-*haredi*, and 25 percent of them were new immigrants (mostly secular) who settled first in Jerusalem and then decided to leave (Choshen 1998). The number of ultraorthodox Jews leaving Jerusalem has also been on the rise, although it is still lower than that of the other Jewish sectors. They leave mainly for more homogeneous ultraorthodox communities such as Betar Elit, Bnei Brak, and Telshe Stone, where housing is cheaper (a reason cited by all sectors for leaving the city).

Due to this process, the *haredi* hegemony in Jerusalem is solidifying and the city's appeal to the secular Jewish population is waning. While the *haredi* population comprises only 30 percent of the Jewish population, four out of seven deputy mayors are ultraorthodox and one is orthodox. The word on the street is that Jerusalem has gone completely *haredi*. The gap between the numbers and the feelings appears to stem from a two-step process: the enlarging orthodox sector of the city translates into a growing feeling on the part of the orthodox that the city is home for them. This notion of home encourages the ultraorthodox to change their habitus and traffic in the city, making them more publicly visible. The result is the feeling that Jerusalem is all *haredi*. Somewhere between the actual numbers and the feelings, the ultraorthodox community is changing its way of city life.

The change was not foreseen by researchers, who pointed to a process of "growth with segregation"[4] (Shilhav 1993). But, the reality is that more and more ultraorthodox people are crossing the lines drawn by researchers in the late 1980s and early 1990s, in activities connected with consumerism and leisure.

Spending time and money and exploring new territories is organized and performed according to social parameters (class, race, gender, etc.). The study of leisure from Veblen to Marxist criticism to feminist scholars reads consumerism and leisure as actions of reproduction. These works strive to unmask the "true motivation" for consumerism and leisure: namely, the stability of capitalism and patriarchy. What seems to be a fun, private, free-will activity is a well-managed act of reaffirming a social order.

Benjamin's approach to both consumerism and leisure is different. It starts with the flaneur, the person on the street, and moves to the cultural system, leaving room along the way for subversion and change (Rojek 1997). Benjamin does not disregard social stratification and neither will we, especially since the ultraorthodox community is generally poor. The family poverty rate in Jerusalem is 8.3 percent higher than the national average (http://www.btl.gov.il, 1999), and is concentrated mainly in the *haredi* and Arab communities. The fact that men tend to stay at *yeshivot* and avoid steady jobs, plus the large number of children per family, both create this poverty and are the impetus for change. The heroes of this chapter who stroll the city malls, parks, and urban centers are signifying both the cry for change, and the change itself.

Before we go into the ethnography of how they do it, we will look at where they can do it.

Prior to the mall era, Jerusalem had three urban centers located about a kilometer apart. These centers served three different communities of the city: Arabs, the general Jewish population, and the ultraorthodox.[5] Before the tremendous population growth of the 1970s and 1980s and the construction of new *haredi* neighborhoods, the *haredi* congregation utilized mainly the northern center in Geula and frequented the other two centers only minimally.

Until the recent construction of Ramat Shlomo, the Jerusalem city planners designed neighborhoods without taking into consideration the needs of the ultraorthodox (Choshen 1998: 39). Thus, the *haredim* were forced to leave their neighborhoods for commercial and recreational facilities as well as public services. Some of the places they went to are the locus of our flanerie and observation. We both (T.E.-O. and E.N.) observed in these places sporadically during different hours of the day in August and September 2000, and revisited them on the holidays of Succoth and Hanukkah in October and December that same year. During those periods, especially the *ben hazmanim* period in August, yeshiva students and teachers are on holiday from school and are expected to spend time with their families in recreational activities.

Our research protocol required that we first explore the city and note the areas in which ultraorthodox people spend time and money. The ethnography describing those explorations has been categorized, edited, and divided.

Malls: You've Seen One, You Haven't Seen Them All

Center One

Center One is situated at the entrance to Jerusalem[6] adjacent to the central bus station.[7] The mall is very accessible, especially to the northwestern *haredi* neighborhoods surrounding it. Center One was built in 1986 as a mini mall, the first of its kind in the city, and subsequently changed its character from secular to more *haredi*: television sets were removed from shops windows and cinemas were closed. The management, realizing that gearing the place to the standards of the *haredim* would diminish its economic feasibility, created a balance between the "spending-time-and-money" mall atmosphere and the *haredi* prohibitions. The center of the mall houses a coffee shop with tables on a raised platform encircled by a shish-kebab restaurant, a Chinese restaurant, a pizza counter, and an ice-cream kiosk. All restaurants are Glatt[8] kosher. The food court fosters practices uncommon in the *haredi* community: men and women mixing in public to spend time and money and enjoy themselves. The coffee shop anchoring one end of the new habitus has couples, families, singles, friends, sitting high up, visible, on a stage, drinking cappucino, eating stir-fried vegetables, engaged in intimate coffee-shop conversations or family birthday celebrations. The pizza/ice-cream stands bordering the other end offer cheaper fast food that can be taken out or eaten at tables near the entrance to the mall and on the central raised platform. Scattered around the food court are toy stores, clothing stores, an optician, souvenir shops – all tailored to the new consumers. Dresses are long, prices are low, the optician is orthodox, and the new Internet café promises a safe surf on the Web. A store on the second floor converted into a synagogue offers services throughout the day, and a *netala* (a place for ritual hand washing).

Another part of the same complex located nearer the central bus station is called The Station Center and has a different, more secular character. It sees more working people from the nearby office buildings and passers-by on their way to and from the central bus station.

Rav Shefa

In the middle of the new northern neighborhoods of the city, an area populated exclusively by ultraorthodox, a courageous entrepreneur built the world's first *haredi* mall. The idea was both appealing and high-risk. Now almost three years later, the mall, whose advertising is directed exclusively to the *haredi* population, has failed to take off. On the face of it, all the elements for success seemed to be in place. The new apartments surrounding it belong to the more well-heeled people of the community, and it is no more than two kilometers from the traditional ultraorthodox neighborhoods. The economic venture appears to be enlightened by cultural sensitivity: "I am the Lord your healer" reads a large inscription on the wall of the pharmacy, photos of rabbis cover the window of the photo shop, and the hairdresser-wig shop window is shielded by a shade to hide the ladies inside. The men's and women's bathrooms are on different levels and each has a *netala*. The supermarket is part of the inexpensive ultraorthodox chain Shefa Mehadrin. All the fast-food restaurants are Glatt Kosher, and while none invite people to sit around, many find chairs and do. No coffee shop was permitted. Despite this cultural sensitivity, most of the stores are vacant; some open for a few hours in the afternoon; others have been rented as office space. Rumor has it the owners are looking to sell.

Malcha

Malcha mall opened its doors in 1993, the Jerusalem branch of Israel's most successful chain of malls belonging to the Canadian-Jewish Azrieli family. It is located at the southern end of the inner-city highway and is easily reached by car from most parts of town. The rectangular three-storey building affords easy access to a mixture of standard mall stores. The food court on the first floor and the several cafés on the other levels offer standard mall fare. Malcha differs from the other Azrieli malls in its fairly large number of ultraorthodox visitors and the Glatt Kosher signs on most of the restaurants.

A Tour

The tour described here is a synthesis of several visits to the different malls. Starting from the south end at Malcha, going north to Rav Shefa, the tour moves from the secular mall to the mixed mall to the designated ultraorthodox mall. It follows in the footsteps of the ultraorthodox flaneurs as they navigate the post-modern mall.

Eran writes: I am wondering whether I should take my notebook with me. While it's the 24th of August, still the *ben hazmanim* period, why would *haredim* come to this place? It's far from any of their neighborhoods, and is known to be a standard mall with movie theaters, large fashion stores, book and music stores, a video game arcade, and the like. I left my notebook in the car and realized my mistake as soon as I reached the entrance. *Haredim* do come to Malcha. Every seventh table is occupied by *haredim*. A couple with a baby stroller sit at the Chinese restaurant; he is tightening the safety strap across the baby's tummy while she is reciting her after-meal blessing from a small prayer book. Three teenagers, a couple with two children and another couple with three children are all sitting near the hamburger stand. Two elderly women from the Sephardic *haredi*[9] community eat falafel. Two fathers speaking English to several children occupy tables in the center of the court. A young couple, his side locks hanging loose and her hair uncovered,[10] have run into another young couple and they decide to sit down together by the hamburger stand. A security guard told me to go to café Neeman-Coros: "It's full of Dosim."[11] And indeed it is. A third of the tables are occupied by ultraorthodox people. Their presence dwindles as I stroll through the corridors. Glimpses into the big fashion stores, Tower Records, and Apropos Café turn up no *haredim*. Children congregate around the main stage, waiting for a show put on by three actors to begin. I spot only two ultraorthodox families in that crowd, and an occasional ultraorthodox parent peeping through the crowd to see what's happening on the stage and then moving away. Gradually I realize that most of the *haredim* strolling the mall are with babies or very small children. One gets the impression they see Malcha mall as a decent enough place for adults but not for older children. I look for the synagogue and find it near the mall offices. The rather fancy room with wooden doors and stained-glass windows bears the name of the mall owner`s father. The chairs are laid out in rows like in a cinema. To get into it you have to ask for the key at the security desk. The woman guard tells me there is no *miynan* (the minimum of 10 worshippers required to hold a public service), that only individuals ask for permission to enter in order to say the prayers required four times a day.[12] Most of the *haredim* in Malcha are dressed in the *Mitnagdim*[13] tradition, very few as Hassidim, and some, mostly those speaking English or French, dress in modern orthodox attire. As I leave the mall, I notice a Hassidic man speaking Yiddish to six small children. They are standing in front of a photo shop advertising the Hebrew new year's calendar decorated with personal photos. Another teenager reads a secular newspaper that is not available in *haredi* shops. I look at my watch. It's time to head north to Center One mall for my appointment with the manager.

Seven minutes on the freeway, a left turn toward the hotels, a right, and straight ahead in the direction of "Exit from town". Jerusalem is the only city I know that has signs all over town pointing the way to Tel Aviv. The mall is full. I run upstairs to the manager`s office. I enter through a small room with a table, a computer, a printer, and an empty chair. Further on, Yoav welcomes me with a big smile but asks me to come back in half an hour because he is busy. I stand on the gallery upstairs and look down. I remember Tamar's first description of the place. She was shocked:

> You wouldn't believe it, ultraorthodox people sitting in a cafe like people anywhere, couples, families, enjoying themselves, ordering from young waitresses wearing pants, drinking cappuccino, eating zucchini quiche and three-layer chocolate cakes. Dates are taking place there between adults 35 and up, maybe divorcees. There are family parties, family get-togethers that include orthodox, traditional, and nonobservant members in the same group.

I look for the groups and individuals she mentioned and count. It is 7:15 p.m. Twenty tables in the central café are occupied. It looks like a place for dates for couples 25 and older, and families. There are no young children. People tend to spend a long time around the tables. I walk down the stairs and stroll around, hearing Hebrew, English, Spanish, French (several times I even heard Yiddish[14] in the café). There are two groups of two couples each; one group of five *Mizrahi* women, three who look orthodox and two who do not. (One is wearing a tight sleeveless shirt.) A big noisy party that appears to be some kind of celebration combines National Orthodox[15] with ultraorthodox, Hebrew with English. They have pulled several tables together and the young ones (those aged 18–25) are at one end and their elders at the other. I notice four Hassidic men with their long coats and characteristic hats. They're eating pasta. Nearby at a smaller table another couple of Hassidic men are eating pasta. They take no notice of each other. All six eat with concentration, drinking cappuccino, and by the time my half hour is up they're gone. There are some nonorthodox tourists (maybe from the nearby hotel), a mother and a daughter, both orthodox, a grandmother with what appears to be her granddaughter of about 25. There are more women than men, as in any café. People are still coming in as I head back upstairs. An elegant couple (looking *Mizrahi),* he in a fine suit, she wearing a long black dress and a beautifully coiffed wig. Another couple speaks English; he has a black yarmulka, a dark suit and a yellow tie, and she is wearing a monochromatic well-cut suit.

"Come in," Yoav says, "sit down." He wears a colorful yarmulka and smokes a cigar. " You can't assume that the visitors to this mall are *haredim,* Even when you see white shirts and black head covers, it doesn't mean they didn't go to the army."[16] When I press him a little he divides the crowds into daytime and nighttime visitors:

> During the day we get all kinds of people, at night I admit it turns *haredi*. It started with boys who left their *yeshivot* and were looking for a place to hang out, and youngsters who came from the US and Europe to study in the *yeshivot* for a year – they have no family here and are accustomed to going out. It's no longer a terrible thing for someone to tell you, "I saw your son at Center One." But when they say, "I saw him in Malcha mall," that's a different story. Youngsters are not supposed to hang out in Malcha. On the other hand, look at the Rav Shefa mall. It's closing down. Why? Because its for *haredim*, targeted to *haredim*. No fun there, no café, no restaurants, just fast food and take out. At the same time, their buying capacity is poor. You can't make money only from *haredim*, you have to have a mix. I won't put an ad in a *haredi* newspaper because it will look bad and cost a lot. But I can spend a pittance and print pashkevills[17] and thousands will come. I've proved it more than once. They don't think of this place as *haredi*, but feel comfortable enough here with *haredim*.

It's almost two hours after I left Yoav's office. The place is still noisy, stores are closed, and the fast-food section is almost empty, but the café still has some thirty orthodox and ultraorthodox people. Tomorrow evening I will visit the *haredi* Rav Shefa mall to check out Yoav's theory, imaging it will be at its best at this time of the year (*ben hazmanim*).

Approaching the Rav Shefa mall entrance the next day around 6 p.m., I maneuver my way through the pack of children racing around, waiting to get into the park of inflated toys. Entrance to this area of oversized inflated trampolines of different shapes and colors is cheap. Exhausted-looking mothers stand nearby supervising their children, others are looked after by older sisters. The "park" is actually a neglected unfinished wing of the mall. The "park" and the poor level of maintenance stand in sharp contrast to the fancier, better maintained, fully constructed center section of the mall. Loud popular Hassidic music fills the air around the "park" and pours out into the streets. There is no background music in the central part of the mall, and the loudspeaker is used only to call people for a *minyan*.

Entering the mall itself, one is met by a hectic vision of Jacob's Ladder. The escalator is treated as a slide and is packed with children trying to run in the opposite direction or running in circles around it. At one point it stopped working and a mother approached the security man: "Can you operate the escalator . . . the children have never ridden on one and would like to experience it." His irritated warning about children who required medical attention as a result of misusing the escalator, and a sign prohibiting usage without an adult, go unheeded. The people seem to see the mall as "home," a place where they can behave as they wish. The absence of food courts and other public areas to hang out or relax in is partially compensated for by plastic chairs scattered around the fast-food shops in the empty corridors and in the main hall.

The hordes of mothers and children in the afternoon hours begin to disappear as evening falls. More men and families are seen, but the number of couples, young people, and singles remains low. Parents leisurely push strollers as their many young children flock around them, making their way down the mall corridors. They practice window-shopping with no windows to look at and hardly any open shops to enter. They demonstrate consumption culture almost without consuming, except at the fast-food shops on the periphery. Around 9 p.m. most of the second floor is vacant, the "park" is closed, and gradually the place empties out until the mall closes at 10:30 p.m.

Throughout the entire afternoon and evening, I can count the number of secular visitors on one hand. Even the *haredi* visitors here look more devout: Yiddish replaces English as the second language, and most of the women's kerchiefs are tied tight around their heads in the stern Hassidic tradition. Of all the sites I have visited for this research, this is the place I feel most alienated. My feelings are shared by the manager, who sends his security man to inquire about my presence in the mall. Ironically, I find myself on common ground with the guy, whose yarmulke is only part of the uniform.

The economic slump was reaffirmed when I set off to purchase a pen. Looking for a place to buy one, I was struck by the number of empty shops. Almost two-thirds of the shops are vacant. The first one I entered had half-price sales because it was moving to Malchi Israel Street. While I am still searching for a pen, a saleslady, crocheting to keep busy, tells me: "There is a shop but it's probably closed because there are no customers, although sometimes it opens for a few hours." When I ask her, "How's business?" she continues, "Let's say no shops here take in more than 6000 shekels a week, and everybody wants to close down." Another worker told me that the builder wants to close the mall but reached an agreement with the shopkeepers to stay open for another three months. The shop selling the pen was, indeed, open with all the merchandise stacked on tables in the corridor under a big sign – *Clearance.*

Up and Down the Streets

Midrachov *Ben Yehuda*

The *Lonely Planet* guidebook tells tourists that Ben-Yehuda Street is located in the center of the city and is considered "the secular heart of Jerusalem."[18] The north end is bordered by Jaffa Road, which divides the ultraorthodox neighborhoods from the inner city. For years researchers considered it a barrier, but following the footsteps of the ultraorthodox flaneur reveals a different story.

The cool summer evenings of Jerusalem compensate locals and tourists[19] for the hot hours till sunset. Hundreds of people from most segments of the Jerusalem population leisurely stroll the *midrachov*. What an easy place for observation, what a classic place to walk after the walkers, to gaze at those who gaze. Walking decisively is difficult; the *midrachov* acquires its own unhurried pace by the strolling masses. Throw a casual glance at the shop windows, watch the beggars and street performers, or take a seat at one of the tables. Be seen and watch the passing parade. The eyes are looking now for *haredim*. Most of those who come here are either Sephardic-*Mizrahi* youth, or non-Hebrew-speaking lads and young couples. The former sit mainly in cheap sandwich bars where some night-shift workers also come looking for conversation. The orthodox youngsters come slovenly dressed, as if they've just come from a hard day's work, but all of them wear a white buttoned shirt. Fashion does play a role, however, and they sport the requisite cellular phone hanging on the belt, a good haircut, and for those who wear them, eyeglasses with thin metal frames. Ultraorthodox American youngsters stroll in groups of three and five. One guy comes up to me, his white shirt half pulled out of his pants. He mistakes me for one of them, but I am still surprised that he addresses me (a secular person) and I chalk it up to his not being a local. His friends wear baseball caps and seem to be enjoying the freedom from the supervising eyes of their parents across the ocean. It is rare for an ultraorthodox person to approach a secular one; when it does occur it is the non-Hebrew-speaking *haredi*, who is more open to secular people than the Hebrew-speaking *haredi.*

The young normative-looking couples tend to stop at the few Glatt kosher cafés and pizza bars in a specific part of the *midrachov.* Some go to the more up-scale Café Rimon. A completely different *haredi* group in that public sphere is the Braslaws.[20] On proselytizing forays to recruit secular Jews to their stream of Judaism, they occasionally put up a booth and hand out pamphlets and stickers, often to the accompaniment of free-style jump dancing to loud Hassidic music. All this fits with their concept of worshipping God with joy, and goes very nicely with the new-age spirit. They attract the attention of passers-by, who look at them as if they are weirdoes or local Hari Krishnas. At 11:30 p.m. the *midrahov* activity is slowing down, there are fewer people on the streets, and fewer still are sitting in the restaurants. The action moves to the nearby night club/pubs/bars area, leaving the ultraorthodox behind.

Malchi Israel Street

Eran meets me at Center One mall and we drive four minutes to Moishe's home near the Rav Shefa mall. Moishe is a friend of my husband and a Karliner Hassid.[21] It is quite cold out, a typical December afternoon in Jerusalem. We arranged to start at 4 p.m. to leave us enough time before lighting the Hanukkah candles.[22] Eran and I are appropriately dressed for a stroll through the ultraorthodox urban center, although my hair is not covered.

The section from between Rokach Square and Yossef Ben Mattityahu Street has no stores and therefore fewer strollers. The rest of the street to Shabbath Circle[23] and into Mea Shaarim Street is crowded. The biggest, most important *yeshivot* in Jerusalem line this street: the Sephardic Port Yossef Yeshiva; the Gur Hassidic Sfat Emet Yeshiva; Haii Olam, the Satmer and Mir centers; and close by in the Bucharian neighborhood, the huge new Yeshivat Or Haaim (Sephardic and mainly for people who become religious) is rising.

"Compared to Friday, it's quite empty today," says Moishe, as we try to pick our way along the narrow crowded sidewalk. "You call this empty?" I say. "Yes, on Friday everyone rushes to do last-minute shopping. There are long lines at every food store, people are buying stuff they used to make at home, like *chale (*Sabbath bread), cakes and cookies, different kinds of salads, and even gefilte fish and chopped liver.[24] Look at this store," he points across the street at some ordinary-looking shop with no special window or sign. "They're the best, their food is so good they broke the tradition of eating only homemade. They aren't expensive, they're clean, let's cross the street and go in." We follow Moishe`s zigzag trail from the delicatessen to a bakery that makes the best Hanukkah donuts, to the popular store for teenagers. The store looks like any other of its kind, with birthday cards, stuffed animals, perfumed candles, little dolls. The aisle is blocked by a baby stroller. The women behind the cash register are speaking English. One wears a wig, the other a hat that exposes some of her hair on her forehead. "Come, come to Gal Paz before they close." Moishe hurries us up, but he meets a friend and we stop. I imagine a regular member of the community must meet several acquaintances walking down this street. Moishe has lived in Israel for only 20 years, and has this afternoon already met four people he knows. One of them sitting in an ambulance[25] called Moishe's cell phone to get him to look where he is waiting at a traffic light. Near Gal Paz, the music store, he meets a good friend, born in the USA, a musician whose stage name is Zuki. Inside the store he shows us several CDs of Zuki & Ding – mainly songs for children. "He's a real artist. It's not easy to be one around here, but he found his way and now he's quite famous, especially among the English-speaking families."

I pay special attention to the shoe and clothing stores to see what's in. It seems one woman's shoe style catches on, becomes "kosher," and appears in abundance in every store. This winter it's a combination of leather and elastic. Scattered along the short strip are three modern-looking pharmacies, photo shops that offer photocopying, and a fancy Judaica store next door to an old-fashioned religious-articles shop.

At one end of Sabbath Circle before reaching Mea Shaarim Street, I look back for a long view of the busiest *haredi* Street in Jerusalem. No one is walking slowly. Each and every person gives the impression of being on the way to somewhere. They know where they're heading, what they're up to, and why they're there. Even groups of teenage girls, who look like any other bunch of girls walking down a city street, are hurrying. Inside the stores it's a little different, especially the music store where people take their time and look around and flip through the CDs, moving up and down the racks of Hassidic, Mizrahi, Cantorial music, songs for children, to the video section and the toy department. Entering the heart of the ultraorthodox section of *Mea Shaarim*, the fast-forward accelerates. People almost run through the alleys. Evening falls, the stores close down, there are candles to be lit. Moishe is going into a Stolin (a Hassidic sect) *yeshiva* to pick up his 11-year-old son Pinchas and take him home with us. As we walk north, we notice people lighting candles in public, in accordance with the custom of "publicizing the miracle of Hanukkah." Pinhas tells me about something they discussed in Talmud that day. It deals with a man who led his camel down the road overloaded with flax. The flax caught fire from a Hanukkah candle on the street. Who should pay for the damage? The candle lighter who performed a good deed but did not watch his fire, or the camel owner who overloaded his animal. Moishe enjoys his son's presentation of the issue and says: "My father never liked 'ostentatious' actions (demonstrative actions done for the sake of the gentiles), and I follow his example."

Fresh Air

Sacher Park

Sacher Park is one and a half square kilometers of grassy meadows situated in the middle of town and easily accessible by foot.[26] The park has the usual Western features: sports facilities, joggers, dogs with their owners, and during Sabbath and holidays it attracts barbecue fans. In August, and especially during *ben hazmanim*, the character of the park changes. To quote one of the regular nonorthodox visitors, "The park turns black."[27]

Going there to observe, I first noticed the high percentage of *haredim*. This surprised me and made me wonder whether I was not used to seeing them there or they had recently begun to frequent the park.

Apart from the sports courts,[28] seculars constitute about one-third of the park's population in August, most of them singles, couples or teams, and very few families. There are fewer secular than *haredim* families. Nevertheless, the predominant feel of the park is secular. Maybe it's the setting. Rising on the hills above is the postmodern building of the Supreme Court, standing across from the Knesset (the Israeli Parliament), and way across the valley are the secular neighborhoods of the city. In the park itself, walkers and joggers still appear on August nights in their tight skimpy attire, teams practice on the central mound, and dog owners continue to walk their pets for lack of an alternative.[29]

The open space seems to tolerate its different visitors, and *haredi* teenagers play soccer next to a women's rugby team in shorts.[30] An ultraorthodox father teaches his daughter to ride a bicycle on the joggers' lane, another father and his sons toss around a ball that sometimes finds its way to a dog's mouth. Women relax on blankets and tend to the food. No one is moving to more remote parts of the park. At least half the ultraorthodox come to the park in groups: older sisters with siblings, groups of mothers with children, youngsters in small groups, and entire families numbering maybe a dozen members. Most eat light dinners, enjoy the evening breeze, and don't bother barbecuing. Around 10 p.m. the *ben hazmanim* visitors depart till the next evening.

Biblical Zoo

The Jerusalem Biblical Zoo opened its gates in 1950 on the northernmost part of the city where a new *haredi* neighborhood now stands. In 1993 the zoo moved to the southern end of the city to a recreation area that includes a football stadium, Malcha mall, and Ein Yael Park. The area, which is not within walking distance of any neighborhood, is easily reached via a new inner-city freeway.

Sprawling over beautifully landscaped grounds, the zoo breeds and shows animals that are mentioned in the Bible. Biblical texts accompany the names and descriptions of the different animals. The paths and a small train take visitors through the grounds, around an artificial lake, a picnic area, and a playground, criss-crossing the natural canyon and its gently sloping walls. During the holidays the zoo offers special activities and lectures beyond the usual explanations and feeding demonstrations given by the staff.

The zoo is a major attraction for the ultraorthodox community, for whom animals and pets are beyond everyday reach. The weight of their massive presence among the visitors is kept in check by several adjustments. A description referring to Darwin's theory was removed at their request, an unwritten agreement was reached with the zoo not to advertise in the *haredi* newspapers, the mini-train "observes Sabbath," even though ultraorthodox are absent on this sacred day, and *netala* sites are available near every kiosk although the level of kashrut is not Glatt. There is no synagogue, and open-air services are a common sight during the summer.

"During *ben hazmanim*, holidays, and even Friday afternoons and other summer days, almost half our visitors are *haredim*," says Sigalit, the zoo's public relation person. "They visit the entire park with no restrictions, You may see fewer of them in the souvenir store because of their financial situation. Having already spent so much on the entrance fee for the whole family, they might buy less at the kiosk and bring food from home and have a picnic. But, other than that they take full advantage of all the facilities." Eran is a little suspicious. He follows a family to see whether they'll stop at the petting corner where children are allowed to touch the animals. Some do, some watch, some move away. The man who gives the feeding demo near the mountain goats acknowledges his audience and lingers on the Halachic characteristics of the goats, which will or will not make them kosher. When the demonstration is over a father summarizes the lesson to his son: "The shofar [the horn blown at rituals] is made from its horn." The zoo is a popular site for young couples who "take walks" as part of their courtship. Fathers taking care of their children might come to the zoo to pass the time. And *haredi* tourists are taking pictures near the lake.

The zoo was not crowded on this chilly Hanukkah morning. I (Tamar) was sitting near the small animal pavilion watching the passers-by. The gardens had a soothing effect. I was attracted by a group of eight girls on their own. The one in charge was about 14, another one helping her was 12, and the rest ranged from a baby in a stroller to a 10-year-old. They had just finished eating and the older girl starts reading the blessing after meals. She can't stop but turns around and bends down so the other girls can see her lips and repeat or follow. Some of them cooperate, others don't. "Esther, we better run or we'll miss the train," says one of the girls. Then she feels uneasy and says one line of the blessing. "It`s already been said," a girl tells her with a serious look. The "bad" girl pushes the "good" one and they start chasing each other. "I don't allow fighting," says Esther, when she is done blessing, "Hannela and Hinda, come back here immediately." Eventually the red-cheeked girls return. Esther bends down to Hinda and says, "You give me too much trouble, come hold the stroller." Near the swan lake I notice a young Hassidic woman with a baby in a stroller. Quite odd, I think to myself, for a woman to come here on her own. I stick around to hear her cell phone ring and her reply in Yiddish:

"*Yo Eich been yeitz do*" (Yes, I am already here). Relieved that she is waiting for someone, I look for the exit. When I leave the grounds people are still parking cars and walking in, and taxis keep pulling up and discharging ultraorthodox, most of whom do not own cars.

Time, Money, Space and Affiliation

> We here encounter a paradox. For though money may represent social labor time, the rise of the money form transforms and shapes the meaning of time in important and specific ways. (Harvey 1985: 170)

The meaning of time is defined in capitalism by its scarcity and usefulness. The common definition is that time=money. Any deviation from this set of meanings reshapes the significance of time (and money) and the community that redefines it. Ultraorthodox people distinguish between two different time cycles: the sacred and the secular. The latter is the time for work, for production and money-making. Via this time, the ultraorthodox community cooperates with capitalism, unites with the world "labor time," and embraces the value system of the contemporary economy. At the same time, this time cycle is never formally approved or positively described. Compliance to capitalistic time is morally presented as a by-the-way action, a constraint, never a chosen or preferred act. The ideal time cycle is the sacred one, the time devoted to the study of Torah. Free from the capitalistic ethos, and dysfunctional in terms of production, it offers an alternative to the taken-for-granted money/social order. The secular community dismantles the division between the two cycles. It sees sacred time as wasted time, and reads the "alternative" order as a cynical exploitation of the working communities. The ability to adhere to sacred time as the real time, and to minimize the power of secular time, depends on . . . money. "It takes money to construct any alternative to the society predicated on the community of money" (Harvey 1985: 185). While the ultraorthodox community in Israel is supported by the state and by its members who do work, the conflict over the social/moral alternative it offers to the capitalist view of time and money might change drastically if more and more people join the "mob," the work force.

The growth of participation in the culture of capitalism, beyond the labor itself, will determine whether or not the ultraorthodox can stand outside the morals (not the praxis) of modernity and capitalism. The ability to refuse those morals is the ability to stay away from the contemporary culture of leisure and consumerism. For the time being, the ultraorthodox walk on their designated public sphere in fast-forward mode. Whenever they expose themselves to others, they make sure to convey a special perception of time – I am in a hurry, I am not spending time. Be it a teenaged girl on an errand to the grocery store, or a man on Malchi Israel Street, everything is done in fast-forward, as if secular time is hallowed by using less of it. Thus, changes in the consumption of time are strongly connected to the space in which it is used and the social affiliation to that space.

> The crowd – no subject was more entitled to the attention of nineteenth century writers. (Benjamin 1970: 166)

> The boundary is not a spatial fact with sociological consequences, but a sociological fact that forms itself spatially (Simmel 1997: 141)

Space and Belonging – or Being in Place

The choice to read contemporary ultraorthodoxy through nineteenth/twentieth-century scholars might look as though we are relegating the ultraorthodox to an earlier time in history, confronting old issues. Indeed, the opposite is the case: the ultraorthodox are completely here in the early twenty-first century, but, rather than taking modernity for granted, they reflect upon it as some of the nineteenth/early twentieth-century scholars_did. Juxtaposing Simmel and Benjamin with a contemporary community that is about to join a major symbolic experience of modern life offers the opportunity for an interesting exercise.

In the rich sociological harvest left us by both Benjamin and Simmel, a matrix is offered that can enlighten the phenomenon under study here. The first dimension of the matrix is *space* and the second is *affiliation*. Rather than reread Benjamin or Simmel, or cover the vast discourse they generated, we will make modest use of their lasting understandings of modernity.

Walking in the city, claims De Certeau, is a speech act. "Walking affirms, suspects, tries out, transpasses, respects, etc., the trajectories it speaks" (De Certeau 1984: p. 99). To walk the city is to say something about oneself and about the city via one's interaction with others, people and objects alike. Choosing a certain path, walking this way instead of that, picking a tempo, regarding/disregarding the scene are outcomes of active decisions. They are part of the make-up of the personal agent who negotiates modern conditions. De Certeau's analysis of these negotiations is a postmodern one, but it echoes the micro–macro analysis that underlies Simmel's modernist understanding of the individual and the metropolis.

The intensity of interactions is at its peak in the metropolis. There, Simmel claims, more than in any other modern site, individuals experience modernity. The quantity of interactions and the variety and richness of stimuli offered by hyper-cities are presented in contradiction to the country-life habitus where one is not confronted with new events every morning. The city-dweller, according to Simmel, develops a "blasé" attitude in order to survive, a kind of individual shield to cover oneself while walking through the city.

As much as one's mode and pace on the sidewalk reconstruct the meaning of one's being in the city, Simmel knows that these are set by and beyond the individual's experience. As a sociologist, he is interested in the supra-individual and in the community. Simmel counts four "qualities" of the spatial form upon which the "structuring of communal life relies" (Simmel 1997: 130): (1) the exclusivity of space; (2) its division into units by borders; (3) the capacity to fix contents to a certain space, and (4) proximity and/or distance in creating (virtual) spaces.

Let's take the city of Jerusalem. Simmel talks about Jerusalem when he looks for a pivotal point that fixes and contains a certain content. He mentions the temple in Jerusalem as the only site for the ritual of sacrifice, a ritual that ceased to exist once the city was destroyed. The destruction of the temple rearranged the relations between space and community for the Jews. The Diaspora was made up of numerous communities, centered around their institutions. Each community offered intense interactions to those in close proximity, while the relations between the communities created an ethnic-holy space beyond distance (Simmel 1997: 150, 157–8). The city of Jerusalem waited. Some waited (and still do) for the Messiah to come before they could build the temple and renew the sacrifice; others got tired of waiting and came to Palestine without him. Several of them built The Hebrew University in 1925 at Mt. Scopus. At a certain point they waited for W. Benjamin to come, but he did not.[31] It's hard to imagine what he would have thought of Jerusalem, but one can try to extrapolate, from his description of Rome, the chances for fun flaneurism in the town of Jerusalem. ". . . in Rome even dreaming is forced to move along streets that are too well-paved. And isn't the city too full of temples, enclosed squares, and national shrines to be able to enter undivided into dreams of passers-by, along with every paving stone, every shop sign, every flight of steps, and every gateway? The great reminiscences, the historical *frissons*, these are all so much junk to the flaneur who is happy to leave them to the tourist" (Benjamin 1997: 263).

A distinction is made here between the tourist and the local flaneur. The former is interested in the history, heritage, and symbols of the city, wishes to collect information *about* it. The latter is into moving along, strolling, looking for an opportunity to be *within* the city like within any landscape, willing "to trade all his knowledge of artist's quarters, birthplaces, and princely palaces for the scent of a single weathered threshold or the touch of a single tile – that which a dog carries away" (Benjamin 1970: 263). It is the landscape composed of living people that can turn into the Promised Land of the flaneur (like Paris, or Tel Aviv: Gurevitz and Aran 1994). Benjamin follows Franz Hessel this time, one Berliner after another. His Berlin/Rome is our Jerusalem, loaded with meanings and memories, trying to hold on to the "cult of dwelling in the old sense, with the idea of security" (ibid.: 264), and block the new architecture of Le Corbusier with its transitional spaces and waves of light and air.

The combination of Simmel and Benjamin juxtaposes the individual and ethics with formation, material and architecture; or where and whom with how and why. The ethnography is analyzed within a matrix formed around this tension. The space is divided into inside (shielded, marked, contains a fixed content, belongs to someone) and outside (open, transparent, exposed to changing uses and meanings); and the blurring of the line between inside and outside (Benjamin's arcade, the contemporary mall). The *affiliation* is divided into ours (a place where we feel "at home," marked as ours by us as well as others, contains our memories, signifies "us," etc.) and theirs (where we are visitors, a new place for us, signifies "another" culture/group, etc.).

A major parameter in addition to *space* and *affiliation* is the act of *Entrance*: whether one enters a place officially, pays admission, moves away from the window and crosses the threshold to enter a shop (to say nothing of buying something), sits down and watches a performance, orders food at the café. Those actions run contrary to those of the ideal flaneur, who remains at a distance and participates just by passing near or by being a potential participant.

The subjects were the guides for our observations in this study. We followed them, as Benjamin went after Hessel and Baudelaire. They mapped out the path of their excursions in the city, they chose the venues for their leisure and shopping. The matrix is applied to our observations in an effort to make sense of the changes that have taken place in the ultraorthodox consumption of time and space, and to decipher the meaning of those changes.

> World exhibitions are the sites of pilgrimages to the commodity fetish . . . It proceeds from the wish "to entertain the working classes, and becomes for them a festival of emancipation" . . . They open up a phantasmagoria that people enter to be amused. The entertainment industry facilitates this by elevating people to the level of commodities. They submit to being manipulated while enjoying their alienation from themselves and others. (Benjamin 1978: 150–1)

Outdoors	*Indoors*	
Malchi Israel Street	Rav Shefa mall Center One mall	Ours
Zoo, Sacher Park, the *Midrachov*	Malcha mall	Theirs

Outdoors/Theirs: the Zoo, Sacher Park, the Midrachov

Consuming an outdoor space that is not designated as ultraorthodox is a complicated action. It offers the ideal experience of flaneurism – exploring streets and alleys, wandering through neighborhoods and around – and at the same time it carries the danger of transpassing. To control the dangers, ultraorthodox people will avoid wandering on their own and will go armed with reasons. At the zoo and Sacher Park, it's the school and work holiday, the kids, the heat, the crowded flats, the lack of means for any other kind of vacation.[32] Like other middle- and lower-middle-class families, they are looking for inexpensive entertainment. The novelty is that they acknowledge the need, the right, the urge to be entertained: to spend time and money, to be exposed to new places and amusement, to explore.

Benjamin claims that what turns merchandise into fetish is the move from symbolism to allegory, the disconnection between the signified and the signifier, the separation between phenomena and their meaning. This is a danger for any moral community, including the ultraorthodox. Thus, they need to make a place Glatt Kosher, to reach a general consensus that the zoo is okay, within bounds, that Sacher Park is okay, that kids riding bicycles is not too *goyish* (non-Jewish). It takes a few pioneers to begin the process, and the masses to follow. The zoo is a signified place; it bears a clear mark meaning, you cannot say that it is for example a place "good for one's health" so you have to tell yourself that you are going to see the magnitude of God's creation. You won't buy food but you'll permit the children to have a popsicle. You'll listen to the secular zookeeper, watch his feeding demonstration, and sum up his words by stressing to your child that the goats' horns are material for the shofar. In the park, fathers can play football with their sons but they keep their shirts on, unlike the secular fathers, and the mothers will restrict themselves to their blanket zone but stretch out on it. The children will race their bicycles on the same lane used by the joggers, whose outfits – a teacher or sister points out to the younger girls – are not *tzanua* (modest).

The *midrahov* is different. It's the inner city, the city center, difficult to pretext, hard to signify as Kosher. Wandering the "triangle"[33] means looking for adventure, watching how the secular people spend time and money, hoping for quasi-interactions with them, or maybe (God forbid) more than that. The flaneurs of the *midrahov* do not come alone as the ultimate flaneur does, but neither do they come in masses. They are there as small groups of liminal people: ultraorthodox tourists (mainly teenagers), Sephardic teenagers who belong to more moderate communities, young couples, or people looking for an evening outing. Mainstream local ultraorthodox families might cross the zone along their way, but they will avoid it as a space for leisure and consumption.

Indoors/Theirs

Malcha mall is the only site that fits this cell. It is referred to symbolically as "their place,"[34] but in the new reality of Jerusalem, the mall recognizes the needs of the orthodox. (One could say this to a lesser extent about many other public places in Israel as well.) The important point is that those needs are met in the market place: the ultraorthodox are recognized as potential consumers. With self-imposed restrictions (no teenagers on their own, and even not with their parents), Malcha mall, with its inside/outside characteristics (like the nineteenth-century arcade), is a good place for flaneurism. The ultraorthodox use it for wandering without buying, for exercising the contemporary experience of leisure in the presence of merchandise, for presenting themselves as potential customers who should be recognized, and for actualizing limited to minor extravagances, mainly food. In a way, this is what most people do in the mall. Most come there to stroll, to hang out, to eat cheap food, and to actualize their right to window shop; to see and be seen, to enjoy the fact that the salespeople have no idea how much money they are ready to spend.

In Benjamin's terms, they are full participants in the contemporary era. By joining the crowds they do not automatically confirm structural capitalism. According to Rojeck's reading of Benjamin, they also practice an act of subversion (Rojek 1997). When they become part of the masses, both their ultraorthodoxy and the secular designation of the mall lessen. They become part of the tribe of potential consumers and blur other cultural parameters that separate them from the mob. They experience the fantasy of consumerism, and fantasy is one of the moral community's greatest enemies. The connections between content, appearances, and meaning weaken, threatening the cultural (not the religious) structure of ultraorthodoxy.

As opposed to those who read consumerism only as a means of control, Benjamin makes room for liberating experiences. The fact that people do not stroll the mall on their own or as couples, tend to come in larger groups, and eat only in certain restaurants restricts those experiences but does not eradicate them.

Outdoors/Ours

In this cell of the matrix, we follow the people on Malchi Israel Street, the ultraorthodox Oxford Street. It runs through the heart of ultraorthodox territory and offers a classic urban stroll, taking in a combination of public institutions, historical sites, modern venues, essential stores, and a few luxurious and fun ones. This is where real shopping is done, for clothes, food, school supplies, medicine, and limited luxuries.

At the same time this classic urban street does not offer its stroller the anonymity of the metropolis. Every individual who exposes him/herself on the pavement can be easily affiliated if not recognized. The clothes, the hats, the hair cover, the stockings – all tell exactly who you are. Thus, the outside/ours experience of flaneurism on Malchi Israel Street is a real phenomenon of the contemporary city, an exhibition of private exploration under social supervision. Every city street has it rules. Here the rules run counter to the culture of contemporary consumption. The people maneuver between the two, knowing how tight the restrictions are and what their bodies should convey. They convey the requisite busy, goal-oriented mode, but capitalize on the fact that no one can really tell why they are out there. They rush on the pavement but take their time inside the stores. They buy some food at the take-out deli, but stop once in a while and eat at the falafel stand.[35] If walking the street is indeed a speech act, as De Certeau claims, and if it "affirms, suspects, tries out, transgresses, respects, etc." (De Certeau 1984: 99), this is what the movements on Malchi Israel Street say:

> I know I am walking within the borders of my community, and therefore I do not allow my body to display time spending, pleasure, strolling, or lack of purpose. I look around and know that I am being looked at. I carry out expected actions but look for new ones. I buy what I need, but look at (and sometimes buy) what I want. I am aware that the fantasies of Malchi Israel Street are limited, but I notice (and affirm by participation) a steady pushing of those limits to accommodate more and more luxury. The zone of Malchi Israel Street offers a vivid urban experience balanced by the social-moral order but not choked or denigrated by it.

Indoors/Ours

If one is looking for the capacity of the moral order to denigrate the culture of time and money spending, look at Rav Shefa mall. The developers of Rav Shefa assumed that the presence of ultraorthodox people at Center One or Malcha meant that mall culture is legitimate. They assumed that once they built a mall suited to their needs, it would be an instant success. But cultural changes are more complicated, and as of now Rav Shefa is a failure. The open invitation to spend time and money in a designated zone requires full recognition of those actions. It demands a clear exhibition of mall behavior with no way out, no blending into a mob, no hiding within the "other culture." Coming to Rav Shefa and keeping it vital means creating a "them" site within "us." It leaves us naked and exposed with no excuses, no way to detach from it. We cannot say we have just come to look at "them," or pass by, or take a peek. Keeping the venue vital means the ultraorthodox have joined the dominant culture. Thus, the only vital spots in Rav Shefa are the orthodox supermarket, the pharmacy, the hamburger stand, and the makeshift amusement park open in the summer. Maybe time will change the current depressed state of the mall, but as of now the only full amusement mall is the hybrid ours/theirs – Center One.

Center One was built for the secular population. The ultraorthodox community does not have to apologize for or explain its existence. Its growing use by the orthodox resulted in elimination of the symbolic[36] secular expressions of the mall: movie theaters, television sets, and regular fashion stores. At the same time it kept alive certain stores, the restaurant, the fast-food stands, and, of course, the café – the only café in Jerusalem where most of the customers are ultraorthodox, where ultraorthodox people display spending time and money action with coffee-shop manners. The scene looks like any other café, unlike, say, the food stands in Malchi Israel Street. The waitresses look like their counterparts in other eating places in Israel, young (mostly students), wearing pants, and obviously nonorthodox. The menu offers the trendy salads, quiches, stir-fried dishes, pastas, and fancy cakes with Italian names found in other up-scale cafés. It does not offer traditional Jewish food. The territory of Center One is not affiliated to the community, but the community has koshered it. It is not an orthodox mall, but they are the majority in it. Mall habitus has not been approved by ultraorthodoxy, but more and more members of the communities participate in it and experience it.

In the middle of winter in 1999, I (Tamar) had to be in the vicinity of Center One and made a date to meet a student of mine there for lunch. It was raining heavily and I was pleased to find a parking spot nearby. I was early and had some time to walk around. The place was not full. After going twice around the ground level and once upstairs, I sat down at a table at the café and continued my observation. When Rina arrived, wet and breathless, I immediately began pouring out my impressions: "That's it, this is the end, they have joined the mob. Look around, a Hassidic couple drink cappuccino? ultraothodox people sitting in clear view on a stage, casually eating spaghetti Alfredo? ultraorthodox mothers with baby strollers eating tri-colored lettuce salad with olive oil and herbs?"

Rina, a modern orthodox herself, listened to my words, and more to their tone, looked around and said, "Now that you mention it, yeah, kind of new, but isn't it to be expected?"

Maybe the community leaders expected it, and maybe this is why they have been attacking the "culture of luxury" for the last 30 years. But what one sees in Jerusalem is a paradoxical change. More secular practice is seen in the city – done by ultraorthodox people. One could say that contemporary Jerusalem is "less holy," not because it lost its ultraorthodox population, but because that population has expanded its habitus, which includes now new practices, many secular in character. A growing number of religious people are carrying out profane activities. At the same time, the "Public Sphere" of the city, zones that were never marked as orthodox, is less lay or secular due to the presence of ultra/orthodox people in them. The power relations between its different inhabitants set the social rhythm of the city. A change in this rhythm affects the appearance of the Public, which in return bears an impact on the communities themselves. The gaps between the secular and orthodox habitus lessen, the border zones of the city are blurred. Crossing them becomes an easier act, although more orthodox people are seen in the secular sections than vice versa. More and more are participating in the same culture wearing different costumes. They meet in the consumption and leisure zone where they are all equal, and diminish the moral differences between them. The fact that they keep their costumes on, and many more aspects of their lives are separate and unique, hides this change and moderates its pace. It does not block it.

References

Benjamin, W. (1970), "On some Motifs in Baudelaire," in *Illuminations*, trans. Harry Zohn, London: Jonathan Cape.

—— (1978), "Paris, Capital of the Nineteenth Century," *Reflections*, New York: Harcourt Brace Janovich.

Choshen, M. (1998), *Jerusalem on the Map – Basic Facts and Trends, 1967–1996*, Jerusalem: Jerusalem Institute for Israel Studies.

De Certeau, M. (1984), *The Practice of Everyday Life*, Berkeley: University of California Press.

Frisby, D. (1977), "The Introduction," in D. Frisby and M. Featherstone (eds), *Simmel on Culture*, London: Sage.

Gurevitz, Z. and Gideon, A. (1994), "Never in Place: Eliade and Judaic Sacred Places," *Archives de Siences sociales des religions,* pp. 4–14.

Harvey, D. (1985), *The Urban Experience*, Baltimore: Johns Hopkins University Press.

Hertzman, E. (1985), Untitled, *Marve Latzame*, vol. 50 (Hebrew).

Rojek, C. (1997), "Leisure' in the writings of Walter Benjamin," *Leisure Studies*, 16: 155–71.

Shilhav, Y. (1993), "Religious Teritorial Extremism," *Mahanaym*, 5: 174–85 (Hebrew).

Simmel, G. (1997), "The Introduction," "The Sociology of Space," and "The Metropolis and Mental Life," all in D. Frisby and M. Featherstone (eds), *Simmel on Culture*, London: Sage.

Wolff, J. (1995), *Resident Alien: Feminist Cultural Criticism*, New Haven: Yale University Press.

–6–

Food for Thought: The Dining Table and Identity Construction among Jewish Immigrants from the Former Soviet Union in Israel

Julia Bernstein and *Yoram S. Carmeli*

The present study concentrates on the immigration of Jews from the Former Soviet Union (FSU), which in the 1990s was by far the largest group of immigrants to Israel. By considering food practices and consumption as a vantage point in cultural analysis, we focus on the ceremony by which the immigrants receive guests at home – the *Zastolie* – which serves as a locus for interpersonal and group interaction. Through observing and interpreting this ceremony we address the chapter's main questions: What are the main dilemmas of this particular immigration of Soviet Jews to Israel? How are "we" feelings and "we" boundaries crystallized vis-à-vis the country's veterans? How is the present interwoven with the immigrants' past? What and where – if at all – is the immigrants' "home"? How are all of the aforementioned expressed in food-related practices? What is the significance of hosting guests for the immigrants in a new society?

For the purpose of the current study, we perceive food as being imbued with symbolic meanings. The chapter therefore analyzes the contents of the images served and consumed at the *Zastolie* table as a kind of "practical solution" which facilitates coping with a new reality. In this process, cultural codes and perceptions brought from the original society are expressed, transformed, and interwoven with new ones by means of material culture in general, and food practices in particular. An underlying assumption of this study is that "culture" is not something one "takes along." Rather, cultural elements are used and interpreted according to the specific context in which they are encountered (Bloch 1977; Gudeman and Rivera 1990; Shilling 1993; Boyarin 1994). Thus, while objects and recipes with decipherable histories play a significant part in this research, emphasis is placed on the activities of people who redefine objects, recipes, tableware, table-manners, and thereby their past(s) and present(s), their individual and collective identities, in various situations and new contexts.

Immigration, Identity, Food

Recent studies on immigration and immigrants highlight the continued importance of maintaining distinct ethnic identities prevalent among immigrants. The continued salience of these identities is carried through cultural, religious, and even political institutions, as well as by means of occupations that rely on ethnic origin (Carmon 1996: 25). The theoretical perspective that allows for the coexistence of various ethnic groups is expressed in the model of cultural pluralism. This is a model that acknowledges heterogeneity in the country of arrival not as a transitional stage, but as a constant phenomenon, and which perceives the various groups in society as affecting each other mutually, simultaneously creating and sharing a national space together (Carmon 1996: 24; Fuchs 1993; Marcuse 1996).

Research in the 1980s and 1990s reflected the legitimization of the diversity and uniqueness of different immigrant groups, and the literature has now expanded to include topics such as the groups' characteristics, their unique traditions, their boundaries and closures (Appadurai 1992; Friedman 1992; Hannerz 1992; Featherstone 1992; Shuval and Leshem 1997). The need to reconsider the term "adaptation" has arisen, and the new concept of "transmigration" has been suggested. This concept conceives of immigrants as living a social reality simultaneously influenced by the state of origin and the state of destination, and the latter's own culture (Schiller et al. 1997). Transmigrants enter the new society preserving their experience, largely hanging on to their social patterns and original concepts, and yet they are ". . . knowledgeable agents, capable of defining their lives within the constraints of the larger social structure" (Kivisto 1990: 47; see also Bodnar 1985). While globalization – in its economic and political dimensions – underlies the process of immigration itself, the particular "postmodern' transmigrant's identity emerges within the context of the international flow of material objects and ideas. Immigrants in Israel can now not only watch live Russian TV broadcasts but also read Russian newspapers, attend performances of Russian theatre-companies and orchestras on tour, and shop in their favorite Russian stores. The issues of their new lives, as immigrants, can be discussed with fellow immigrants living in other countries such as the USA, Canada, and Germany, or with relatives and friends who remained in the Russian Federation and are now visiting Israel. Consequently, this study aims to understand how people conceive of their "new home" and how they define themselves both within and outside it.

A theoretical consideration of migration, transmigrants, and the latter's experience of their past and their new commitments entails a reconsideration of the central concept of "identity." Identity is no longer considered in holistic or dichotomous terms – "adaptation," "desocialization-resocialization" – (see for example Park 1950; Gordon 1964; Lieberson 1961; Ben-Rafael and Sharot 1991), or as a fixed – "primordial" – characteristic (see Weingrod 1985; Smooha 1986; Swirski 1989).

It is rather a "strategic presentation of self" (Schoenfeld 1991: 4) and can be considered to be dynamic and changeable. To paraphrase Inowlocki, it seems more useful to consider a person not as "being" Russian, Jewish, or Israeli, but "doing" Russian-ness, Jewish-ness or Israeli-ness (see Inowlocki 2000; and see Sack 1997). Moreover, the underlying assumption is that "[I]dentities are multiple. No person has a single identity. Each . . . [person] has many identities, but which of these is salient in which situation profoundly influences thinking and behaviour" (Gitelman 1995: 29). Immigrants' identities – their autobiographical constructs, their facing of "others" – are changing according to social conditions, circumstances, and the specific contexts in which they are located (Benske 1994; Goldstein 1985; Neeman 1994; Shabtay 1996; Shuval and Leshem 1997).

Consequently, in studying immigrants' identities via their hosting and food consumption in Israel, one should attend to the situational and highly differential character of the inquiry. In the present chapter, we will consider a part of the immigrants' self-definitions: those construed while joining together around a festive table to enjoy a favored and familiar atmosphere. Within this framing, different identities emerged, depending on the hosting of various groups of guests: immigrants who have lived in Israel for the same period of time; veteran immigrants who emigrated from the Soviet Union in the early 1970s; emigrants from the Russian Federation who migrated to other countries, such as the USA and Germany, and are visiting Israel; groups of friends and relatives who continue to live in the Russian Federation but are currently visiting Israel; and groups of Israelis, who were rarely invited as guests in the homes of the people we studied.

As food is a symbolic medium par excellence, the significance of food and eating in the construction of identity has already played a significant part in Classical Anthropology as well as being a focal point of more recent studies in the Sociology of Food (for example Barthes 1979; Bourdieu 1984; Goody 1982; Douglas 1975; Lupton 1996; Beardsworth and Keil 1997; Lévi-Strauss 1966, 1970; Mennel 1985; Mennel et al. 1992; Morse 1994). Food types are considered to be signs in a semiotic communication system shared by a group of people (Barthes 1979). We not only consume the food's nutritional value but also acquire the experience of its taste, as we consume the significance and symbols behind the product (Beardsworth and Keil 1997: 51). Lupton (1996) goes beyond cognition as she addresses choices and preferences in the field of food in the context of "embodiment and subjectivity." Food consumption is a phenomenon of "supremely physical presence," and within this framework people's interactions take place through the senses. We smell, taste, see, and touch food, and sometimes we even hear it (as in food sizzling in a pan) (Lupton 1996: 13). Through conversations about food and their non-verbal experiences, people seek to reach and understand their selves – which is particularly relevant in terms of the condition that accompanies immigration.

In analyzing food consumption, history and context are important, as they shed light on how one food-type was historically given preference over another, how this and other items have become symbols – i.e. a component of identity – and how meanings and identities are contextually transformed. According to Barthes, foodstuffs often symbolize continuity and tradition thereby maintaining a connection with the consumers' past (Barthes 1979: 171). We must therefore investigate the importance, for immigrants, of the present uses of pre-migratory food-images, alongside the forms and meanings which food images and significances acquire in the present changing context.

It is particularly significant to address the emotional aspects of these food-images, as immigration is a particularly sensitive condition experienced by adults who are moving to completely new locations. Thus, it is interesting to consider how memories of taste, smell, and outward appearance are reconstructed in the combination of dishes displayed on the *Zastolie* table, and to analyze the Russian dishes in the Israeli context as they now incorporate new ingredients and symbolic contents. Equally interesting are the rituals, the festivity, and the discussions that occur around the hosting-table, as they constitute the framing and vocabulary for the immigrants' negotiation of old-new identities, and for new definitions of self. In the case of "Russian" immigrants to Israel, a change in social status, embodied (in large part) in the immigrants' present-day non-professional occupations, affects the desire to recuperate the past, to confirm one's sense of identity with the native group, to tie up past and present vs. locals or "others" in a dignified way. The immigrants' usage of the basic idiom of food and of food consumption – in the private sphere – may thus offer an analytical insight into the phenomenon of "Homo Sovieticus' (Glants 1997) in Israel.

At this point it is necessary for us to briefly outline the Jewish identity and other general characteristics of the latest immigration-wave from FSU to Israel. Between 1990 and the year 2000, Israel received a mass influx of immigrants that significantly increased its population: between 1989 and 1994, Israel's population increased by almost 1 million people (14 percent of the country population) (Lewin-Epstein 1997; Carmon 1996; Ritterband 1997). Most of these people were of an employable age (45–64). However, the most educated among them – 70 percent of those employable (as, indeed, were also the majority of the population in our particular study) – were not employed in their original professional field (Carmon 1996: 5–7; see also Leshem and Shuval 1997; Lewin-Epstein et al. 1997). The majority of these immigrants to Israel tended to live in the large urban centers, where – due to financial constraints – they resided in the less attractive parts (Carmon 1996). In our case, it was "Hadar" neighborhood in Haifa which was the focus of this study.

A large proportion of the immigrants (especially those who arrived from the European parts of FSU) came from towns and cities, where they lived in relatively small middle-class families, often with a fraction of an extended family sharing one household. Numerous immigrants worked in professional as well as academic occupations. The commitment to academic learning, and to high culture – in social life, at home, and in children's education – was, both for them and for the outside world, a central characteristic of their "Jewish" identity – an identity which lacked any religious component and for many included only minor significance of nationality or ethnicity. According to the interviews conducted for this research, the immigrants left the Russian Federation due to a multiplicity of negative factors, such as limitations on civil liberties, discrimination and anti-semitism, concerns over the children's and the family's future due to increasing uncertainty accompanying the disintegration of the USSR, and socio-economic difficulties. The picture derived from our research corresponds to the data collected in many studies on this topic (Rivkina 1996: 162; Lewin-Epstein et al. 1997). The participants of our study also reported other motivations for the move, including the growing number of relatives in Israel and visits there, as well as a reaction to the "open gates" policy that was adapted as part of the process of "Perestroika" (Gitelman 1997: 32).

Most of the literature on the recent immigration influx concludes that Jews from the Russian Federation, who for three generations had no involvement of any kind with Jewish cultural traditions, left for negative reasons or for new individual opportunities rather than coming to Israel for ideological reasons (Rivkina 1996; Lewin-Epstein et al. 1997). Thus, this truly was a process of "immigration," as opposed to being an occasion of "repatriation" (the term used was "*Aliya*" which, in Hebrew, literally means "ascent"), since this was the relocation of a population whose affinity to the Jewish collective in their country of origin and in Israel was relatively obscure. This characteristic affected these immigrant's lifestyles in the new society, both in terms of how they were perceived by the local population, and in their structuring of their material and spiritual world. Asked about their identity in Israel, 81 percent chose "Russian Jews" and only 12 percent chose "Israeli" (ibid). In the present study the immigrants often referred to themselves as "*Alimi*" or affectionately as "*Alimchiki*" (as a Russian – from the Hebrew "*Olim*," meaning Jewish newcomers), a term which was contrasted with "*Vatiki*" (from the Hebrew "*Vatik*," meaning veteran) which they used to refer to the 1970s immigrants from the USSR.

The *Alimi* group is unique not only in name. The size of the immigrant population and their motives for emigration, the arrival of Russian tourists and performing companies, the accessibility to Russian broadcasts (Russian cable channels) and press, as well as the understanding exhibited by the Israeli society, and the immigrants' right to cultural expression – have all led to the creation of a Russianspeaking subculture in Israeli society. The existence of such a Russian-speaking subculture, of "cultural ghettos" (Gitelman 1995: 8), or more neutral "cultural enclaves", is easily observable. These cultural enclaves include a variety of institutions necessary for its individual members and for community life. They are struggling within themselves, as well as with the Israeli society, to formulate their own identity and to foster unique status symbols that are distinct from those used by the locals. These symbols should be studied through the informal connections which exist among families and friends who gather at the *Zastolie*.

The present research is based on fieldwork conducted between 1998 and the year 2000. The population studied – Jewish immigrants from Russia and the Ukraine – comprised 70 people, consisting of three main family networks and their guests, who were close friends and relatives. The participants' ages ranged between 48 and 58. Most of the middle-aged individuals convened at the *Zastolies* which we observed had a higher-education degree (either in technical fields or in the humanities) but in Israel their jobs were unconnected to their professional training. Their current occupations with, on average, low incomes typically required fewer qualifications and skills. The majority of the participants emigrated from FSU in the period 1990–1992, a period during which, despite the fact that the super-power had already started to disintegrate, the image of a strong and large Russia persisted, and this was the image that the immigrants brought with them to Israel and which was expressed in the *Zastolie* discussions.

During observations and throughout the interviews participants were highly cooperative. All of the interviews were conducted in Russian – Julia's native language – which contributed to the participants' openness. In effect, the language barrier and low social status of their present occupations prevented them from presenting themselves as they would have liked to.

The *Zastolie* Gathering

Between Hosts and Their Guests

Alongside the important custom in the USSR of offering a meal to anyone who enters your home – regardless of the time of day, weekday or weekend, or the guest's relation to the family – a *Zastolie* hosting was usually (and in Israel still is) planned in advance. Musya Glants, who wrote about the meaning of food in art in the Soviet context, describes the *Zastolie* as "having a party and sitting together for a long time, enjoying food, drinks, and conversation" (Glants 1997: 229). A main characteristic of the phenomenon was that the entire visit was spent around the table. Due to crowded housing conditions in Soviet Russia, once prepared, the table took up the entire space of the room. The guests were physically bound to their seats for the duration of the event. A *Zastolie* hosting usually took place on the weekend and lasted half a day. When celebrating a birthday or a similar event, the number of guests in the *Zastolie* was approximately fifteen. In addition to the gatherings for special events, a *Zastolie* also accompanied a gathering of friends over the weekend. In this case, the composition of the *Zastolie* table depended on the frequency of the group's social gatherings: the more infrequent the gathering, the more splendid the array of foods.

Among the immigrants studied, the traditional form of a Russian *Zastolie* and its symbolic significance were perceived as being diametrically opposed to "eating out," particularly at a restaurant. Eating in restaurants in Russia was a very special and rare event. A *Zastolie* ceremony – which must be characterized by an abundance of foods – held in Israel in the late 1990s cost in the range of NIS 800–1000 ($180–240). However, it continued to be the most economical of gatherings. Inviting friends and relatives to a restaurant, even eating "fast food" (among the immigrants this usually entailed one person or a couple inviting the others), would have been considered expensive by the immigrants, as well as wasteful. It flaunted the organizers' high economic status and placed them within the circle of the locals (*Izrailtyane*), distanced from the Russian tradition. Even upon their arrival in Israel, eating out was therefore reserved by the immigrants for celebrating a circumcision or wedding events (in Russia, even weddings were celebrated in the home), while all holidays and other occasions, including routine weekend gatherings of friends and relatives, continued to be celebrated by *Zastolie*, which took place at home, in the main living room (the Israeli "*Salon*").

Nonetheless, the holidays themselves and the mode of their celebration were significantly reshaped by immigration. In the previous context the *Zastolie* was associated first and foremost with events "at home" (family occasions) and political holidays. (In the atheist USSR there were no religious holidays.) To these had been added, of special importance, the celebration of the Gregorian New Year. With the move to Israel, most of the Russian original holidays and the original manner of celebrating them faded. At the time when our research took place, the immigrants were, in general, quite indifferent to the Israeli political and religious holidays, although they did celebrate these days with a *Zastolie*. Another important change that occurred is that in the Israeli context the celebratory foods which had previously been specially bought and prepared for the holiday's *Zastolie*, became accessible, easily attainable and, to an extent, an ordinary habit. Because of the public holidays' lack of significance and because prestigious foods are easily available, the distinction between the quotidian and the celebratory has been blurred. In Israel, rather than being reserved only for a yearly family event or a holiday *Zastolie*, an abundant array of dishes and specialties might easily appear at a *Zastolie* among friends who have not seen each other in two months.

To the *Zastolie* occasions in Israel one should note an exceptional and important case – that of the Gregorian New Year's Eve. Being the only "real" holiday – according to all participants – this holiday and its associated *Zastolie* are particularly splendid and festive. At this time of the year, each home changes according to the tradition brought from abroad, bringing in fir trees, ornaments of colored glass, woven goods, decorated chains, and red ribbons. This holiday unites the immigrants, and wherever the Russian language is heard, so is the repeated "*S novim godom*!" ("happy holiday" in Russian).

As observed in Israel, a *Zastolie* has a clear structure of gathering, which begins and ends around the dining table. It is also characterized by an additional selection of elements, such as the quality of the serving dishes, the composition of the dishes served, and people's behavior throughout the occasion. To begin with, complying with an unwritten script of manners and particular practices conveys the participants' adherence to a certain elite-like or upper-class genre. The first of the conventions states that the guests are not to arrive at the stated time, and certainly not earlier. The time set for the gathering usually assumes that guests will arrive within the hour. When the guests – properly dressed – appear, the appropriate greetings are extended. The guests, as a rule, hand over gifts to the hosts, in a manner not unlike the punching of a clock to confirm arrival. The gifts – unless the *Zastolie* celebrates a special occasion – are expected to consist of alcohol or boxes of chocolate.

Once seated around the table, particular rules of etiquette and avoidance are a matter of course. One should not begin eating before the ceremony of the first toast has been completed, or serve oneself before serving the neighboring person. One should not touch any food-items with one's hands or ask about the ingredients of a dish before tasting it, or express any hint of dissatisfaction with the dishes one abhors during the meal. One should not lick one's fingertips, place elbows on the table, pick one's teeth (or use a toothpick at the table), or purse one's lips. Note that while in the previous society participants belonged to middle social class, they nevertheless earned (as per socialist ideology) the same low salary as factory workers. Table manners and expected behavior thus elucidated symbolic class distinctions as they so often do in other places and times (see Bourdieu 1984; Elias 1994).

The unwritten rules of the *Zastolie* also upheld a cherished Russian in-group tradition. When we visited on Lara's birthday, an interesting situation arose as conventions were violated, following the suggestion to arrange a buffet-style table ("Swedish style" in Hebrew) for the *Zastolie.* This suggestion was made by Reuven, Lara's husband, who was the only participant born in Israel, was married to the daughter of one of the participant families and spoke fluent Russian. We set about the task of setting tables in the corner of the room, leaving a large space in the center. As the guests arrived, they all waited for the beginning of the event, which is usually signalled by laying out the table in the room's center. "So, when do we start?," Nicolai, Lara's father, dared to ask. Lara apologetically explained that they had decided on eating buffet-style this time. "But why?", inquired all of the guests, making it absolutely clear that this was all a silly mistake. They immediately began returning the tables to their "proper" place. Once it was all properly rearranged, they all finally took seats and Lev, Lara's uncle, in an effort to relieve the tension, said jokingly: "We'll have our Russian, not a Swedish, table!"

In a *Zastolie* meeting, immediately following arrival, men and women move on to their separate tasks. The men organize the tables in the main living room (or in the prize possession, the yard or veranda – a Soviet's dream and the embodiment of the capitalist image). They bring in the chairs, open bottles of alcohol, put bottles in the refrigerator or freezer for quick cooling, and open the cans of sardines for toast. The women, on the other hand, offer to help in the kitchen. They deck the table with a cherished cotton tablecloth (especially kept for such occasions and which is often the grandmother's), arrange the Russian flatware – heavy decorated items made of an alloy of copper and nickel – and the crystal serving bowls. At this stage, what remains to be done is to transfer the cooked dishes from pots and pans into the fancy serving dishes, adding last-minute ingredients (such as mayonnaise in salads), laying the tableware and carrying the dishes to the table. Women are expected to offer their help throughout, helping to serve the warm dishes and replacing plates with new courses.

A Russian *Zastolie* meal (in the USSR and in Israel) was traditionally divided into two main parts: main course and dessert. The first usually included cold dishes and appetizers as openers. Fifteen to thirty different small dishes were usually placed on the table in a *Zastolie*. Following the appetizers, hot dishes were later served in the *Zastolie*. Occasionally, with more intimate company, the hot and cold dishes (the appetizers and the main course) were served together. Last was the dessert, served as the sweet conclusion of the meeting.

When a *Zastolie* meal is being offered, the men seated at the table pour alcoholic drinks for their wives and themselves while the hostess, the *hoziyaika*, presents them with the various dishes and begins to serve them and pass the food around. Women who remain seated help by serving the salads to their husbands and themselves. (Occasionally, men help transfer the dish to the individual plates.) During the long meal the participants at the table would alternately split into small parties of two or three, each holding their own conversations. Common toasts (initiated each time by someone different) repeatedly unite the people convened. More frequent still are the compliments to the *hoziyaika*.

The host and hostess both encourage their guests to eat. As expected, their encouragements are loaded with humorous scolding and overrated emotional pleadings, all in a Russian-Jewish familiar manner that an outsider may find nagging and annoying. This encouragement is expressed in sentences such as Nicolai's "I see you're only talking and not eating," and Alla's comment, "Please eat, the main course will be ready soon." Paina made comments such as "Can I serve you some of this salad?" and "Please pass this one down to the other side of the table – they haven't even tasted it yet." Felix, hosting, contributed: "This sausage is extremely good, try it, I'm telling you it's superb, from the Russian store, believe me, just try it, if you don't like it just leave it, you've got nothing to lose." And in the form of a statement rather than a question, Alla said, "I'm serving you some of this one," and in an attempt to convince the guest, "I'll give you a little of this one, there's only a bit left, we must finish it." Since the table is overloaded with items and there are always leftovers, Paina playfully threatened/pleaded "I won't let you leave the table until everything has been eaten."

In response to the hosts' attempts to please the guests, the latter are "obliged" to express their amazement at the abundance of dishes and the effort invested, and to praise the hostess. Often an apologetic remark can be heard, as from Lyuba, one of Lena and Nicolai's guests: "Wow, I took too much – but it looks so delicious!" or from Sophia (one of Alla and Felix's guests): "My eyes could go on eating . . . I probably took too much!" In the intimacy of the group, a transgression of an elitist rule – one which bans one from filling an entire plate (or stomach) with food – thus turns into praise for the hosts, phrased in the idiom of apology.

In the tranquil spirit that fills the *Zastolie* gathering, discussions of topics from the participants' present lives were interwoven with memories from the old country. The people seated at the table discussed their life in Israel. Discussions centered on political affairs in Israel, current work-related topics, events currently taking place in Israel as well as in FSU (the latter being followed through local and Russian TV channels, and in the Israeli Russian-language press). Friends consulted each other on existing sales and the best and cheapest places to purchase goods, veterans passing information to the more recently arrived newcomers when they need to complete a formal application or approach this or that government official. Among women, the subject of food was often common. One could hear discussions on the use of unfamiliar Israeli ingredients or the alterations made to familiar recipes. Phaina: "For the truffles to come out hardened, you have to leave the mixture refrigerated for at least two hours . . . but it still tastes different because the powdered milk here is different." Lena: "For potato salad here [in Israel], you do not need to add the mayonnaise and sour cream together, the mayonnaise is so tasty here, that you can use it without the sour cream, but use only the [Israeli] "Telma' brand or American kind."

During the *Zastolie,* friends and relatives discussed their leisure pastimes: Russian books recently published in Russia and bought in special book stores in

Israel, and cultural events such as concerts, theater performances on tour from Russia. (These had been followed through local and Russian TV channels, and in the Israeli Russian-language press.) A favourite subject was often that of travel abroad. Throughout the *Zastolie* the hosts often showed photos of their recent trips, sharing stories with guests that have already visited that particular destination and relating details to those who had not yet been there. For the participants, a trip abroad, although financed with difficulty, was one of the important "side effects" of immigration, enabling the realization of a previously unattainable dream.

As observed in Israel, the *Zastolie* meeting – the meal and its discussions – thus continues and lasts for hours. As the *hoziyaika*, usually with the assistance of female guests, collects the main-course dishes, a dessert is always served and indulgently feasted upon. This often involves beverages being served with home-made cakes. Candies or fancy chocolates purchased from the Russian specialty store follow. Occasionally, instead of the homemade cakes, an impressive purchased cake from the Russian store might be served, which in the Russian context occurred only on the most exceptional of occasions.

So far, throughout the event, and according to the *Zastolie* conventions, people have rarely left their seats, except for occasional cigarette breaks. (Going somewhere, especially when leaving food on the plate, requires an apology or excuse.) Now everyone is excessively full. Comments are increasingly being heard such as Alik (Lena and Nicolai's guest) saying, "I can't move I'm so stuffed," and Sveta (Lena and Nicolai's guest) commenting, "No, don't offer me anything more, I've been full for the last two hours, I just can't have another bite." Besides punctuating the event, which draws nearer to its end, these late comments at the table are additional declarations of gratitude to the hosts, and approval that a *Zastolie* meal has indeed been fully accomplished.

The women now clean the table and wash and dry the dishes. People who leave the table during the dessert are hinting at their imminent departure. When parting, each guest repeats leave-taking statements. Sentences such as "we enjoyed ourselves," "we had a nice time," and "it was great seeing you again" are always accompanied by the expected "it was all very delicious," "thanks for everything, it was extremely tasty" and "thank you very much, everything was delicious". To these the hosts usually respond: "Please come again" or "we'll be in touch."

The reception described above was repeated at the home of each of the hosting participants when its turn came, with the hosting family presenting its own style of hosting. Nevertheless, if the gathering did not celebrate a particular event (such as a birthday), the hosts did not expect any of their guests to hold such a gathering in the near future. Often it was one family that traditionally hosted such gatherings, until it became a custom within the group to meet at a certain home.

On Friends, Relatives, and the "Others"

A *Zastolie* ceremony in Israel can be seen first and foremost as a social gathering as well as a form of leisure entertainment to which the participants are accustomed. This tradition, which uses the table and food as the gathering axis, and which welcomes the "immigrated" along with the newcomers, includes the interaction among friends, acquaintances, and relatives in the home environment. At all times, all of the *Zastolie* participants were native speakers of Russian so that only Russian was spoken, adding to the sense of the familiar. Intimacy and solidarity were encouraged by the offering of food, of "gift-giving relations" between hosts and guests, performed generously and in abundance (Mauss 1990 [1950]; Cheap 1988: 18; see also Carrier 1990).

The friends and relatives seated around the table helped each other in getting acquainted and coping with the new circumstances (Gold 1997: 264; and see Leshem 1997). Friends helped in matters of language and offered advice to those who had been in Israel for only a year or two. Frequently heard requests from recently arrived immigrants might be: "please call or find out for me . . .;" "I might not understand what they say . . ." Later still, after a significant period of living in Israel, veteran-immigrant friends and relatives acted as spokespeople for those who had arrived later, helping them with their applications and dealings with various ministries and institutions. (Indeed, even after several years in Israel, most immigrants rarely entered the home of *Izrailtyane*, except to do odd jobs there.)

A gathering of family and friends, and vis-à-vis the locals' otherness, the *Zastolie* fosters a group spirit. It has been formed as a unique microcosm vis-à-vis the "world outside". Whereas in Russia there was once the hostility of an oppressive political regime, coupled with racial and nationalistic antagonism, the Israel "outside" is experienced as an alien world, reserved, hard to communicate with, and in some significant ways inferior and jealous of the newly arrived immigrants. In the context of the familiarity, the support and the gift-giving invoked through the *Zastolie*, central identities threatened through immigration and life in Israel are experienced as symbolically, even if just temporarily, recovered and sheltered: gender identities, parent–child relations and, on a collective plane, the immigrants' sense of belonging to a social elite.

Zastolie gatherings were, and still are in Israel, highly gendered events. In the *Zastolie,* men and women who have lived together for long periods of time displayed their selves within a sympathizing and familiar arena. The immigrants from urban environments in European FSU imported traditional middle-class gender relations, male dominance, and a relatively strictly structured division of labor. In many cases, almost all of these features were put under threat by the loss of social position, of meaningful employment, and of public face. With the festive gendered clothing and the celebration of the various tasks around the table, however, these gendered features were now symbolically tied together once again.

The hostess is the main figure in the *Zastolie* preparations – and she is praised by all for her traditionally feminine culinary accomplishments. Women bring in the dishes, they prepare and serve the men at the table and they clean up afterward. Men undertake the designated masculine roles – they carry the heavy table and they open the bottles. Their hegemony is celebrated in the chivalrous and ritual pouring of the wine, and in guiding those parts of the discussions which deal with "serious (work, politics) matters." Given the immigrants' present stage of life, and their being surrounded by old friends, acquaintances, and relatives in the *Zastolie*, this performance of gender was not only a restatement of the past *Zastolies*, remembered from the FSU. Gender here was also invoked as a safe "given" ground, something acknowledged by age and reassured through long acquaintances. In a world of lost social positions it is a part of one's identity which is invoked and regained through the matter-of-factness of its manifestations.

People who had gathered around the table were often close and distant relatives, among them the hosts' – and sometimes the guests' – elder children, who had already moved out and were again invited along, to recreate an old-fashioned family gathering. Parent–child relations are a fragile and sensitive sphere, as emigration (as is often the case) has depleted parental resources. In urban middle-class Russian-Jewish families, these past resources had included parents' experience and understanding of their environment, their material resources, their position, their pride, and the parents' social connections that helped their children at critical junctures.

Not only were parents now deprived of these resources, they had lost language skills and indeed now needed as much help as their children. From being authoritative figures, parents had suddenly and irreversibly become incapable of understanding the outside world, and were being pushed into hard competition for lower positions in a new labor market. That they could hardly support their children was a source of agony, as well as being a distressful mirror for their condition.

In the *Zastolie* scenario, preparing the table and the food on it provides one of the few occasions whereby parents may symbolically reaffirm their past role in the family and in society. This emphasizes the importance and uniqueness of the *Zastolie* in which a family ceremonially unites around the table as they have done in the past. Parental care, as in the country of origin, is invoked and distilled from the present hardships. It is nevertheless true that this past parental image is now precarious. It is shaken in areas beyond the table and the home, disrupted by any contact with the present world. And yet throughout the *Zastolie* gathering, the sense of intimacy and worth was pervasive. It was also reinforced as the hostess, taking on the maternal role in a supposedly extended family (i.e. composed of the relatives and friends), obliged the guests to taste and eat the various dishes, and spent the evening demonstrating her concerns and commitment to the welfare of the guests.

In Russia's recent past, both gender and parental identities had been firmly shaped – in terms of the immigrants' social standing, their class position, and networks. For the immigrants at the table, this standing and "*intelegenzia*" image were captured in their academic education, their professional standing, their affiliation to Russian high culture – all, as it were, encapsulating and constituting much of their being "Jewish," in the country of origin.

In a sense, more than the influence on the private aspects of gender and parenthood, it is here, in the sphere of public and collective images, that the immigration to Israel and facing the *Izrailyane* has turned into an uneasy experience. As experienced by many newcomers from the FSU, Israel is largely looked upon as being a mixture of the Oriental and the American-like cultures. In addition to their cultivated affiliation to Russian culture now being irrelevant and strange to locals, their encounter with Israel's fierce competitive economic and social regime entailed – besides an economic threat – a sense of frailty, of loss of dignity, and of alienation. These feelings pervaded many aspects of the immigrants' life in Israel (as expressed in the "Russian enclaves") and were suffused throughout the *Zastolie*'s proceedings. Dining and eating are of prime importance as a "true upper-class" idiom: the late arrival, the specially prepared food, the use of the central living room, the festive silverware, the haute cuisine, the restraints (and apologies) related to food consumption, the demonstration of cultural capital – embodied, for instance via the connoisseurship of European (rather than Israeli) culture – all energized and symbolically revived the immigrants' dignity and the lost images of respectable social positions.

In the *Zastolie*, "original" – and now precarious – identities of men and women, of parents and their children, or of the elite's dignity, were invoked and imbued with an aura of authenticity. With its reflexive significance, the *Zastolie* also reflected a degree of friction vis-à-vis the Israeli realm in which they presently lived. Providing shelter and a period of recuperation for original identities, participation in the *Zastolie* was also a claim of continuity in terms of "what we really are."

The *Zastolie*, its Walls and Their Cracks

An Old-New Table

We now look more closely at the food served at the *Zastolie*. All of the dishes on a *Zastolie* table should be characterized as "haute cuisine" – hours of special preparation at home are infinitely preferred to ready-made shopping. In the historical context of immigrants from FSU, this strenuous home preparation was not only a matter of "Russian" tradition, unique to the *Zastolie,* but also of cooking patterns formulated by the unstable conditions of the Soviet economy. Buying, cooking, and preparing the *Zastolie* dishes at home is always considered to be cheaper, not only than eating out, but also compared to buying ready-made food. In the Israeli conditions of the early 1990s, prior to the appearance of Russian specialty stores, the *Zastolie* table was still laden mostly with home-cooked dishes prepared with raw products. Items processed at home even included soft cheeses, certain kinds of sausages, jams, or fruit or meat dumpling (called *varenik or pelmeni*). By the late 1990s, the conditions had changed. The *Zastolie* included many ready-made items purchased especially in honor of the occasion. Yet, the esprit of haute cuisine continued to be salient. Home preparations and delicacies especially made at home were still prominent. The process of putting together a meal, and preparing the table for an event such as a birthday, required an average of two days of constant work on the part of the *hoziyaika*. She knew expectations would be high. In addition, she also knew that on the day of the gathering her guests would refrain from eating their midday meal.

The composition of an average *Zastolie* table as it was set in Israel combined the habits of "festive eating" in the Russian context – which formed a part of the guests' expectations at any gathering – with other, newly added components from the country of origin. These were all joined by ideas of festivity to which the participants had been exposed in Israel.

While an ordinary Russian family meal always begins with soup, the cold dishes and appetizers laid on an average *Zastolie* table in Israel were abundant. Components included potato salads, tuna salads, beetroot, herring, mushroom and corn salad, liver pâté, cabbage salad, sauerkraut, different kinds of hams and sausages, stuffed fish (gefüllte fish), marinated peppers, stuffed eggs, and more. In the Russian *Zastolie* in Israel, the hot dishes which followed this opulent abundance of appetizers usually included meat and potatoes – usually chicken, meat and vegetable pies, meat paste, sometimes *pirozhki* patties with meat, potatoes or cabbage, and eggs, and sometimes *bliny* (pancakes) with meat, mushrooms, and potatoes. Meat – fried and baked (especially grilled chicken) – symbolized the festive table, and toast with sprats or caviar was associated with the prestige of a special event. These were opposed to fried or boiled potatoes, which were recognized as simple, everyday food and thereby inappropriate for special occasions. (For similar symbolic perceptions in France see Lévi-Strauss 1966: 930–40.)

One of the new "Russian' features of the *Zastolie* in Israel was the addition and display of food-items that had been known and yet were unaffordable in the country of origin. (In the appetizers' display these included items such as sardines, bread with butter and caviar, smoked salmon, squid, trout, and anchovy salads.) While some of these were regular and popular, even "cheap," in the West, they were rare in the USSR. They now carried particular significance for the immigrants and in turn shaped the significance of the whole *Zastolie*. Other modifications which reshaped the *Zastolie*'s significance in Israel, and to which we shall later return, included the preparation of dishes which were traditional not only to the immigrants' particular native Soviet Republic (as it used to be in the past) but also of other republics in FSU, alongside the appearance of "Russian" food products, which had recently been popularized by the Russian TV.

In addition to all of the above, the adoption of new Israeli elements, considered "exotic" by the *Zastolie* participants, should also be noted. For instance, broccoli, celery, basil, hummus, tahini, savory pies, cheesecakes, and filo-dough savory pastries were included. On particular Israeli-Jewish holidays one could also observe the addition of national-religious symbolic foodstuffs, such as doughnuts on Hanukkah or matzah at Passover.

Both the hot and cold dishes served at the main parts of a *Zastoli*e meal were accompanied by a large variety of "compulsory" alcoholic beverages as well as soft drinks. The latter, in Russia, included compote and lemonade, while in Israel they included carbonated drinks such as soda, Sprite, and Coke. As for the first, a new regime of alcohol consumption permeated the *Zastolie* in Israel. Sitting at the table Faina and Roman told of their astonishment when their local supermarket rejected their returned beer bottles because they did not believe that a single family could have consumed that much beer. Participants of the *Zastolie* pointed out that in the Israeli *Zastolie*, alcohol consumption among the immigrants had decreased, which they explained by the need to be "overly responsible" regarding the next day's work. They additionally mentioned that the hot weather in Israel was not conducive to alcohol consumption. As Roman put it: "In an Israeli *Zastolie* I have yet to see someone get completely drunk," a component that was never missed in any Russian *Zastolie*.

While the diminishing role of alcohol was a source of some dismay and reminiscence, other modifications of the *Zastolie* menu, as we will later further discuss, were generally perceived in terms of an elaboration and expansion of the old tradition. Moreover, while many of the *Zastolie* dishes – old and new – were repeated from one gathering to the next, there were also occasions in which the repertoire would be changed according to the guests invited. The matching of a particular setting of the table to the specific set of guests can be considered a dynamic text of relations and meanings (Lupton 1996; Mennell 1985). At a gathering with veteran immigrants, more prestigious products and dishes were displayed as a sign of the hosting family's success in the new society, demonstrating their ability to compete with the veteran group. When tourists from the Russian Federation were the guests, in addition to the prestigious items – which now indicated the host's success in the capitalist world – other products and dishes were laid out on the table, such as Israeli traditional hummus, thina, avocado, pita, indicating the "Israeliness" of the hosting family, which does not actually consume these items on a daily basis. However in the very unique instances when a native Israeli was among the guests, the hosts prepared special dishes that symbolize their

Russian identity, such as cherry-filled pastry puffs or *pirozhki*, which would not have been prepared for a gathering composed only of fellow *Alimi* immigrants.

Recollections

According to Lupton, food and eating constitute an intense emotional experience that is intertwined with embodied sensations and the most varied emotions, from loathing and hatred, fear and anger, to happiness, pleasure, gratification, and desire (Lupton 1996: 36). Insofar as immigration is considered a strong emotional experience that requires the redefinition of the self, the traditional Russian part of the *Zastolie* – the old-favorite cooked dishes, the tastes, the smells, the conventional manners and behavior by which food is consumed – was an axis for the invocation and embodiment of the country of origin and of the immigrants' life in it.

Throughout the long, drawn-out meal, participants in the *Zastolies* we studied recalled old common friends and acquaintances. They constantly recollected street names and addresses where they had lived, jobs previously held (particularly noting those which had entailed moonlighting, and regularly discussing the sums earned). They related and recounted their pastimes, vacations, and events they had attended. Significantly, they constantly and repeatedly referred to the metonym of food, cuisine, and foodstuffs.

In their experience of self, Russian food and the country of origin largely constituted an inseparable part of the present. Through the act of eating, the immigrants' present in Israel has been imbued with reminders of the past, and with the continued influence of their affiliation to their country of origin. Karina: "taste the pickles, they're from the Russian store, really tasty;" Lena: "spread the butter on the bread, it's real butter from the Russian store, look how yellow." Felix: "try this sausage, it's just like the one I brought from Moscow when I was there on business." Emphasis is thus placed on the particularly Russian origin of a dish, or its similarity (". . . turned out just like . . .") to an original Russian dish. Repeated comments given as encouragement and as thanks to the hostess are: "Wow! Just like there!", "a true *Zastolie*", "just like at home, in Russia."

A special degree of reflection on the past and present accompanied the Russian ambiance invoked during the particular festivity of the *Zastolie* celebrating the New Year's Eve. In the Hadar area in Haifa, where our study was carried out, not only were their own New-Year's *Zastolie* and their own decorations especially "home-like" for the immigrants. On this day the immigrants felt a particular affinity toward the nearby Christian-Arab streets of town. This area, which on a daily basis played no role in their lives, now glittered with the holiday provisions, images of Santa Claus and Christmas trees. These all infused the immigrants with a feeling of "home," as it used to be. It was a unique situation in which the "world outside" (just the most immediate, and hence a small part of Israel) celebrated along with the inner world of the *Alimi*. "This is a real Holiday. Now I get it!" (Vladimir), "the street suddenly got a facelift" (Irena), "This is just like home" (Christina).

Comments characterizing events, objects or food as "like" or "turned out just like" the original Russian, revitalizing living bonds with the former country, have never quite disappeared in *Zastolie* conversations. At the same time, these constant reminders, the constant reference to the other place, enfolded the present in yearning. While participants talk about familiar food items, memories of searching and consuming in the USSR were recalled, and stories of the ventures undertaken to obtain the desired foods were told and retold: the "proper connections" with people of a certain commercial chain, the price per kilogram, market vs. shop prices, the names of shops and streets, or remembering particular locations where there were better chances of "getting" certain products at certain periods. In many of these reflections, the previous life and old country were talked about in terms of longing; however, as memories, they were something that had been left behind. Tamara to Alla: ". . . do you remember when we were traveling together on business to Minsk, we suddenly saw those boxes of concentrated milk. It seems unbelievable now that on a night's train-trip home each of us was carrying twenty boxes . . ." Alla continued: "Never mind that, that was only the milk. Remember the rest? It was so heavy! And now it seems ridiculous." Felix: ". . . and how much worrying, and arguing, and shouting in lines; you stand there and wonder: 'will it or won't it be enough?' To make it last, the vendor or the people in line would decide on a certain quantity for everyone . . . [A]fter spending hours in line, you don't get to choose, you take what you get and feel great! You've got it and it's enough! You'll bring it home, unexpectedly, and everyone will be thrilled!" Ina: "It's unbelievable how much time we spent 'collecting'." (Ina applies "*kolekzionirovanie,*" ordinarily used for stamp or coin collecting, to refer to food which was bought by chance and kept – i.e., "collected" – for special occasions.) Igor: "Yes, everything we got by struggling, and it made you so happy! Each time – an event, realized expectations, the pride of success; whereas here – you buy it, and – nothing! You can buy more, as much as you want and – nothing."

During their conversations, the "authentic" "Russian" products – brought from Russia, and served and consumed at the present table – were particularly cherished and in a sense were also over-glorified by the immigrants. However, the perception of the food's "likeness" to the Russian original, and its over-glorification by the immigrants, experientially also encapsulated a self already distanced from the original place and time. The country of origin was conveyed at the table as having been relinquished and as the past. Despite the search for the commonly admired authentic food, matters of taste varied among the people convened. During our observations there were several incidents when a certain product was described as "just like" ("*tochno kak*") by one person and as a "miserable fake," "not the same" ("*Zhalkoe podobie*," "*ne to*") (i.e., having nothing in common with the original item) by another. In addition, the desired original, such as bread brought as a gift by a visiting tourist, sometimes remained on the table while the local sliced bread was happily consumed. On one occasion, during a conversation around the table Yuri, one of Lena and Nicolai's guests turned to Lena saying: "Do you remember those *belyash* (fried *pirozhki*, pockets filled with meat) that they used to sell at the entrance to the Metro? I can still taste their flavor." Lena responded: "What's the big deal, they're easy to make!" Yuri then responded: "No, that wouldn't be the same . . ." to which Lena, pondering, commented: "It's you who are no longer the same."

The Unreconstructable Image of "Home"

In the *Zastolie*, immigrants gather with old friends from the "previous life." (The *Alimi's* use of "*predyduschaya zhizn*" – meaning reincarnation – emphasizes the separation between life before and after migration.) By providing shelter, enabling the symbolic revival of their "true" identities, and suffusing their present with the presence of the country of origin, the Zastolie participants here conjure and harbor a private sphere in which one expresses one's private, personal experience, and in which one is charged with renewed energy and emotional support for venturing forth from the private to the public. Murcott's metaphor of the meal as "something to come home to" (Murcott 1982: 80–1) is of particular interest in this context. Constituting the walls of this "internal home" (Marcuse 1996) through the gathering, the recalling of food, and its preparation and consumption, the *Zastolie* is itself much like a real home. It is, temporarily, where (what) we really are.

Indeed, "home" and "homeliness" (the researchers' metaphors) were also among the main subjects of the immigrants' own conversations. This was *clear* not only through their references to the *Zastolie* and reminders of the old country ("true Zastolie", "just like home"). Rather, the association made between the *Zastolie* and home permitted it to be a place where the immigrants could openly reflect upon the roles of "homeliness" and "home" in their present, in their new life.

Israel – the *Alimi's* new country – has had a particular significance as "home" for Jews of various past immigrations. In the Zionist ethos, Jewish immigration to Israel is conceived in terms of *Aliya* to "The Country" – ascending being originally related to the "*aliya la'tora*" (a privileged synagogue ritual), and "The Country" connoting the Jews' return to a cosmic-historical homeland (see for example Rozenzweig 1971 [1930]). In practical daily life, acquiring an apartment (i.e., "having a place") in Israel is financially particularly difficult. For the immigrants from FSU, owning an apartment in the new country is an economic achievement as well as an autobiographical statement. As Roman, in a *Zastolie* discussion, noted: "your own fortress [compared to a rental], your home, where you can drive a nail in the wall where you wish." (This was an image that was frequently repeated in the immigrants' rhetoric.)

However, the context of the intimate and homely *Zastolie* was where doubts were also expressed regarding the possibility of having one's real "home" in an Israeli apartment. Some of the apartment-owning participants expressed their feelings in the following manner: Olga: "A home, but not quite;" Nicolai: "not exactly home;" Vera: "here you don't feel like the apartment's yours, that it's part of you till the end of your days"; Lena explains: "everything around, outside, isn't home – nature, people, climate. The home you've built [here] . . . can't keep out all these things, it can't stand against them: these things infiltrate your life. That's why, no matter how hard you try to create something of your own here, it doesn't feel like home." Felix touches upon the experience of immigrants: "Now if I move to another country, I won't have the feeling of being disconnected from my home because I've already been disconnected and that sense stays with me."

In the context of Israel, the immigrants' perceptions are characteristic of the newcomers' discontentment, of the *Alimi* being experientially deprived of the place they deserve. They are characteristic of the immigrants who came to Israel without any religious-national Jewish conviction, or any Zionist ideological affiliation. The term "*Aliya*" as used by the immigrants lacks the "homecoming" connotation, and immigration is called "arrival in Israel" rather than "return to Israel" or to "The Country." And yet, in the context of global migration and the phenomenon of transmigration, Felix's and the others' perceptions should perhaps also be understood as representing the experience of transmigrants, i.e., the experience of "home" as being divided between "here" and "there," or "home" as possibly anywhere and nowhere. To paraphrase Boyarin: the only place in this universe where immigrants might feel at home is with the realization that they are not at home (after Boyarin 1994: 4).

Further indications that this may be an accurate portrayal of the experiences of these immigrants are their perceptions that it is not only Israel and one's own Israeli apartment which are not fully a home. As described above, the *Zastolie* itself – the temporary "walled" home in the new country – is not quite a home either. In the case earlier referred to, Yuri's memory of the taste of *belyashi* could not be recaptured – "wouldn't be the same" – once removed from its original context: sold at ten kopecks in the underground of the city where a person was born and where they had lived for approximately fifty years. While reflecting on the conditions in the country of origin, people themselves were mindful of the difficulties related to earning a living in the previous FSU context, of the change in their conditions, and of the appropriateness of their decision to emigrate. Hence, the nature of their longing and of their nostalgia had not been an outcome of happy experiences in the FSU, as was also supported in the comparisons made between their current condition to that reported in letters received from Russia. Their own past experiences, embodied in the food's "likeness," was "sanitized" (Stern 1992: 11) and "fictionalized" (Lupton 1996: 50). The traditional food, and its present significance, thus encapsulated the precarious walls of the "original home" invoked through the *Zastolie*.

This, however, did not deter the immigrants from time and again seeking out the original food, or one "just like it." This is so, because "likeness" (i.e. similarity), in addition to sameness, points to difference(s) as well.

"Here I Can Get Anything"

With all of the references made by the immigrants to the past and to the original home, the *Zastolie*, as structured in Israel, was not simply a new construction of the original home. This is indicated not only by the clear nostalgic and distancing dimension. Through the *Zastolie*, life after "reincarnation" was also admitted and, in an important sense, celebrated.

This, to begin with, could be noted by the explicit admission and serving of Israeli food, the penetration of Hebrew words and local terms into the immigrants' dialogues as well as the prevalence of discussions on topics concerning daily life in Israel. In the immigrants' lives, these, beyond their particular Jewish/Israeli import, had higher-order, more general significance. They were signs of living outside the FSU, of joining in with the (Western) world. Israel, the new country, constituted in this respect a condition and a vantage point for a new framing of identities – both present and past.

For a start, the hosts carrying on the *Zastolie* tradition were no longer constrained by limited availability, as they had been in the FSU, due to the wealth of products that characterized the new society. In spite of their present economic condition, they could – for the first time – compose a meal as they chose. This freedom to choose was, by itself, a new social and existential condition. In the Western tradition it has meant living the experience of freedom itself (as the West would have it) (see for example Slater 1997).

For Russian immigrants to Israel in the 1990s, this condition in their new country was not only a source of "freedom." In the context of a globalized, postmodern world, the freedom of choice in addition appeared as a vehicle for a complex transmigrant identity. In the new country, with its freedom of choice, the traditional *Zastolie* has turned into a theater of variable identities. The identity markers cast in these meals included not only the *Zastolie*'s traditional dishes, or Israeli typical local ("exotic") dishes, but also other categories – new performances, and variations – of being "Russian" (or "Israeli," or both) within the new condition.

Among the new performances, one recalls the dishes characteristic of different republics in the FSU. In the *Zastolies* observed for our study, participants happily prepared dishes such as *plov* from Uzbekistan, *Leche* from Georgia, *Borsht* from the Ukraine. In the context of the new condition in Israel, these, in the past alien to the Russian *Zastolie*, are of interest. As noted above, most of the participants in the *Zastolies* under study emigrated to Israel just a short time after the dissolution of the USSR. The novel custom of serving an all-FSU repertoire demonstrates the immigrants' sense of belonging to a strong and powerful state. (Genis and Vail 1992: 134) call it "patriotic gigantomania;" (see also Solodkina 1996.) At the same time, this re-invention of a state – and of identity – which no longer exists, of an already imaginary space of a "USSR home," was itself plausible due to the crumbling of the superpower as well as to the physical distancing of the *Zastolie* participants from their original home and society. Among the hosts and their guests, the discussions of Russian current events, and the comparisons with local Israeli events, were managed (from the "here and now", according to Gudeman and Rivera) from the point of view of Israeli citizens who are not directly affected by the internal political and economic woes of Russia (Gudeman and Rivera 1990). Notions of "the past" and of the "country of origin" were then expanded and played out in the new-*Zastolie*, and through the negotiation of new present identities.

The "original" identity has also been distanced and enacted in the display of the present through other *Zastolie* practices. The nostalgic and glorifying attitudes focused on even the most simple, familiar and typically "Russian" foodstuffs; these have blended in the new country – as we discussed earlier – with a fascination and pride for the free economy and of its associated dreams. Thus, Nicolai in hosting one of his visitors from the Russian Federation stated: "Here [in Israel] I can 'get' anything." The guest asked disbelievingly: "Anything?" and Nicolai responded: "Yes, I'm telling you! If I feel like having "*Kobachkovaya Ikra*' [a cheap Russian zucchini salad eaten by "simple workers" in the USSR] from a can, you know, like they serve at cafeterias in a factory – I go ahead, or if I want for example a sprat in tomato sauce (also canned), no problem! I go to the Russian store and buy it!" According to this example, the immigrants living in Israel are able to flaunt their economic status by drawing attention to the surprising possibility, so unexpected by the visitor from the FSU, of obtaining simple Soviet food items – the epitome of Russian present ordinary life – in Israel.

The same combination of living the Russian present, playing and displaying its remoteness, and celebrating the present in the new country, can be followed in the immigrants' enthusiastic discussion and use of products recently advertised for the first time on Russian broadcast channels. Thus the immigrants prepared and displayed dishes presented on famous cooking and entertainment shows, such as "Smak" ("Food of Passion"), "Tasty Hysterias," "Women's City," and "From a Woman's Life." Much like the previous examples, the celebrating Israeli/Russian immigrants compared themselves on an imaginary level with the socio-economic class of their friends who remain in the Russian Federation, who cannot afford most of the recipes featured on these television shows.

And last, of great significance to the immigrants currently in the new country, was the fact that the meal might now include not only traditionally festive dishes, or new local items or FSU and newly advertized Russian items that the host has managed to find, but also particular items that in the past were altogether rare and hardly ever found on the same table. Many of these items were associated with capitalism and were considered a luxury in the USSR. In spite of modest incomes, these now appeared on the *Zastolie* table. The use of specialty and luxury items symbolized not only the communist ideal of abundance (as represented in Russian cookbooks brought by the immigrants to Israel), but also the capitalist image of food, as it was described in the closed-off USSR. Thus, among the new items that could be discerned on the immigrant's table in the new country, alongside the trout, smoked salmon, and caviar, were coleslaw and pineapple salads, which in communist Russia were a major symbol of the capitalist world – as per the renowned words of a Soviet poet, Vladimir Maykovsky: "Eat your Pineapple, chew your hazel grouse, your final day has arrived, bourgeois" (cited and trans. Glants 1997: 19).

The Israeli context made it possible to attain an image of an ideal and abundant Russia that did not exist for the majority in reality. It was also a symbolic realization of a past Russian fairy-tale about a "spread tablecloth," magical in its ability to produce an abundance of delicacies, fruits, dishes, meats, and wines. In Israel, the use of local "exotic" products as well as prestigious and modern foods thus intended to demonstrate (particularly to Russian guests) the lifestyle of a capitalist world and the achievements and economic status of the immigrant hosts. In gatherings that included visitors from Russia, and in those including only the group of immigrants, the cultural symbols were perfectly understood by all.

The identity of the "Russian" immigrants or transmigrants in Israel combined a simultaneous participation in the life of two societies, the original one and the new. An active participation in the original society (by following the news shows and literature, hosting visitors, eating Russian food, celebrating the *Zastolie* occasions) was combined with its being perceived from a distance, becoming an object of nostalgic longing, of over-Russification, an object of display and experimental presentations. In addition to being about the "original"-home and the continued relevance of Russian identity, the Israeli *Zastolie* has therefore also been about their perception of present life in FSU and on the past as a bygone. It was simultaneously about the predicament of immigration to Israel, and also about the present, confirming that past-dreams have come true.

However, Israel was certainly not where they felt they "really" belonged. A capitalist, technologically and economically modern country has both been explored and incorporated. Nevertheless, relations between the immigrants and the *Izrailtyane* were highly strained, and the immigrants were unwilling to perceive themselves as a part of the local community. While the immigrants displayed the benefits of their new life, the locals – perceived as inferior in terms of their culture – were far better off in terms of these same benefits. Therefore, the displays were mostly directed toward the immigrants' own compatriots (*Alimi*, *Vatiki*, guests from Russia). Furthermore, Israel's Jewish national-religious and Zionist dimensions were largely alien to the immigrants. It was noted that *Zastolies* were used to celebrating local religious-national holidays, although without much excitement. Further, the *Zastolie* repertoire was on these occasions slightly distinguished by the addition of traditional Jewish elements. On the one hand, these do not indicate an "absorption of immigrants" or a too highly significant change in the "Russian" character of the *Zastolie*. Among the Russian immigrants the introduction of matzah on the Passover table did not preclude the appearance of bread (forbidden by the Jewish religious rule). In the same context, we also witnessed the nostalgia for the celebration of the Gregorian New Year. In the eyes of the Jewish *Izrailtyane* neighbors and in the general context of the "Jewish state," this Slavic nostalgia was perceived as highly peculiar. And yet, the mixing of matzah and bread, or even the mood set by the New Year's Eve, did not indicate a non-Jewish identity. They were rather indications of the particular Jewish identity of these immigrants from the FSU. During the late 1990s these immigrants, and their condition vis-à-vis the locals, made the immigrants' interests and their life connections focus largely on Russia, on group-inclusion, as well as crossing – when affordable – beyond Israel, to the European cultural home. Yet identity, as shown in this chapter, was differently experienced and differently presented in different contexts, perpetually being combined with other identities, and largely in flux.

References

Appadurai, A. (1992), "Disjuncture and Difference in the Global Cultural Economy," in M. Featherston (ed.), *Global Culture,* London: Sage.

Barthes, R. (1979), "Toward a Psycho-Sociology of Contemporary Food Consumption," in R. Forster and O. Ramun (eds), *Food and Drink in History,* Baltimore: Johns Hopkins University Press.

Beardsworth, A. and Keil, T. (1997), *Sociology on the Menu*, London: Routledge.

Ben-Rafael, E. and Sharot, S. (1991), *Ethnicity, Religion, and Class in Israeli Society*, Cambridge: Cambridge University Press.

Benske, T. (1994), "Ethnic Convergence Processes under Conditions of Persisting Socio-Economic Decreasing Cultural Differences: The Case of Israeli Society," *International Migration Review*, 28(2): 256–80.

Bloch, E. (1977), *Tubinger Einleitung in Die Philosophie*, Frankfurt am Main: Suhrkamp.

Bodnar, J. (1985), *The Transplanted: A History of Immigrants in Urban America*, Bloomington and Indianapolis: Indiana University Press.

Bourdieu, P. (1984), *Distinction: a Social Critique of the Judgement of Taste*, Cambridge, MA: Harvard University Press.

Boyarin, J. (ed.) (1994), *Remapping Memory: The Politics of Time Space*, Minneapolis, London: University of Minnesota Press.

Carmon, N. (ed.) (1996), *Immigration and Integration in Post Industrial Society*, Basingstoke: Macmillan.

Carrier, J. (1990), "Gifts in a World of Commodities: The Ideology of the Perfect Gift in American Society," *Social Analysis*, 29: 19–37.

Cheap, D. (1988), *The Gift Economy*, London and New York: Routledge.

Douglas, M. (1975), "Deciphering a Meal," *Daedalus*, 101(1): 61–81.

Elias, N. (1994), *The Civilizing Process*, trans. E. Jephcott, Oxford: Blackwell.

Featherstone, M. (ed.) (1992), *Global Culture*, London: Sage.

Friedman, J. (1992), "Being in the World: Globalization and Localization," in M. Featherstone (ed.), *Global Culture*, London: Sage.

Fuchs, L. H. (1993), "An Agenda for Tomorrow: Immigration Policy and Ethnic Policies," *Annals of the Academy of Political and Social Science*, 530: 171–86.

Genis, A. and Vail, P. (1992), *Lost Paradise, Immigration Autoportrait*, New York: Columbia University Press.

Gitelman, Z. (1995), *Immigration and Identity: The Resettlement and Impact of Soviet Immigrants on Israeli Politics and Society*, Los Angeles: The Susan and David Wilstein Institute of Jewish Policy Study.

—— (1997), "From a Northern Country: Russian and Soviet Jewish Immigrants to America and Israel in Historical Perspective," in N. Lewin-Epstein, Y. Roi, P. Ritterband (eds), *Russian Jews on Three Continents. Migration and Resettlement*, London: Frank Cass.

Glants, M. (1997), "Food as Art: Painting in Late Soviet Russia," in M. Glants and J. Toomre (eds), *Food in Russian History and Culture*, Bloomington and Indianapolis: Indiana University Press.

Gold, S. (1997), " Soviet Jewish Aliyah 1989–92: Impact and Implications for Israel and the Middle East," *International Migration Review*, 31(3): 754–5.

Goldstein, J. (1985), "Iranian ethnicity in Israel: Reformance of Identity," in A. Weingrod (ed.), *Studies in Israeli Ethnicity*, New York: Gordon and Breach.

Goody, J. (1982), *Cooking Cuisine and Class. A Study in Comparative Sociology*, Cambridge: Cambridge University Press.

Gordon, M. M. (1964), *Assimilation in American Life*, New York: Oxford University Press.

Gudeman, S. and Rivera, A. (1990), *Conversation in Colombia: The Domestic Economy in Life and Text*, Cambridge: Cambridge University Press.

Hannerz, U. (1992), "Cosmopolitans and Locals in World Culture," in M. Featherstone (ed.), *Global Culture*, London: Sage.

Inowlocki, L., (2000), "Doing 'Being Jewish': Constitution of 'Normality' in Families of Jewish Displaced Persons in Germany," in R. Breckner, D. Kalekin-Fishman, and I. Miethe (eds), *Biographies and the Division of Europe: Experience, Action and Change on the "Eastern Side,"* Opladen: Leske and Budrich.

Kivisto, P. (1990), "The Transplanted Then and Now: the Reorientation of Immigration Studies from the Chicago School to the New Social History," *Ethnic and Racial Studies*, 13(4): 455–85.

Leshem, E. (1997), "The Israeli Public's Attitudes Toward the New Immigrants of the 1990's," in E. Leshem, and J. Shuval (eds), *Immigration to Israel: Sociological Perspectives*, New Brunswick NJ and London: Transaction Publishers.

Lévi-Strauss, C. (1966), "Culinary Triangle," *New Society*, 12: 937–40.

—— (1970), *The Raw and the Cooked*, trans. John and Doreen Weightman, London: J. Cape.

Lewin-Epstein, N. (1997), "Introduction," in N. Lewin-Epstein, Y. Ro'i, and P. Ritterband (eds), *Russian Jews on Three Continents: Migration and Resettlement*, London: Frank Cass.

Lewin-Epstein, N., Ro'i, Y. and Ritterband, P. (eds) (1997), *Russian Jews on Three Continents: Migration and Resettlement*, London: Frank Cass.

Lieberson, S. (1961), "The Impact of Residental Segregation on Ethnic Assimilation," *Social Forces*, 40: 52–7.

Lupton, D. (1996), *Food, the Body and the Self*, London: Thousand Oaks, New Delhi: Sage.

Marcuse, P. (1996). "Of Walls and Immigrant Enclaves," in N. Carmon (ed.), *Immigration and Integration in Post Industrial Society*, Basingstoke: Macmillan.

Mauss, M. (1990 [1950]), *The Gift: The Form and Reason for Exchange in Archaic Societies*, London: Routledge.

Mennell, S. (1985), *All Manners of Food: Eating and Taste in England and France from the Middle Ages to the Present,* Oxford: Blackwell.

Mennell, S., Murcott, A., and Van Otterloo, A. N. (1992), *The Sociology of Food: Eating Diet and Culture,* London: Sage.

Morse (1994), "What do Cyborgs Eat? A Real Logic in Information Society," *Discourse*, 16(3): 86–123.

Murcott, A. (1982), "On the Social Significance of the 'Cooked Dinner' in South Wales," *Social Science Information*, 21(4/5): 677–96.

Neeman, R. (1994), "Inverted Ethnicity as Collective and Personal Text: an Association of Rumanian Israelis," *Anthropological Quarterly*, 67(3): 135–49.

Park, R. E. (1950), *Race and Culture*, Glencoe: Free Press.

Ritterband, P. (1997), "Jewish Identity among Russian Immigrants in the US," in N. Lewin-Epstein, Y. Ro'i, and P. Ritterband (eds), *Russian Jews on Three Continents: Migration and Resettlement*, London: Frank Cass.

Rivkina, R. (1996), *Jews in Post-Soviet Russia. Who Are They. Sociological Analysis*, Moscow: A.R.S.S. (in Russian).

Rosenzweig, F. (1971 [1930]), *The Star of Redemption*, London: Routledge & Kegan Paul.

Sack, R. (1997), "Geography, History and Social Science Progress," *Human Geography*, 21(3): 431–2.

Schiller, N. G., Basch, L., and Blanc-Szanton, C. (eds) (1997), *Towards a Transnational Perspective on Migration: Race, Class, Ethnicity and Nationalism,* New York: New York Academy of Sciences.

Schoenfeld, S. (1991), "Interpretive Social Science and The Study of Jewish Identity: Inside the Black Box," paper presented at the Third Israel–Canada Conference on Social Scientific Approaches to the study of Judaism, Bar-Ilan University, Israel.

Shabtay, M. (1996), *Identity Reformation among Ethiopian Refugees in Israel: The Case of Ethiopian-Israeli Soldiers,* unpublished PhD dissertation, Department of the Behavioral Sciences, Ben-Gurion University.

Shilling, C. (1993), *The Body and Social Theory*, London: Sage.

Shuval, J. and Leshem, E. (1997), "The Sociology of Migration in Israel: A Critical View," in E. Leshem and J. Shuval (eds), *Immigration to Israel: Sociological Perspectives,* New Brunswick, NJ and London: Transaction Publishers.

Slater, D. (1997), *Consumer Culture and Modernity*, Cambridge: Polity.

Smooha, S. (1986), "Three Approaches to the Sociology of Ethnic Relations in Israel," *Jerusalem Quarterly*, 40: 131–61.

Solodkina, M. (1996), *Zivilizovannyi diskomfort: Sovetskie Evrei v Israile v 90 godi. Statii po Sociologii Alii i Sociologischeskaya Publizistika* (Civilized Discomfort: Soviet Jews in Israel in 1990s. Sociological Essays, published in Russian). Tel-Aviv: Ivrus.

Stern, B. (1992), "Historical and Personal Nostalgia in Advertising Text: the fin de siècle effect," *Journal of Advertising*, 11(4): 11–22.

Swirski, S. (1989), *Israel, The Oriental Majority*, London: Zed.

Weingrod, A. (1985), *Studies in Israeli Ethnicity: After the Ingathering*, New York: Gordon and Breach Science Publishers.

Zukin, S. (1995), "Place, Modernity, and the Consumer's World: A Relational Framework for Geographical Analysis," *Contemporary Sociology*, 24(1): 70–1.

–7–

"Doing Market" across National and Gender Divides: Consumption Patterns of Israeli Palestinians

Amalia Sa'ar

This chapter documents practices of consumption among Palestinian citizens of Israel from a variety of communities.[1] In Israel, and particularly among the Palestinian minority inside it, the massive influx of consumer goods and the burgeoning consumer culture that has surrounded them are relatively recent phenomena.[2] They are direct consequences of globalization, the rise in national wealth,[3] the spread of multinational commerce, and the significant cheapening of goods that were formerly beyond the reach of the masses. Among the Palestinian citizens of Israel mass consumption is even more recent, expanding rapidly mainly in the last decade of the twentieth century.

A salient characteristic of Israeli-Palestinian consumption is that it extends across a range of markets, which are located within the state and beyond, and which offer varied types of goods, price levels, and interactions.[4] To some degree, nearly all households combine purchases from different markets, sorting them according to a host of considerations such as cost, luxuriousness, convenience, satisfaction, or accessibility. This daily exercise of getting and assessing the value of goods attainable from different locations involves potential and actual crossing of gender, ethnic, and national borders. It vividly embeds consumerism in concentric circles of power, and induces consumers to position themselves actively, though not necessarily consciously, with respect to these powers.

Like older forms of exchange, consumption by Israeli Palestinians constitutes a token of social relationships (Douglas 1996; Miller 1995), and through them allows articulations of personal and collective identities (Friedman 1994; Halter 2000).

At the particular historical moment that this chapter records, Israeli Palestinians faced simultaneous openings of multiple borders: ethnic, national, regional, and cultural. These openings coincided with a booming economy of mass consumption, into which they were drawn along with the rest of the Israelis. Having relatively easy access to both Israeli-Jewish and non-Israeli Arab localities, they utilized the openings of regional and national borders to diversify their material and cultural consumption. Like ethnic populations elsewhere in the world, who reside on opposite sides of national borders and are consequently frequent crossers of these borders,[5] Israeli-Palestinian consumers could thus save or spend, adjusting their budgets and their social statements according to changing ability, accessibility, context, and need. In the process they have negotiated their position vis-à-vis the different reference groups that inhabit their lives. For Israeli Palestinians, shopping in the Palestinian Authority (PA), Egypt, or Jordan yields more than an opportunity for cheap material consumption. Likewise, Israeli shopping centers offer them more than high-quality products. Rather, these very different shopping environments furnish them opportunities to participate in the various cultural settings that comprise their social world.

A second prominent theme that emerges in Israeli-Palestinian practices of consumption, alongside frequent crossing of physical boundaries, is experimentation with cultural boundaries, most notably those of gender. In the fast-emerging consumer culture among Israeli Palestinians, gender symbolism is especially prominent because the moral discourse of authenticity usually lumps together mass consumption and women's liberation as the major causes of Westernization.[6] This moral interpretation, moreover, is reinforced by the historical coincidence of the advent of mass consumption on the one hand and the expanding economic, educational, and civic opportunities for women on the other. Patterns of consumption tend partly to reaffirm traditional gender roles, but they also represent innovation with regard to the gender division of labor and notions of manhood and womanhood. Since many consumption practices involve new goods and resources, their gender classification is not obvious. Therefore, consumerism often yields opportunities to experiment with gender identities.

As in the case of doing market across geopolitical boundaries, the experimentation with gender through consumption has implications beyond personal matters. In this respect too, consumption constitutes an avenue through which the community molds its collective identity. Consumption has become a major vehicle for the production of modern men and women (see Abaza 2001; Abu-Lughod 1995; Forte 2002) who in turn serve as major embodiments of the modernity, and of the morality of their community.

The Consuming Community

In the 1990s, the years in which I did my research, the life of the Palestinian citizens of Israel seemed to evince improvement. After decades of political acquiescence they started to gain some prominence on the state's parliamentary scene. Their freedom of movement increased significantly compared with that in the first two decades of Israeli statehood, when they lived under military government. Their public discourse vis-à-vis Israeli-Jewish society has become sophisticated, demanding the civil rights that were theirs according to the state's liberal-democratic ethos. A new generation of intellectuals, who were still denied access to employment in the public sector, turned instead to establish numerous non-governmental organizations (Ittijah 1998), through which they managed to raise funds and produce community services that the state had neglected to offer. Economically, the majority of this population still occupied the lowest echelons of the Israeli class system both as individual households and as communities (Israel 2000; Kraus and Yonay 2000; Swirski and Conur 2000). Nevertheless, they became increasingly able to afford a variety of consumer goods – including cars, electronic appliances, and leisure activities, which only a decade before would have been very far from the reach of most. In this atmosphere of rising civil and political salience, and improved personal welfare, the Palestinian citizens seemed to have acquired a sense of confidence, which fed back into already existing ideas of individualism, personal freedom, and open opportunities, and through them to a general collective image of modernity.

However in 2002, when this chapter was being written, this sense of expanding possibilities was less strong, and at times seemed to be actually regressing. Amid world-wide economic recession and two years of political tensions with the PA, Israel experienced a deepening economic depression that had a particularly acute effect on the poorer segments of its population, including the Palestinian citizens. Rising nationalism reframed the latter as a potential fifth column and eroded the legitimacy of their claims for liberal rights. The most stark instance of this turn of events took place in October 2000, when political protest of Palestinian citizens instigated a violent police crackdown. In the following two years, escalating violent clashes between Israel and the PA brought about increasing restrictions on the passage of people and goods across the borders. Consequently, the movement of Israeli Palestinians into Arab localities outside the state became ever more difficult or even ceased altogether. Moreover, owing to intensifying public hostility toward Arabs, their movement in and out of Jewish localities too lost much of the ease it had acquired over the previous decade or two.

Since an acute state of war exists at the time of writing, it is difficult to predict whether the recent decline in consumption among Israeli Palestinians, both in expenditure and in spatial range, will mark a new phase or whether the wide array of consumption activities evident in the 1990s will be restored. Whatever direction it may take in the future, such periodical turns of events do not render obsolete the symbolism outlined below that I have discerned in the practices of consumption. Rather, they highlight how much symbolic meaning-making is embedded in history and at particular economic and political junctures. As I hope to show in this chapter, the theme of modernity that features very highly in the local discourse about consumption, including the seemingly apolitical notions of individualism and materialism, is strongly ingrained in the political-economic conditions of the community. While the latter do not always come up explicitly in the context of consumption, they still figure very clearly in the symbolic texts that it produces.

In the 1990s then, and to some degree already in the 1980s, Israeli Palestinians were assimilated into a fast-increasing national and global consumerism. For them as for people the world over, this created a certain atmosphere of democratization,[7] as a wide variety of consumer goods and practices that had been too expensive and therefore served as class markers became readily available for the masses. Nevertheless, the intensity and scope of Israeli-Palestinian consumption is not uniform, as they are not a homogeneous population. Christians generally tend to have smaller families, higher levels of education, and higher occupational prestige than Muslims (Kraus and Yonay 2000), three parameters that influence household economies, including consumption. Likewise, urban communities tend to have higher rates of female labor-force participation, which again affects family-income levels and the scope of household consumption. For the purpose of the present chapter it is also important to mention the economic disparities between Palestinians in Israel and in the PA, which as we shall see have clearly affected the patterns of consumption of the former.

Israel is a rich country with a relatively high standard of living. For example, in 1998 the GDP in Israel was $16,754, compared with $1,322 in the neighboring Arab countries (and $22,184 in the EU) (Swirski and Conur 2000: 5). This general affluence, although far from being equally divided – in fact, social inequalities in Israel have increased sharply – is intertwined with expanding consumerism. Matras (2001: 13) identifies the intensification of consumer activities across the Israeli class system as social embourgeoisement, by which he means a general expansion of levels and qualities of consumption, increasing appreciation of the value of schooling and training, especially of post-secondary training, and a rising demand for leisure opportunities and pursuits. This phenomenon, he stresses, is present in all ethnic groups and has occurred despite widening income inequalities. Indeed it is remarkable that while by conventional measurements of social class the Palestinian citizens of Israel have always been classified in the lower-middle and poor strata of society,[8] they too have nevertheless been increasingly drawn into the broader process of social embourgeoisement.

Going Out in Natania: Affording to Stop and Shop at Jewish Localities

Mūsa is a 42-year-old Christian. He is married, a city dweller, and a self-employed accountant. Here is his description of how he manages the economics of his domestic consumption:

> My gross income is about NIS 10,000 and I estimate that my wife's household expenses are about NIS 3,000. I give her small sums on an irregular basis, a few hundred here and a 50-shekel bill there, whenever she asks or even without her asking. I am her walking money machine. These sums are for food and household expenses and they do not include clothing and entertainment, for which I pay separately with checks or credit card. I separate personal expenses from household expenses. In fact, it would be cheaper for me to give her a set monthly salary [*sic*] of say NIS 1,200 and have her manage on that . . .
>
> I really like going out. We go to restaurants and cafés here in town or in other cities, such as Tiberias, Natanya, or Tel Aviv [Jewish-populated cities]. We also go on week-long vacations to hotels in Israel or in other Mediterranean countries.

Mūsa, his 33-year-old wife Nawāl, and their only child live in an apartment building where his elderly parents and three married brothers also live, in separate apartments. The construction of this building was a shared enterprise between Mūsa's father and his sons. Today each nuclear family functions as an independent economic unit, although they still spend much time together on a daily basis, sharing meals and often going out to restaurants or on vacations. At work Mūsa is his own boss, running an independent firm of accounting and tax consultancy. He employs some of his relatives, namely his wife Nawāl as his unsalaried secretary and his sister-in-law and niece as salaried clerks. In the past one of his brothers worked for him for six years, as did his father for a short while after he retired.

Typical of family businesses, Nawāl's employment constitutes an expansion of her domestic work. She receives no independent income and her work is framed as "help." Mūsa remains the sole owner and manager of the family capital. Nawāl is given relatively little leverage with regard to spending money on consumer goods. While she is a regular participant in the consumption of goods and entertainment, and has a certain say as to what items she wants to buy, her consumption is largely mediated through a man. A wife's being given set sums of money for domestic and personal expenses, as in Nawāl's case, is a rather common practice. It applies not only to wives of business owners but also to women who are married to wage-earners. Many of these women do not participate in paid labor because they have small children at home, because there are no suitable jobs available for them, or because their husbands insist that they do not become employed.

In terms of class, Mūsa and Nawāl's is not a typical family. Rather, Mūsa being self-employed and his relatively high income place their circumstances well above those of the average Israeli Palestinian household.[9] Throughout the 1990s, however, habits of going shopping in a mall, sitting in a restaurant, or even going on vacation at a hotel became increasingly popular and spread into more and more segments of the population, largely due to a diversification of sites and prices. Shopping centers, in particular, have turned into attractive recreational sites. Located at short driving distances from most Arab settlements, they appeal mostly to adolescents and married and unmarried people in their twenties and thirties, and to a lesser degree also to people in their forties and fifties, who use them as sites for family excursions.

Hunting for Cheap Products in Expanding Territories: Israel, the West Bank, Gaza, and Beyond

The bulk of daily purchases of most Israeli Palestinians, however, takes place elsewhere. Inside Israel, people buy mainly in open-air markets, wholesale stores, and local neighborhood stores, or from peddlers who visit their neighborhoods. Goods at these different markets themselves cover a wide price-range, and the lowest prices among them are significantly cheaper than those in the air-conditioned shopping centers. In all-Arab localities, such stores/markets serve locals of all income levels, including the better-off in the community. In mixed cities, such as Tel Aviv-Jaffa, Ramla, Lydda, or Haifa, cheap stores and open-air markets are usually located in the poorer areas, where families reside amid industrial workshops, garages, offices, and brothels, and their customers are poor people from diverse ethnic and national backgrounds.

Cheaper products still can be found across the borders in the PA and to a lesser degree also in Jordan and Egypt.[10] Historically, the region now divided by national borders was one cultural domain, where communities maintained marriage relations, political alliances, businesses, and cultural exchange. These relations were abruptly severed following the creation of the state of Israel in 1948 and the sealing of the international borders between it and its Arab neighbors. Following the 1967 war and the Israeli occupation of the West Bank and Gaza, much of the historical exchange between Palestinian communities on what had become opposite sides of the border was gradually restored.[11] After the peace agreements between Israel and Egypt in the early 1980s, and then Jordan in the mid-1990s, exchange relationships were established/renewed with other Palestinian and Arab communities.

In Arab stores inside Israel and in many of the Jewish-owned cheaper stores, much of the merchandize originates in the PA, where the merchants travel regularly to buy the goods. Transactions by Israelis across the borders are by no means unique to the Palestinian citizens of the state, but they are more common among them than among Jewish citizens in terms of scope, regularity, and directness.[12] Whereas Israeli Jews purchase from the PA territories mainly through mediators, for Israeli Palestinians direct contact is easy and even rewarding. Not only do they speak the language, many of them have relatives and friends in the West Bank and Gaza, with whom they already maintain an elaborate network of exchange. The relatively new phenomenon of large-scale movement of consumer goods between Palestinians from both sides of the border is therefore incorporated into an existing and active network of social relations.

Suha, a 25-year-old Muslim woman from an urban community in the center of Israel, has become highly skilled in making the best of cheap markets, tending to visit more and more of these as she became an adult. At 18, after she got engaged, Suha traveled alone to markets in Tel Aviv, Ramla, and Lydda (all inside Israel and less than an hour's drive from one another), to buy her dowry of bedclothes and home accessories. By the time I knew her, Suha, then a university student, was already a mother of a two-year-old. Like Nawāl, she lived with her husband Zeidān in a unit adjacent to his parents and married brothers, and since Zeidān was also still a student, they depended heavily on his father's financial support. This, in turn, was given within a strong patriarchal mode of relations, including ongoing attempts by Zeidān's mother to monitor her daughter-in-law. While she fiercely resisted her in-laws' attempts to control her, Suha did use their money – or, as she put it, her husband's money – to pay for tuition, for a car, and for driving lessons. Older and more confident that she had been when she first got engaged, she started using their car for shopping expeditions in towns in the West Bank, usually in the company of another woman or a child. On one occasion, for example, she invited an unmarried female neighbor to go with her to the West Bank city of Tūl Karem, where she took some of her gold jewelry to be repaired. During that one morning's trip the two women visited the jeweler and then dined at a restaurant before they drove back home.

Producing to Consume: Creating more Markets at Home

At the same time as they take their consumption activities farther away into old and new sites and territories, Israeli Palestinians are also creating new markets at home. At the core of this process lies a dynamic relation between consumption and production. Material goods for daily consumption, from food and clothes to dwellings and home appliances, are increasingly purchased rather than made or processed at home. Yet self-production of some of these goods for consumption or barter continues to exist on a small scale. For example, women buy bread but may also bake it at home; likewise cakes and other foods. Some women, especially in rural settlements, keep livestock, grow vegetables and fruits, or make clothes for their families; men build, renovate, and maintain the infrastructure of their own and their brothers' houses. Overall, the proportion of self-produced goods in the cycle of familial consumption is diminishing and that of ready-made ones is growing. But the possibility of reverting to self-production and self-service has not disappeared. The persistence of this option constitutes an important factor of consumerism, for it gives families leverage to cut down on household expenses according to changing needs. It also allows them to venture into business enterprises, mainly in the food, recreation, and gift industries, which in turn feed back into a growing cycle of consumption.

This connection is particularly prominent in the case of women, whose increasing and diversifying participation in consumption has been historically related to their changing participation in production, in that they have more cash to spend and they themselves produce new goods for other women to consume, mainly through their work in the informal sector.[13] Muna, about 40 years old, a Muslim, is a mother of six who resides in one of the villages of Galilee. Some years after her marriage Muna, who had only five years of formal schooling, decided that she needed to earn a living. She took a sewing course, bought a sewing machine, and started doing small mending jobs for her neighbors. Gradually she started sewing and selling new clothes too, and within a few years she managed to establish herself as a fashion designer specializing in wedding gowns and party dresses. Two years before I met her in 1998, Muna opened a store in the street-level room of her house, where she sells her dresses, lingerie, and accessories. The goods that she sells, as well as the material for the dresses, she buys on special trips that she makes to the city of Nazareth.

Muna, who is one of a relatively small group of women small-business entrepreneurs, affords an example of a cyclical link between women's production and consumption. Through her business Muna responds to an existing demand for women's luxury consumerism, but at the same time she contributes to nurturing and broadening this demand. Because she works from home, and because her business is largely informal, she is able to supply luxury clothes that are cheaper than those attainable outside the village. Also, her selling from home makes her merchandise attractive to village women, whose movements are restricted to walking distances and to domestic visits inside the village. Similar small businesses run by women and geared mostly to women consumers are home-based hairdressing salons, children's nurseries, fortune-telling, or handicrafts and home-made food. The success of all these relatively new business enterprises depends on the entrepreneurs' ability to convince their neighbors to purchase goods that were traditionally home-made. Such convincing, however, usually does not mean creating needs where none exist. Rather, it is a by-product of the broader mass-consumption that takes place outside the Palestinian enclaves, in which these women already participate on a small scale, but where costs are still too high to make them regular customers.

Going Out in Ramallah: Crossing the Border for Fun

An important and growing branch of consumerism that thrives on regional border crossing, besides the purchase of products and raw materials, is recreation and entertainment. Here are included short vacations in nearby Mediterranean and Arab countries or at hotels inside Israel, traveling to attend concerts by famous Arab musicians (mostly in Jordan or Egypt), and nightly recreational gatherings in restaurants in the PA that offer food and live music (*sahrāt* in Arabic). For large segments of the Israeli-Palestinian public, these forms of recreation have become financially and technically feasible only in recent years. This is a direct result of economic globalization, which has brought down the prices of flights and hotels and has produced an abundance of packages and group deals, as well as of the changing political conditions in the region. The Israeli peace agreements with Egypt and with Jordan yielded an abundant flow of Israeli tourists to these two countries, which owing to the significantly higher standard of living in Israel has been very much one-directional. Within this stream of tourists the Palestinian citizens are very prominent. Alongside the attraction of visiting countries that share their culture, language, and relations, the low costs incurred in visits to the neighboring states are an important factor enabling Israeli Palestinians to travel abroad for vacations.

Another, relatively small-scale branch of cross-border consumption is the pilgrimage to Mecca, which is officially sanctioned by the state of Israel for its Muslim citizens. Local Palestinians travel to Saudi Arabia in chartered buses, and during their short stay in the holy city they pay for accommodation and for the rituals. These include the purchase of a sacrificial lamb, and sometimes also of additional lambs on behalf of relatives and neighbors at home, who entrust them with this mission. The returning pilgrims usually take back small gifts, such as colorful clothes and beads or ritualistic items.[14]

The growing branch of leisure consumerism accords an interesting role to women as they, and not only men, engage in organizing trips and entertainment evenings. As mentioned, for most Israeli Palestinians, trips and vacations at hotels have become affordable only in the past decade or so. This mass influx of new clientele into the local and regional tourism industry created a plethora of small-scale entrepreneurships, in which Palestinian women enjoyed a relative advantage from the start. First, a (small) number of highly educated Palestinian women were already incorporated into tourist agencies in the Jewish sector, so that when the market ripened they became useful middle persons for these agencies, which wanted to draw in Arab customers. Alternatively, having acquired the skills and the connections, some of these women themselves took the initiative and started organizing private trips for groups of relatives and acquaintances. A second advantage for women lay in the norms of gender morality and gender segregation, which cast suspicion on women who traveled without their husbands. In light of these factors, women entrepreneurs began organizing trips and entertainment evenings for women only, marketing their personal good reputation as a guarantee of propriety. As in the case of Muna, the fashion designer, these women simultaneously responded to and created a demand in ever widening circles of low-income women, for whom until quite recently vacations and trips had never been an option.

Wafa is a 38-year-old divorced mother of four who lives in an urban community. Her income consists mostly of welfare benefits and some irregular alimony payments. For a period during our acquaintance, Wafa was engaged in organizing trips and entertainment evenings for people in her community. I first met her during a four-day organized women's trip to Jordan, which we both joined. During our stay, Wafa participated very little in the group's activities, and it was clear that she had independent local connections. (People she introduced as relatives would come to pick her up from the hotel.) Later I understood that she used this visit to establish business connections, for after we got back she started inviting people in the community to go on similar trips with her for cheaper prices. Beside the packages to Jordan, Wafa also organized several one-night outings (*sahrāt*) to restaurants in the West Bank city of Ramallah. Unlike the trips abroad, these *sahrāt* were gender-mixed, and as she invited certain unmarried individuals to participate, Wafa made a point of telling them that they would have an opportunity to meet available members of the other gender.

As a woman in the community commented to me, there was something peculiar, even uncanny, about Wafa's organizing this kind of activity because she was religious. Shortly after her divorce she had started wearing religious Muslim attire, which consisted of long-sleeved full-length dresses of opaque material and a headscarf. For Israeli-Palestinian Muslims, entertainment evenings that include music and are attended by unrelated members of both genders are somewhat borderline situations. While many attend them gladly, as they would wedding celebrations, others, especially religious people, tend to avoid them, claiming that they harbor potential immorality. In fact, the case of Wafa's organizing *sahrāt* was doubly contradictory, because besides being religious she was also divorced. Divorced women are supposed to be particularly careful about attending secular entertainment events, let alone organizing them, for they are regarded as potential suspects of immoral behavior almost by definition. As it happened, Wafa's religious attire, which normally indicates overall religious observance, actually gave her a certain protection from such suspicions. The factor that should presumably have prevented her from engaging in the entertainment industry was what enabled her to do so. From an analytical point of view, Wafa's highly ambiguous involvement in entertainment consumerism is not surprising. It reflects the inevitable ambiguity that accompanies the parallel expansion of mass consumption on the one hand, and of gender categories on the other.

Women, in Particular

In the growing consumerism of Israeli Palestinians at the close of the twentieth century, women have been particularly prominent as consumption and women have become historically and discursively intertwined. Historically, the intensification of mass consumption has coincided with dramatic changes in women's social and economic opportunities. Women have entered the culture of mass consumption at the same time as they have started to gain visibility in the public sphere in other respects also. The relatively recent phenomenon of Israeli-Palestinian women driving, moving about on their own, running bureaucratic errands, or speaking on their own and their families' behalf, is closely related to their consumer participation in that it facilitates it and emanates from it. Women move about more freely when they drive their own cars, have cellular phones, and can use credit cards. These, along with their familiarity with the codes of consumer society, increase their independence and self-confidence. They encourage women to venture into ever-expanding territories, which, in the end, enhances their participation in consumption even more. In response, local discourses on morality and modernity have assumed strong causal links between consumption and what people habitually call "the liberation of women."

In many of my formal interviews, especially those conducted with male notables such as sheiks, priests, or community leaders, consumer culture was popularly depicted as a source of collective malady, which entailed hyper-materialism and moral deterioration, by which most meant deterioration of gender morality. This verbal moralism was often a response to unarticulated messages that resonated in the conduct of many in the community, which connoted that consumerism was a sign of modernity and cultural sophistication. People extensively displayed consumer goods and skills, such as cars and driving licenses, cellular phones, fashionable dress, or recreational outings, to communicate cultural refinement and personal advancement.

A widespread local assumption, then, is that being part of modernity, consumption entails profound changes in gender relations. However, ethnographic documentation reveals that the transformations in gender relations often tend to be less striking than they appear. To a degree, mass consumption has followed and even strengthened the traditional gender patterns that assign large spending and purchasing away from home to senior family members, primarily men. Despite the short distances and generally smooth journey, and although increasing numbers of women drive cars, traveling across the border is still more legitimate for men than it is for women. For example, bulk purchases of fresh food (meat, vegetables, and fruit), which is significantly cheaper on the other side of the border, are more likely to fall to men. Men are also the ones who are more likely to buy expensive goods, such as jewelry, furniture, or construction materials. In many cases, when they wish to make such purchases, even women who have cars still ask their husband, brother, or son to take them.

Yet as we have seen ethnographically, this norm is flexible, even though it remains widespread. Suha, Muna, and Wafa, as well as 'Abla, whose example below will conclude this section, are in many senses exceptional individuals. These are women who dare to behave in ways that are not firmly within the consensus of gender morality. In the context of consumption, they not only act in an economically resourceful and entrepreneur-like way toward their family, which is fairly common behavior in women; they take their initiative on to the public sphere, and in the process they do not hesitate to cross borders, literally as well as metaphorically. While they are not necessarily representative, examples of such women are interesting here because they mark directions of change as well as the fluid boundaries of normative behavior. On the one hand, such women embody the idea that consumption and modernity indeed bring about revolutionary change in the status of women. Yet on the other hand, being exceptional they also denote the limits of such change, which in the experience of most women is much less radical.

When I tried to establish whether or not women going shopping in the PA on their own was considered normative behavior, the answers revealed that "the norm" was diverse and rather inclusive. Most women I spoke to said they did not feel safe or comfortable doing expensive purchases in the PA without the company of men. They would, however, happily join a female friend for half a day's trip across the border in the latter's car when the opportunity arose, and would come back with small bargains, such as toys or children's clothes. It all depended on the family, people asserted, by which they meant the degree of each family's conservatism (*taḥaffuṭh*). Indeed, different families within the same village, neighborhood, or clan (*ḥamūla*) may adhere to very different standards in this respect, some prohibiting their women from leaving the village or the neighborhood unescorted, others allowing them to travel alone to any destination inside and outside the country, and for any reason. Moreover, it is not uncommon to find different interpretations of normative feminine behavior even within the same household, where one sister may feel that she cannot allow herself to take the bus alone, say from Jaffa to Tel Aviv, while her sister readily drives herself all over the country, and stays overnight with relatives or friends (see Sa'ar 2000).

Aside from what local people call families' conservatism, traveling alone to large shopping malls in Israel or to the PA depends also on whether or not a woman can drive; still more on whether she has her own car. It depends also on her age and family situation (for example, elderly women are less likely to travel alone; young unmarried women may not be allowed to travel for fear for their reputation), and on her lifestyle in general. Women who work outside the house or study in a different city are more accustomed to being out on their own. Their Hebrew is usually more fluent, they feel confident dealing with strangers and, if seen by a relative or a neighbor, are more likely to have a legitimate excuse for being out in the first place. Women who manage to appropriate the prerogative of independent across-the-border consumerism usually are sustained by a combination of some basic material means, a social environment that is at least partly supportive, and most importantly, a very assertive personality.

For the majority of women who travel to the PA, Egypt, or Jordan, with male relatives or in groups of women, the borders still constitute a significant factor in the articulation of gender and consumption. Even so, the encounter of citizens and non-citizens in consumer transactions still gives these women some significant edge. This is particularly evident when they meet with salesmen and peddlers from the West Bank and Gaza *in their own neighborhoods*. The products that women can buy from these non-citizens are usually cheaper than what they can get in the local stores and markets, and this gives them a sense of power. Many women become exceptionally assertive in bargaining and take much pride in managing to bring the already low prices further down. Likewise, when displaying goods purchased across the border, women emphasize the good bargain they made, interspersing their discourse with paternalistic expressions of pity for the poverty-stricken people who sold it to them.[15] Lastly, even when no physical or political borders are crossed, consumption still offers opportunities for bending and crossing the boundaries of gender morality. An obvious example in this respect is watching television, an item that is found in the vast majority of households, usually with a wide selection of satellite or cable channels. When they come across sexual or erotic scenes on television, some women switch to another channel in embarrassment, while others make a point of watching and even adding interpretations.

I conclude this section with a story of one last outstanding woman. 'Abla is a 33-year-old unmarried professional Muslim woman, a neighbor of Suha. In 1998 'Abla took over a small unit in a compound in which her extended family, namely parents, two married brothers, and two other unmarried sisters, had lived as protected tenants. That unit became vacant after one brother moved to an apartment he had newly purchased. While at once there were various contenders for the new space, 'Abla managed with her father's support to claim it for herself. She decided to renovate it, and hired one of her brothers-in-law to do the work. Most atypically she did not give this brother-in-law a lump sum to buy the necessary materials, but instead did all the purchasing herself. She would travel frequently to Ṭul Karem to inspect the available merchandise, then to bargain, and finally to arrange for the transport of blocks, tiles, faucets, sinks, and such appliances. On these trips 'Abla, like Suha, would take a younger companion with her, usually a boy or an adolescent girl. However, she never took men and she did all the negotiating herself. Indeed, 'Abla told me that on these trips to Ṭul Karem she soon became noticed and got many reactions of wonder and flirtatious behavior from local men. Apparently she handled these very skillfully, for she managed to complete all the transactions to her full satisfaction without ever being assaulted or seriously harassed. Although she had given some of the merchants her private phone number for technical arrangements, none of them abused their possession of it to pursue her romantically.

'Abla is an exceptional individual in many respects. She herself said when I asked her about the trips to Ṭul Karem: "I don't know anybody who does what I do." She is exceptional not only with regard to *where* she chose to buy, but also to *the kind of goods* she bought by herself. Normatively, Palestinian women do not undertake to renovate homes on their own, and when they do they tend to be content to choose a subcontractor, usually a relative, and let him go about the actual purchasing of materials. It is precisely because of her exceptionality that 'Abla constitutes a good example of the point at issue, which is that at the junction of three historically new roads – mass consumption, modernizing gender relations, and changing political borders – the practical meanings of gender and ethnicity/nationality are amenable to creative shaping.

Statements about Identity in the Discourse of Consumption

Anthropologically, the exchange of goods through consumerism can be seen as an exchange of images and meanings (Bourdieu 1984), and therefore as a form of discourse (Sahlins 1976: 286). Israeli-Palestinians use consumption to negotiate their position vis-à-vis Palestinians in the PA, other Arabs, Israeli Jews, and in a more generalized sense also "the modern world." The web of movements spun in this process produces a commentary on their relationships with these groups, hence a discourse on collective identity. Practices of consumption create "an unstable field of floating signifiers" (Baudrillard, in Featherstone 1987: 19), which unravels simultaneous possibilities of difference and sameness *within and without* the national collectivity. Thus, Israeli Palestinians approach material and more so cultural consumption in Arab localities outside Israel with a combination of romantic ardor and the relaxation of those who have returned home. This wishful position, however, is rendered significantly more complex by the fact that they come from and return to their actual homes inside Israel. In actuality, when Israeli Palestinians go for shopping, holidaying, or entertainment in the West Bank, Egypt, or Jordan they vacillate between two contradictory positions: of a deprived minority at long last reuniting with its native culture, and of privileged customers who stand to make a nice bargain.

The map of Israeli-Palestinian consumerism presents a particular construction and experience of space, which are different from the state's hegemonic construction. In certain important respects this is a subversive alternative space as it provides the Palestinian citizens with avenues for cheap consumption that are not available to the Israeli-Jewish public. More than that, through cultural exchange and collective communication with other Palestinians it provides them with avenues to evade the state's control and its attempts to isolate them. Yet despite its subversive potential, this alternative space is by no means protected from the forces and logic of national exclusion. For one thing, Palestinian citizens who cross the borders are periodically subjected to inspection, arrest, and related methods of control. A more subtle form still in which the hegemonic order penetrates the alternative space is the partial internalization of Israeli ethnocentrism, which the Palestinian citizens willy-nilly tend to adopt in their encounters with the poverty and less modern technology on the other side of the border.

Regardless of the explicit or conscious political identifications with which they approach their consumer transactions, the interchange of Israeli Palestinians with Israeli Jews and non-Israeli Arabs alike is invariably affected by their multiple affiliations. While at it, they shift among contradictory positions of affinity, strangeness, power, and disempowerment. Consumption-related interactions with other Arabs are informed by a conglomeration of cultural closeness and a sense of shared history, alongside the paternalism of those who live a more comfortable life. Likewise, their interactions with Israeli Jews are fashioned by a mixture of the affinity of co-consumers on the one hand and feelings of alienation and hostility on the other.

Consumption then, especially when it takes place on some Other's turf, provides daily opportunities to grapple with the meanings and implications of being Israeli Palestinians. In a similar vein and maybe even more intensely, it also creates opportunities to experiment with ways of being a man or a woman. These two issues are closely linked, because gender is a popular key symbol in articulations of collective identity and because in practical individual experiences, being a woman/man and being Palestinian (or Arab) are inextricably connected circumstances. The utilization of gender as a key symbol in representations of national and ethnic identity is well documented in the literature (see Haeri 1999; Katz 1996; Kelsky 1999; Peteet 1993, 1999). Especially popular in this respect is the role of gender as carrier of modernity and authenticity.[16] For example, analyzing advertisement images in the Arabic press in Israel, Rekhess (1987) points out a conflict between what he calls "traditional" and "Western" influences. In all his examples the controversial images are always those of women who are either too exposed or too covered for the taste of the readers. He cites similar findings from a study conducted in the Arab Gulf states, according to which Arab consumers reacted negatively to the implantation of Western images and values, which again revolved around the representation of women's bodies.

For Israeli Palestinians, because of their multiple and conflicting affiliations, modernity represents many things at once. It stands for both the relatively advantageous and disadvantageous components of their existence. In respect of the Jewish majority inside the state, modernity represents a form of cultural takeover, whereas in respect of non-citizen Palestinians and other Arabs it represents a form of cultural advancement. We could see an example of this duality in the case of Mūsa. His tight control of his wife's expenditures clearly reflected traditional masculine role definition. At the same time, his consumer choices, such as taking his wife out to have a good time or orienting her to run an up-to-date household, also suggested that he was re-creating himself as a *modern* man. Unlike verbal debates about identity,[17] consumerism allows far more subtle negotiations of ideological constructs such as national authenticity and modern civility, because it translates them into a series of practical daily behaviors. The observations of such behaviors that were presented in this chapter have revealed continuity rather than a break between the various moral codes and identity components of the group in question.

Acknowledgments

Fieldwork for this project was largely made possible through the financial support of the Wenner Gren Foundation and the Lady Davis Fellowship Trust, and I would like to extend my gratitude to these two institutions. Nurit Bird-David, Debbie Bernstein, Tally Katz-Geru, and the editors of this volume Yoram Carmeli and Kalman Applbaum made very helpful comments on an earlier version of this chapter. I thank and appreciate Tania Forte for sharing with me her unpublished work on consumption among Israeli Palestinians, and Murray Rosovsky for his careful editing of this chapter. Last but not least, I am grateful to my Palestinian friends and acquaintances for speaking to me about their lives openly and willingly.

References

Abaza, M. (2001), "Shopping Malls, Consumer Culture and the Reshaping of Public Space in Egypt," *Theory, Culture and Society,* 18: 97–122.

Abu-Lughod, L. (1995), "The Objects of Soap Opera: Eyptian Television and the Cultural Politics of Modernity," trans. M. Strathern, in D. Miller (ed.), *Worlds Apart: Modernity through the Prism of the Local (The Uses of Knowledge: Global and Local Relations),* London: Routledge.

Balas, T. (2000), "The Third Authority: Radwan Abu Ayyash Deals with Arafat, Pirates, and Tnuva," *Otot,* 233: 20, 26 (Hebrew).

Berdahl, D. (1999), *Where the World Ended: Re-unification and Identity in the German Borderland*, Berkeley, CA: University of California Press.

Bourdieu, P. (1984), *Distinction: A Social Critique of the Judgement of Taste*, trans. R. Nice, Cambridge, MA: Harvard University Press.

Cohen, L. (1998), "The New Deal State and the Making of Citizen Consumers," in S. Strasser, C. McGovern, and M. Judt (eds), *Getting and Spending; European and American Consumer Societies in the Twentieth Century,* Cambridge: Cambridge University Press.

Douglas, M. (1996), *Thought Styles: Critical Essays on Good Taste*, London: Sage.

Eshet, T. (1996), *Cultural and Symbolic Meanings in a Shopping Center (Mall)*, M.A. Thesis: University of Haifa (Hebrew).

Featherstone, M. (1987), "Consumer Culture, Symbolic Power and Universalism," in G. Stauth and S. Zubaida (eds), *Mass Culture, Popular Culture, and Social Life in the Middle East*, Boulder, CO: Westview.

Forte, T. (2002), "Saving and Spending, Cooking and Cleaning: Shopping and the Making of Women, Homes, and Political Persons in the Galilee," *City and Society*, 13.

Friedman, J. (ed.) (1994), *Consumption and Identity (Studies in Anthropology and History)*, Chur, Switzerland: Harwood Academic Publishers.

Haeri, S. (1999), "Woman's Body, Nation's Honor: Rape in Pakistan," in A. Afsaruddin (ed.), *Hermeneutics and Honor: Negotiating Female "Public" Space in Islamic/ate Societies*, London: Harvard University Press.

Halter, M. (2000), *Shopping for Identity; the Marketing of Ethnicity*, New York: Schocken.

Israel, C.B.o.S.I. (1996), *Statistical Abstract of Israel 1996. Number 47*, Central Bureau of Statistics.

Israel, N.I.I. (2000), *Annual Survey 2000*, National Insurance Institute, Research and Planning Administration (Hebrew).

Ittijah (1998), *Arab Community-Based Associations*, Haifa: Ittijah.

Katz, S. H. (1996), "Adam and Adama, Ird and "Ard: En-gendering Political Conflict and Identity in Early Jewish and Palestinian Nationalisms," in D. Kandiyoti (ed.), *Gendering the Middle East: Alternative Perspectives*, London: I.B.Tauris.

Kelsky, K. (1999), "Gender, Modernity, and Eroticized Internationalism in Japan," *Cultural Anthropology*, 14: 229–55.

Kraus, V. and Yonay, Y. (2000), "The Power and Limits of Ethnonationalism: Palestinians and Eastern Jews in Israel," *British Journal of Sociology*, 51: 525–51.

Lewin-Epstein, N. and Semyonov, M. (1993), *The Arab Minority in Israel's Economy* (Social Inequality Series), Boulder, CO: Westview.

Matras, J. (2001), "Economic Reform, the Turn to Globalization, and Impacts on the Labour Market and Stratification in Israel," paper presented to the ISA Research Committee on Social Stratification, RC28 Meeting, Mannheim, 2001.

McGovern, C. (1998), "Consumption and citizenship in the United States, 1900–1940," in S. Strasser, C. McGovern, and M. Judt (eds), *Getting and Spending;*

European and American Consumer Societies in the Twentieth Century, Cambridge: Cambridge University Press.
Miller, D. (1995), "Consumption and Commodities," *Annual Review of Anthropology*, 24: 141–61.
Peteet, J. (1993), "Authenticity and Gender, the Representation of Culture," in J. Tucker (ed.), *Arab Women: Old Boundaries, New Frontiers*, Bloomington: Indiana University Press.
—— (1999), "Gender and Sexuality: Belonging to the National and Moral Order," in A. Afsaruddin (ed.), *Hermeneutics and Honor: Negotiating Female "Public" Space in Islamic/ate Societies*, London: Harvard University Press.
Rekhess, E. (1987), "East and West in Advertisement," *Otot*, 87: 20 (Hebrew).
—— (1989), "Israeli Arabs and the Arabs of the West Bank and Gaza: Political Affinity and National Solidarity," *Asian and African Studies*, 23: 119–54.
Roberts, M. L. (1998), "Gender, Consumption, and Commodity Culture," *American Historical Review*, 103: 817–44.
Rosenhak, Z. (1998), "New Developments in the Sociology of Palestinian Citizens of Israel: an Analytical Review," *Ethnic and Racial Studies*, 21: 558–78.
Rouhana, N. (1989), "The Political Transformation of the Palestinians in Israel: From Acquiescence to Challenge," *Journal of Palestinian Studies*, 18: 38–59.
Sa'ar, A. (2000), "'Girls' and 'Women:' Femininity and Social Adulthood among Unmarried Israeli-Palestinian Women," Ph.D. Dissertation, Boston University.
Sahlins, M. (1976), *Culture and Practical Reason*, Chicago: University of Chicago Press.
Semsek, H.-G. (1987), "Popular Culture versus Mass Culture: the Social Dynamics in a Popular Cairene Quarter. A Case Study," in G. Stauth, and S. Zubaida (eds), *Mass Culture, Popular Culture, and Social Life in the Middle East*, Boulder, CO: Westview.
Smooha, S. (1989), *Arabs and Jews in Israel*, Boulder, CO: Westview.
Swirski, S. and Conur, E. (2000), *Social State of Affairs, 2000*, Adva Unpublished Report (Hebrew).
Weaver, T. (2001), "Time, Space, and Articulation in the Economic Development of the U.S.-Mexico Border Region from 1940 to 2000," *Human Organization*, 60: 105–120.
Wilson, T. M. (1995), "Blurred Borders: Local and Global Consumer Culture in Northern Ireland," in J. A. Costa, and G. J. Bamossy (eds), *Marketing in a Multicultural World: Ethnicity, Nationalism, and Cultural Identity*, Thousand Oaks, CA: Sage.
Zayed, A. (1987), "Popular Culture and Consumerism in Underdeveloped Urban Areas: a Study of the Cairene Quarter of Al-Sharrabiyya," in G. Stauth, and S. Zubaida (eds), *Mass Culture, Popular Culture, and Social Life in the Middle East*, Boulder, CO: Westview.

–8–

Consumption under Construction: Power and Production of Homes in Galilee

Tania Forte

This chapter is about the consumption of resources as seen through the production of homes in Israel. Making a home is a central concern for most Israeli citizens, one in which they invest time, thought, hopes, money, and work. Indeed, "putting a roof over one's head" is a pervasive, often-discussed aspiration leading to momentous decisions about making a home. On the other hand, "paying the mortgage," a long-term obligation, is the often inevitable corollary.[1] Yet, while Israeli citizens at the turn of the century may dream of red-roofed houses, they rarely articulate the fact that their personal decisions about home-making, and the obligations these entail, are inscribed within political, economic, and social power relations. In this chapter, I discuss the production of homes in relation to three underlying macro-level trends: state land control; home financing policies; and global consumption trends as represented in Israel. Each of these is very much at work in Israeli citizens' everyday life, Palestinian and Jewish alike; each has also contributed to transformations in the cultural constitution of an Israeli sense of home at the end of the twentieth century. Through these three trends, state and global patterns of power shape the very homes and lives of Israeli citizens. They enter into decisions such as where to make one's home, how to pay for it, how to plan and furnish it, as well as how to live within it – that is, into personal, intimate consumption decisions. I briefly discuss these trends before showing how they are materialized in the home and life of Palestinian citizens of Israel in the Galilee.

State and Global Power: Land Control, Home Financing, and Consumption Trends in Israel

Territorial Control: Placing Homes on the Landscape

Critical studies have highlighted ways in which state land control has constrained the access to land of Arab citizens since the foundation of the state (Jiryis 1976; Zureik 1979; Lustick 1980; Falah 1989; Yiftachel 1991). Access to land controlled by the state is indeed a prominent site in which difference between citizens is manifested.[2] Land expropriations, for instance, have repeatedly targeted Palestinian citizens of Israel, linked to repeated efforts to expand the "Jewish" presence over territory. In addition, resources earmarked for infrastructural development of Arab settlements notoriously lag behind those for development of Jewish ones. As Palestinian citizens of Israel have organized into a political presence, such inequalities are increasingly more visible in the Israeli public sphere. In the terms of Michel Foucault, the state project of territorial control is indeed an attempt to bring together specific "truths" with specific applications of power construed as legitimate (Foucault 1980a).[3] In the case of Israel, then, truths expounded by Zionist narratives reinforce territorial control, and tools of territorial control in turn strengthen these founding narratives.

In addition, the relation between citizens and the land on which they live has been mediated by administrative means which condone and perpetuate difference. Of course, like those in states all over the world, Israeli officials employ specific technologies of land surveying and planning in order to formalize, standardize, homogenize control over state land (see among others Anderson 1991; Scott 1998; Gottdiener 1994). But here such tools have been specifically used to constitute material differences between Palestinian and Jewish citizens (Falah 1989). An added, recurring dimension of land policy in Israel is that Jewish citizens have been encouraged to settle in particular areas which are either heavily populated by Palestinians (such as the Galilee) or considered "empty" (such as the Negev desert). Thus population settlement is a tool of control as well, and has been used as such by government officials over the years (Kimmerling 1983; Yiftachel 1991).[4] At the same time, incentives to settle in particular places have taken different forms. Intermittently, land has been released for settlement free of charge in specific areas considered strategically important or in some way peripheral; there have been higher subsidized mortgages or grants for people who choose to settle in particular areas. Likewise, more subsidized public housing is available for rent in these areas (Dadon 2000; also Kallus and Law-Yone 2000). These factors have entered into decisions of citizens, especially those of moderate means, as they decide where to live.[5]

What is manifest here, then, is that ways in which state institutions control and plan land affect the settlement of citizens on state territory. Two major patterns are evident. Palestinian citizens have been discouraged from moving to "Jewish" settlements and towns, and building space within Palestinian settlements has been constrained, lagging far behind the demand. On the other hand, since the 1950s Jewish citizens have been encouraged through financial incentives or land grants to move to "less desirable" areas, which are also in fact areas more heavily populated by Palestinian citizens. This pattern is also reproduced in the Israeli press and popular discourse. While Palestinian citizens have been perceived to "take over" state land, Jewish citizens are seen, in contrast, to "guard" it or to hold on to it. Tools of control, therefore, are used to constitute very differently the relationship between land and citizens.

Home Financing

Since the foundation of the state of Israel, policies have consistently encouraged citizens to buy property rather than to rent (Lewin-Epstein and Semyonov 2000). This has been accomplished through two means: by discouraging renting and by providing incentives to buy. There is comparatively little public housing for rent in Israel, and private rental companies have been discouraged through consistently high taxes throughout the history of the state. By contrast, state officials have encouraged home-ownership through subsidized mortgages.[6] Considering the conditions of renting versus owning constituted by state policies, it is not surprising that home-ownership is an aspiration of Jewish and Palestinian citizens alike, and quickly becomes that of new immigrants as well.

Finally, government officials have a great deal of control over real-estate prices in Israel. A major mechanism of control has been the government's policy of releasing public land for housing and development in limited amounts so as to maintain a constant surplus demand, and therefore to sustain high land prices (Almagor 1996: 183, cited in Dadon 2000).[7] Thus while citizens claim their "right" to state-subsidized mortgages, they are simultaneously unaware of the ways in which the state works through land institutions to affect the price they pay for land.

Consumption and Privatization

Because of mass immigration from the former Soviet Union and greatly increased subsidies from the United States coupled with tariff reduction on consumer goods, the state of Israel experienced an economic boom in the early to mid-1990s. Since that time, consumption has increased dramatically, manifested on the landscape by mushrooming shopping malls, large chain stores, more spacious and more numerous homes, and a growing capacity for people to own cars or travel abroad. Visits to the malls, advertising, and trips abroad provide citizens with experiences through which they re-imagine themselves as global citizens and autonomous persons.[8] Such experiences, in turn, have given rise to new experiences of place, and have helped foster aspirations to new homes, new objects, and new selves.

The demand for homes and commercial expansion have modified the landscape. Interest in the development of Israeli real estate has grown with demographic expansion and the influx of private capital from abroad, as well as new, more flexible institutional policies that released land for development. Concurrently, as some actors have been attempting to appropriate lucrative state land for their own benefit, debates about "privatization" of land and its attendant political implications have emerged (see Shenhav 2000; Saporta and Yonah 2000; Yiftachel and Kedar 2000). But while the discourse about land has shifted from debates about a national project to debates about commercial real estate, political agendas continue to be materialized through them. At the same time, socioeconomic difference is growing. There is an emerging tension, then, between new consumption patterns and new allocation of resources in land.

The making of a home, from construction to decoration and domestic practices, results from interactions with state institutions and economic transformations on the one hand, and from multiple understandings of self and other on the other. Homes are, then, processes by which resources are consumed and selves and sociopolitical relations are renegotiated. I explore how these diverse elements are manifested as they weave themselves into the homes and lives of ordinary people. Because of the very detailed data necessary to sustain such an analysis, I have decided to focus my ethnographic description of home-making upon the citizens among whom I conducted extended fieldwork in the early 1990s, and to whom I paid repeat visits in the late 1990s. The people I describe here are inhabitants of a Palestinian town in the Western Galilee.[9] This analysis is not intended as representative of the experience of all citizens of Israel. Instead, it highlights the fact that as people make intimate decisions about home-making, whether in the fancy neighborhoods of Tel Aviv or in the foothills of the Galilee, they have to contend with state policies, with changing social norms, selves, needs, and desires. It is through this process that resources are mustered and consumed, and relations of power made manifest. Consumption then emerges as a channel by which tensions of power work themselves out.

Negotiating Land Consumption in Deir al-Asad

Sayideh and Hassan are going to build

They have been married for 24 years, and as first cousins they grew up close together. Their parents built houses in the 1950s on a common plot of land that once belonged to their common great-grandfather, Othman. The plot is now a crowded street, inhabited by Hassan and Sayideh's brothers, male cousins, and uncles. There is little room for expansion.

But Sayideh and Hassan are lucky: they have gotten hold of a piece of land. Among Sayideh and Hassan's relatives from the same generation, four families have so far managed to get land and build elsewhere, and an additional three – including Hassan's – are planning to build on the same newly acquired piece of land, much further up the hill. All the other households, it is expected, are saving and working in order to buy land and build. As they do, the houses they leave behind will be remodeled for younger brothers or nephews who are coming of age.

In 1999, Sayideh and Hassan's oldest son Mahmoud, who is working as an electrician and finishing his computer engineering degree at the Technion, got engaged to his mother's brother's daughter, who lives four houses down the street and is studying to become a kindergarten teacher. He entered the lottery for plots of state land designated for young couples.

It was rumored that that land would be sold to the winners at about 35 percent below the current town market rate. This is part of a new program, which the government is supposed to be testing in the town. One lottery for 60 plots was held in 1996, but no one is sure when the next one will be, and the list of registrants is getting longer. In 1996 the odds were one in three; in 1999, according to town people who repeatedly and anxiously check the numbers of candidates registered with the local council, the odds were about one in ten or twelve. As of 2001, the lottery had not yet been held.

Anyone who has seen recent Palestinian houses on the landscape, even from afar, remembers them as multistoried square concrete structures that often look bare and unfinished. Here and there a more elaborate villa stands out, with a fancy red-brick roof, marble columns, or a stone facade. Such houses in themselves tell stories about distinctive land-consumption patterns that various people and institutions have inscribed in them. The fancy homes are those of a few successful entrepreneurs, professionals or landowners who can – and according to local social norms, must – make their success stand out in the town social landscape. Unlike other Israeli citizens who are successful, Palestinians are rarely able or willing to move into fancy town neighborhoods or build a home in a suburb.[10] Neither do their houses stand in a separate neighborhood – since building land is hard to come by in most towns, the house building itself – not the place where it stands – is the concrete means to visible social distinction. These houses distinguish the owners as wealthy; on the other hand, their constrained location in a Palestinian settlement also mark them as Palestinian within the Israeli sociopolitical landscape.

Sayideh and Hassan, like most people of average means, are building a square concrete building which will hold four apartments: one for themselves, and one each for their three elder sons. First, they will "close" two apartments, their own and that of their married son. When the other sons marry, they will close the other apartments as well. Most homes, unlike most homes in Jewish settlements, are a concrete manifestation of households. Like households, they are processes rather than finished products.

What these houses also represent are the changes in consumption patterns of Palestinian citizens of Israel in the Galilee over the past three generations. In that time, people in Hassan and Sayideh's extended family have gone from having a room for their family in their father's mud house to living in their own 30-square-meter concrete homes in the 1960s, to building 90-square-meter apartments in the 1970s and 1980s, and now to planning 160- to 300-square meters per "nuclear" household (Forte 2000). Such increases in household space are consistent with changes in ideas and actual surface of a proper home in Israeli Jewish society (compare Werczberger 2000). For many, it is the ultimate "Western," or "modern" home, representing individual tastes and lifestyles – two bathrooms, at least one with a Jacuzzi, three bedrooms, a large living room, the latest appliances, American kitchens, and Italian bedroom sets, and perhaps a "traditional," "oriental" corner. Clearly, Israeli Palestinians have joined global consuming trends. Personal desires and local social norms are increasingly being reshaped by cable TV, magazine advertisements, or satellite dishes, and people increasingly manifest the selves they desire and imagine by putting together a patchwork of objects and styles that display these imagined selves. There is here a sense of entitlement: as many women explain, they are free to go and shop "like Israelis, to sit where they sit and buy what they buy" – and they mean in the fancy malls of Israeli towns. This is, in a way, what social scientists have called the triumph of the market over the state.

And yet, the market for land in Israel doesn't reflect the same openness to the desires of Palestinian Israelis. The ability to buy land and to move are more heavily over-determined for Palestinian citizens of Israel than for Jewish citizens. Space is at a premium in Deir al-Asad. Since the 1980s, demand for building land has consistently exceeded availability on the town master plan. One main tension in securing land for building involves government land-control policies on the one hand and local demographic expansion on the other. Because of this tension, people live in increasingly crowded conditions. Most courtyards were used into the 1970s for gardens and animals, but were gradually built up into homes for younger generations. People wanted and were expected to produce larger homes of "their own," and since the mid-1950s found the means – financial and otherwise – to bring them into being. In addition, the town population grew tremendously. Moreover, the government severely restricted building zones in most Arab towns in such a way that the area available could not accommodate the inhabitants' present numbers and aspirations.

Whether or not they are aware of this, most state officials couch control within a scientific discourse of planning and land rationalization which masks the fact that they impose state power through differential practices (Foucault 1980a; Lefebvre 1991; Anderson 1991; Scott 1998). Thus in the late 1990s, on a visit to the area, the district engineer and the engineer of a nearby town (both Jewish) deplored the few planted areas still visible in the building zone and advocated that the local landowners should sell these plots rather than holding on to them for their children. Further areas could only be open for expansion, they argued, when such "wasted" space was filled. Town landowners, on the other hand, were concerned with safeguarding future building space in a context in which it is made both scarce and expensive. Thus the tension between state land control and Palestinian demographics stood out as a pressing and explicit concern, marked as a "problem" while Jewish demographic expansion on the land was perceived in a positive light. Addressing architecture students from Tel Aviv University in 1999, the [Jewish] district engineer responsible for planning and implementation in the area described the land/demographics situation in the area thus: "There are 40,000 inhabitants in Karmiel, and 40,000 in the villages in the area. Well, between you and me, *they* are slightly over 40,000, but I don't usually tell people this." Thus for this man, as for many more who worked for land institutions in the area, citizens were conceived in terms of their positive or negative presence on the state's geopolitical landscape. This was taken as commonsensical, as was the idea that there are abiding "cultural differences" and diverging "political interests" among Palestinian and Israeli citizens.

These days, it is very hard to buy land from private owners in Deir al-Asad, mostly because, in the state-designated building zone, there is little such land to be had. People hold on to whatever land they own as much as they can, since, as many tell it, it represents "their children's future." In 1999 the price had reached $150,000 a dunam, more than the cost of building land in the nearby town of Karmiel and three times what it cost ten years before. In the past 15 years, people in Deir al-Asad and other settlements in the area have been talking about building tall apartment buildings, but so far no funding has been made available, no building codes have changed, and none have been built. People who don't have building land are either tearing down old houses and building larger, three-storey buildings on the same plot, or using makeshift additions. Yet for many young men their ability to marry depends on their ability to build houses. So why don't people move elsewhere?

People from the area, and especially from the nearby town of Majd al-Krum where land in 1999 sold for $300,000 a dunam (if it was available for sale at all), have been thinking about this. Some have even bought land in a couple of neighboring Palestinian towns where land is available at cheaper prices. The hard part, of course, is leaving behind the major reciprocity network upon which people rely, their own family. Certainly, land is also relatively cheap in the nearby (Jewish) town of Karmiel but so far, Palestinians are not welcome to buy there; few Palestinians live there at all, and most in rented homes. What many Palestinian professionals in the area are demanding is an "Arab town" – that is, a new town with buildings and proper infrastructure, but made specifically to solve the housing problem of Palestinians. Such an idea is also often associated with Arab cosmopolitanism, that visible in cities of the Middle East, or discussed in books about the period before the foundation of the state of Israel, which are familiar to Palestinian intellectuals and sometimes discussed in the Arab press in Israel. Yet even these aspirations, ironically, are set today in the terms of existing spatial segregation of Jewish and Arab citizens, segregation that land policies and state institutions have established and perpetuated. The desires and aspirations of Palestinian citizens, then, have also been shaped by state land policies.

The political tension at work here determines local land consumption in very specific ways: it establishes the availability of land, and the capacity of people to move within state territory. Moreover, it affects the everyday life and even the hopes and aspirations of ordinary people.

Thus, when people like Sayideh and Hassan make "personal" choices about where to live, or aspire to particular kinds of homes, they are in fact subject to very specific restrictions based on their position as Palestinian citizens, restrictions which are effected through land policies and practices. Within such a context, what kind of choices do people have, and make, about how to constitute selves, how to make a home, how to live within the contemporary world as they imagine it and as it is dealt them? Such questions can be explored further through a very careful look at seemingly insignificant, mundane details of everyday thoughts and practices through which consumption is manifested and negotiated.

According to national census data, most Palestinians are located on the periphery of the Israeli economy, working in low-paying jobs. Yet they share with other Israeli citizens aspirations to large homes and up-to-date appliances, and in fact often follow similar patterns of consumption. A home, be it among Palestinian citizens in the Galilee or among Jewish citizens in other areas, has equally become a means of signifying personhood, household status, and social transformation. What is remarkable here is that so many People in Deir al-Asad are able to build at all, despite the lack and expense of land, and despite their more limited economic means. The capacity to realize one's aspirations implies the ability to channel power. How is it, then, that people manage to build these homes? What resources are specifically being consumed to produce houses? What follows here is an exploration of how consumption works in Deir al-Asad – how people negotiate their relationship to the state, how they develop what they perceive as housing "needs," how they manage to finance and fulfill them, and how, in this process, they develop new moral values, households, and senses of selves.

Consuming Resources, Producing the House: Of Mortgages, Gold, Love, and Changing Selves

Let me start a while back, in the 1970s, when Sayideh and Hassan built the home in which they currently live on the courtyard of Hassan's parents' house. Sayideh remembers how tight their budget was, even after she sold the gold

> from her wedding to build. On days when she took her infant son Mahmoud to Karmiel to see the doctor, she walked the five miles because she didn't have bus fare. At that time, she started the sewing workshop she has maintained ever since on the ground floor of their building, and made extra money to pay for the household expenses.
>
> In 1972 Mohammad [Hassan's brother] and Hassan's households paid for the foundations and the shell of the three-storey structure. Then each household "closed" its own apartment in time, paying for these expenses separately. Neither household sought the low-interest mortgages available through the housing ministry. At the time, remembers Sayideh, people were afraid to borrow from Jewish banks.

In Sayideh's account of the building of the 1970s home, as in many others I heard in the 1990s, government mortgages are conspicuous by their absence, and women's gold by its presence. Why were some things considered as resources to be consumed in order to build a home, and others not? I briefly explore below what these resources meant, how they were experienced, and how sociopolitical power was channeled through them.

The question of whether or not to take government mortgages reflects particular ways in which the state has marked its Palestinian citizens, and in turn the way they have responded to practices connected to this categorization. Between the 1950s and the 1970s, state-subsidized low-interest mortgages were available to all Israeli citizens. Yet few Palestinian citizens took advantage of these mortgages at the time. Government control practices, in the 1950s and 1960s, included surveillance of Palestinians' lives through local informers. In addition, the legitimacy of Palestinian claims to land ownership was undermined as much of their land was expropriated, and their entitlement to land systematically questioned through the courts in the 1950s, with some court cases lingering into the 1980s.[11] Unlike Jewish immigrants, Palestinian citizens were not encouraged to use government mortgages. Ordinary people who didn't have privileged connections with government or political figures saw mortgages or bank loans in general as strings attaching them to the state in dependency relationships, which in turn made them vulnerable because they could be used as leverage against them. Their fear of state-subsidized loans was, to a great extent, connected to the experience of the entanglement of state control into their personal, political, and economic lives. Most people in Deir al-Asad started to use government mortgages in the 1980s. By that time government surveillance had become less aggressive and people felt more confident in establishing their civil rights. By then, government money was not widely perceived to endanger household status. Instead, it was seen as enhancing the capacity to establish one's home. These perceptions were directly linked to how people experienced government practices toward them.

In addition to differential access to mortgages, government policies work to allocate smaller loans to Arab citizens. In the 1990s, the amount of the mortgage was systematically less for most Palestinian citizens of Israel. There were higher sums available for new immigrants, for Jewish religious-seminary students, and for people who had served in the Israeli armed forces, or whose relatives had served. This effectively included all the Jewish population, and excluded a large majority of Palestinian citizens of Israel. Most people in Deir al-Asad were aware of such differential treatment, but as far as building houses went they accepted it as part of the reality in which they lived.

A resource most often consumed in Deir al-Asad in the process of home financing in the 1970s was a woman's jewelry. Sayideh's gold, which she contributed to the house, is also a string attached that entails specific sociopolitical meanings, status, and personal commitments. Most important here is the fact that it is both money and adornment. According to local ideology, the jewelry was given her by her husband's household and she can dispose of it as she sees fit after the wedding. Jewelry is sometimes given with the wish that a young woman may never "need" to sell it, reflecting the importance of its financial value. At the turn of the century a woman's necklaces, bracelets, and headdresses, part of her wedding costume, often consisted of gold and silver coins which could be displayed to index family status, but also strung together or pulled apart when needed later on.[12] They were both money and adornment, a potential resource that might be consumed in time of "need."

The same ambiguous meanings are present in a woman's jewelry today. On the one hand, it reflects the ability to provide of the family she is entering, and thus their social status – it is an object of substantial value displayed on the new bride or mature woman. On the other hand, it is money, since it can be sold and converted into other things – thus many women reported having sold at least some of their jewelry in the 1970s in order to build a home. While it is explicitly presented as belonging to a woman personally, it can be put to the use of her husband's household. So the gift, in fact, is not necessarily made to the woman herself, as an individual, as is often portrayed both by local people and by anthropologists and historians. It becomes meaningful through a woman's actions over time – in this case, in the 1970s, as perceived "needs" started to center around new, larger, and more expensive apartments, women saw fit to convert it into a contribution to the house for her new household. But why would a woman contribute something that is seen as "her property," her own financial security, to something that is seen as property of her household, that is, of her husband's family? What was most important for her and for the household then, as I will show below, is not the gold itself, but the way she as a woman had the capacity to use it to transform the house, the social relations, and the selves within.

Sayideh sold her jewelry in the 1970s. In the early 1990s, she criticized one of her husband's brothers because he kept buying gold for his wife to show how much he loved her, but as a result he could not afford to build a house. This remark reflected changes in moral economy, as a larger, fancier concrete-block apartment had by then become a norm. In the late 1990s, at a time when her household's financial situation was good, Sayideh, who had earlier asserted that she didn't care about gold, started to explain that a man who bought gold for his wife was "romantic." Since her husband had not taken the initiative, she then pressured him to go and buy her several heavy gold bracelets. At the time, she justified this by reminding him that she had sold her jewelry in the first place for the family, and it seemed only right that she should now be "given" gold again. In her remarks in the late 1980s and in the late 1990s, she made the jewelry mean different things: when she sold it, she was doing what was morally and socially proper for the household, unlike the relatives criticized for buying jewelry instead of building a house. When she made her husband buy her gold, she elicited it as an expression of love and romance. The gold she received then was not simply a replacement for what she had sold, though indeed it did have an important financial value. It was a "romantic" gesture, an expression of his attachment to her which returned the attachment she had shown to the household when she had sold her jewelry. It was, then, an action replacing her own action of twenty years previously. Together, these actions reshaped their relationship. The money she contributed in the 1970s was not simply an object or a quantity of money: it was her own capacity to act and to shape the household, the new home, and her relationship to her husband. In turn, it allowed her to develop a new sense of self and to make new judgements and demands: she could criticize her brother-in-law for buying jewelry instead of a home, and she could demand gold as a romantic gesture from her husband. It was not a simple debt that was being repaid, but rather a person and a relationship that were being recognized, enhanced, and transformed.[13] Herein lay the women's choices and aspirations.

So, what do state mortgages and women's jewelry have in common? First, they are both resources that channel power, enhancing people's ability to act – in this case, to consume resources on the one hand, and to produce homes on the other. Both these means of financing a home are used as the result of people's conscious decisions, which are made within the historical circumstances in which they find themselves. In this sense, they are not things in themselves; rather, they are potential practices which, at specific times, can be mustered as the capacity to realize the home of one's aspirations. Thus consumption activities – be they getting a mortgage from the state or selling one's jewelry – enter into the financial production of the house. They show how power is exercised through particular choices at particular times, through people themselves, and how in turn people re-position themselves as the wielders of the power which the potential consumption of these resources gives them. Once more, a tension between "obligation" and "choice" highlights an underlying paradox. People see themselves as free to realize new aspirations, and transform themselves by wielding them through particular means, be it the new use of a mortgage or of a woman's jewelry. At the same time, they become subjected to these aspirations and to the activities through which they produce them: houses have to be larger, women have to sell jewelry, men have to save to build, families have to take out mortgages. This, then, is the twofold nature of consumption, which I will continue to explore below: while it allows for transformation and creativity, it also constrains people to channel power in specific ways.

Consuming Land and Labor: Using and Displaying Households and Social Selves

> As far as getting hold of building land goes, Sayideh and Hassan were lucky. In mid-1998, they were able to buy a small plot of land to build on. It happened like this: Sayideh's brother Qassem was doing good business into the mid-1990s and had bought a plot of 1.4 dunam, on which he intended to build a large new home. Business difficulties compelled him to sell at the end of 1997, and his brother Ahmad bought the land for the going rate. Ahmad's meat factory was booming then, and he had just built himself an over-$300,000 home on one dunam of land he had purchased from another town in the early 1990s. He bought Qassem's land, he says, so that it would not go out of the family. In 1998, he agreed to sell it as follows: 0.4 dunam to Sayideh and Hassan (his sister and cousin), and 0.5 dunam each to his brothers Qassem and Adib. Sayideh and Hassan bought their piece for the equivalent of $120,000 a dunam, slightly below the market rate (because "Ahmad is our relative, and we help each other"), which they agreed to pay in full within the year (because "Ahmad has large expenses on his own house"). Adib bought his piece for the equivalent of $80,000 a dunam. His discount is larger, Sayideh explains, because he is Ahmad's brother rather than his cousin, and he works for Ahmad as well.

The extended household's land and money are also resources that may be consumed as people produce homes. In this case, Sayideh and Hassan secure land through Hassan's father's brother's son, Ahmad, who is also Sayideh's brother. As money and land change hands, social relations and their meaning are very much present. While Ahmad and others mention causes for the exchange, another unspoken cause for this selling at less than the going rate is plain. Ahmad's gesture preserves, and even enhances, the extended household's dignity. He gets his brother Qassem out of financial difficulty and enables him to build a home, albeit a smaller one. He helps his sister and cousin to build. Sayideh insists that it is because her husband is a cousin (father's brother son) that they get the discount from Ahmad, rather than because she is his sister. Indeed, as a sister she holds an ambiguous status here. On the one hand, she should not expect preferential treatment when it comes to property division since she is not part of the exchanges usually expected between brothers. Under normative circumstances she would have been expected to share a plot with her husband's brothers rather than with her own, since the local custom is overall patrilocal. On the other hand, Sayideh is especially close to her brothers, and very much involved in "helping out" in myriad informal ways. Her own actions and personality have a great deal to do with her brothers' agreement to have her and Hassan buy into the plot. Yet she must be very delicate about the formulation of this transaction. If she says that they received the plot because of her, her husband might be branded as "weak." It is therefore important to explain the deal in terms of Hassan's relationship to her brother rather than in terms of hers. This slightly unusual arrangement is reframed as inconspicuous consumption.

Indeed, while people in the town are expected to conspicuously display their ability to consume land and the financial help of the extended family, some resources have to be downplayed.[14] Because she is a wage earner and a strong woman herself, Sayideh has become particularly aware of the problem of representing her role in the household through overt statements. When she first started earning money in her tailoring shop, she boasted to relatives that her earnings allowed them to buy a new refrigerator, a freezer, a washing machine. Rumors then flew around the neighborhood that Hassan was not able to provide adequately for his family, and as a result he insisted that she close down the workshop. When she started to work again a year later, she suggested that she would use her earnings for routine expenses such as food or utilities, and that he would use his to purchase new furniture or appliances. In the same way here, she presents the discount Ahmad gives her household as the result of his connection to Hassan rather than to her. The fact that the discount is less than it would be had Hassan been Ahmad's brother supports this assertion and discourages rumors as well. Here it is not simply connection that is expressed through the financial arrangement, but a socially proper connection. Highlighting this connection effectively downplays Sayideh's contribution to the procurement of land in one case, and to the purchase of appliances in the other. Here Sayideh's capacity to act is hidden so that the status of the nuclear and extended household can be enhanced in the normative terms of local discourse. It is possible, though not certain, that this discourse may at some point be stretched to include Sayideh's now somewhat eccentric – though obviously socially and economically powerful – actions. Meanwhile, they are hidden.

In the same fashion, Sayideh and Hassan can say that they are helping Ahmad make payments on his home. And best of all, no one in fact had to sell the land on a public market: it remained "in the family." In this way, Ahmad can enhance his status as a wealthy, wise, and generous person within his own family as well as within the community. Thus statements about consumption highlight the contribution men (especially wealthy ones) make to the status of the extended family, and downplay that of women.[15]

> So Sayideh is taking in extra work. Fancy curtains have become fashionable and she is doing brisk business in them. In addition, "bridal parties" with bridesmaids have become the norm at the end of the 1990s, and Sayideh is quite busy in the summer making sets of bridesmaids' dresses. Hassan found a second job on some nights and weekends, and Shadi and Fadi, the 20-year-old twins who dropped out of college the previous year, got jobs in a factory and in construction. In order to pay for the building itself, the three older boys and the parents will take mortgages from the housing ministry.
>
> Hassan can get cheaper iron from his job. Sayideh's brother Said, who operates a quarry and deals in balat [floor tiles] and sheish [Heb. Marble] can help provide cheaper floors. Their son Mahmoud, who got an electrician's license before going to the university, will purchase materials wholesale and lay down the electrical system. Since he has helped others to install electricity in their new homes, people skilled in plumbing and masonry can be expected to return the favor. The household will hire workers, especially for digging foundations and carting away dirt, but will also work on the house. As someone commented, there isn't one Darawi (inhabitant of Deir al-Asad) who has not worked in construction.
>
> Of course, Hassan and his sons will work on the building. And cousins will help with building as well. Many indeed have worked in construction, and most young men have experience helping out on relatives' house-building projects. This kind of work is informal, sporadic, irregular, fluid: when relatives help out, sometimes they are paid, especially if the relatives who are building are more well-off than their own family and can afford to hire them full time. But most often they work with the unstated understanding that the relatives will help when they in turn have to build. In 1999 on a cool spring day, for example, I saw one of Sayideh's brothers, in his late forties, working on his nephews' new home. He himself has taken almost 15 years so far to build his over-$400,000 home, which will house his family and those of his two sons. The nephews have been helping. While he has paid some of them at least, he also helps them work on their building.

Though discounts, mortgages and gold may help to produce the house, one main resource consumed in the process is people's own labor and that of their extended family. For most Jewish citizens of Israel, home-building is done by developers or hired contractors. Whole neighborhoods, or even towns, were developed and sold to the (overwhelmingly Jewish) public. Those who want to build their own home do so by hiring one or several contractors, and cost in the late 1990s was estimated at $800–1000 a square meter. But construction has been a major sector of employment for Israeli Palestinians, who also know how to procure materials cheaply. For the amount of money it would take to finish one 160-square-meter apartment in a Jewish area, Sayideh and Hassan intend to build two or three apartments. Two apartments, Mahmoud's and their own, will be finished right away. The others will be completed when the twins marry. Now the twins "help" their older brother; later, he will "help" them.

Unlike most Jewish Israelis who are building their own homes, Sayideh and Hassan are not calculating cost in square meters nor working through one contractor. Certainly, the size of apartments, indexing social status, is constantly discussed and compared in square meters. But when calculating costs they add up the cost of making the foundations, of the materials for the building shell, and of other materials they will use in the coming year. They tend to buy these materials themselves, and to hire contractors separately. During the period of house construction, most family members are working overtime (often on the grey market) in order to pay for the heavy expenses. This concerted effort is seen as a source of power: the greater the amount of labor mustered, the better the house. Throughout, all are aware of and motivated by the fact that that the resulting house will reflect their own social standing.

> First Sayideh and Hassan thought they would build quickly, so that Mahmoud could marry and move in. But then, calculating wedding and building expenses, they decided to wait until after the wedding. Sayideh's brother Ahmed has an extra apartment on the first floor, which his brother Said and family used for eight months in 1998–99. Said's son is also getting married soon, so Said's household is rebuilding and enlarging his building's shell to provide three apartments for himself and his two sons. He is coordinating this with the completion of the house of his brother Samih, who used to live downstairs from him. Mahmoud's wedding coincides with Said's move back to his renovated home, so that the new couple can move into the vacated apartment. Neither Mahmoud, nor his uncle Said, are expected to pay rent. Said tiled the apartment floor as a favor to his brother Ahmad. Ahmad is doing well financially; the apartment will be used for his son later. Ahmad is praised by relatives, whom he knows will not hesitate to help out if the need arises later on.
>
> The exchange of labor within extended households, while very frequent, cannot be entirely taken for granted nowadays. Sayideh prides herself in the fact that she has taught her sons to help each other out. She contrasts this approach, favored by her brothers who have been partners in business, have exchanged money and work when building their homes, and have bought agricultural land in common, with that of her husband's family: "My aunt [her husband's mother]

> didn't teach them to help each other; Hassan and Mohammad, and the others, all saved separately and didn't share their money; many others in the village don't help their brothers build. They are each poor, all work for other people. My brothers have succeeded in business because they work together, they are stronger."

Many people consider the labor of the extended family as a resource to be consumed in common when they build homes. Yet the use of this resource entails balancing tensions. Indeed, family members aspire to autonomy on the one hand, and are mindful of the family's social status on the other. In addition, people want "modern" and "independent" homes, but in order to produce them within limited means they have to coordinate consumption of resources. This particular type of consumption emerges here, again, as ambiguous: while it is the means to become more autonomous, it nevertheless appears to replicate "traditional" patterns of behavior. How then, are these tensions played out, and how in turn can consumption be understood in this transformative context?

The word Sayideh uses for her brothers' partnership is *sherkeh* (spoken Palestinian; *Sharika* in literary Arabic). It means company, partnership, but it is also the word used in the old days for cultivation and goat-raising agreements.[16] It often implies a long-term business relationship in which profits are divided and reinvested. The term, then as now, covers a variety of formal and informal arrangements, to which people have attributed different values at different historical periods. Here Sayideh chooses to give them a socially positive connotation for a particular reason.

Success, as she presents it here, stems from the ability to consume the resources of the extended household to further the ends of "nuclear" households. Indeed, until recently, her brothers put all their income in a common bank account out of which they paid themselves monthly salaries. Recently, as some of their sons became of marriageable age, their expenses greatly increased and they decided to establish separate accounts.[17] According to Sayideh, tensions between the wives were at the core of this. She explains that "when there are problems like that, that's it, everyone goes by himself, it's better that way (*lema bsir fi mashakil hek, yallah, kull wahad iruh lehalo, ahsan.*)" Here the intention is not to promote individualualism, but rather to loosen the financial pressure by dividing up the common bank accounts. What is understood is that the brothers are likely to recreate the same arrangement with their own sons once they come of age and need to build a house and get married.

Such an arrangement is not unusual: several sets of brothers or father-son teams in the town bring together their incomes and share expenses for extended periods of time. This is Sayideh and Hassan's current arrangement. Hassan, Mahmoud, and his brothers have their salaries directly deposited in a common bank account, and each of them gets some pocket money. Sayideh cooks for everyone, because buying in bulk and cooking quantities saves time and money. She is happy that Intisar, Mahmoud's wife who is a student teacher, goes along with this, because "some girls don't like it." Indeed, many young women and men consider that eating at one's parents' house or not having one's own bank account are signs of "backwardness" and dependency. But Sayideh is adroitly promoting Intisar's cooperation by "spoiling" her: Intisar keeps her salary for her own expenses. In addition, the household has recently bought a car out of the common bank account "for Intisar," so she can get back and forth to work independently. (Mahmoud, meanwhile, has the use of a company car through his job.) Thus through the "traditional" arrangement of the extended household with a common bank account, Intisar can display the outward signs of consumption that make her a "modern" woman: she has money to spend on herself and leisure activities, and a means to circulate independently.

Common financial and extended household arrangements, explains Sayideh, is what one household in five does in Deir al-Asad at any given time, especially during periods when large expenses are at stake. But she does not see this arrangement as permanent. When they enter the new house, she declares, Mahmoud will be independent/free (*hurr*): "Finished, he lives alone, he can do what he wants." Mahmoud will still be obligated to help his younger brothers through his own labor as well as financially, and the reciprocal relation through which resources are perceived as "common" will likely continue to be nurtured through large and small exchanges of financial assistance, labor, gifts.

On the other hand, others, like Hassan's brothers, have opted to keep their finances "separate."[18] The fact that such different arrangements exist in towns has often been portrayed in terms of "traditional" versus "modern" household arrangements, or again in terms of the rise of "Western," self-interested individualism. It would be easy to see Sayideh and Hassan, and Sayideh's brothers, as simply repeating traditional arrangements.

I argue here that Sayideh's description demands another interpretation. What has happened is that Sayideh and Hassan's family – together with all the other households who have used this approach, albeit temporarily – have chosen to use some patterns resonating with the social and economic relations of "the old days" in order to economize and to transform their household. These arrangements do not hold persons in "traditional" relationships, but rather in negotiated ones that satisfy both present means and present aspirations: Intisar is a case in point. As she and others describe it, they are not trapped in the webs of custom. Rather, they have come up with a system through which more resources can be harnessed and consumed, and thus enhance the power of households to produce and transform themselves within their limited means and circumstances.

Conclusions

To sum up, the diversity of economic arrangements existing in Deir al-Asad does not simply show a movement toward greater "individualism." Rather, it reflects changes in building and housing practices on the ground, which resonate with changes in material and social aspirations as well, and changes in notions of what constitutes persons and proper social relations. While most people at times couch these practices in terms of aspirations to "privacy" or household independence, this very privacy or independence is most often achieved through pooling common resources for a time.

Aspirations for large, "modern" homes are consistent for Jewish and Palestinian citizens of Israel alike. On the other hand, the ways in which they are brought about for average-income people in Palestinian towns in the Galilee is often through the consumption of various resources, among which the extended family's economy – encompassing all that pertains to running the household – is currently prominent.

Sayideh and Hassan's new home, according to its size, layout, and projected furnishings, will stand for the achievement of a middle-income home in contemporary Deir al-Asad. It will represent their standing within local society, their own personal tastes, their innovations. Like all the new homes I visited since 1999, its furniture will be overwhelmingly new and relatively expensive. The prices, like those of wedding furniture, will be made public, simultaneously signaling and defining the owners' current status. What I have aimed to highlight here was the ways in which people produce homes by constituting resources for consumption out of reciprocal relations, objects, and various forms of labor. These resources, as I have shown, are never neutral quantities of money. Rather, they are shaped and enacted through social and political relations, and in turn are put to work to constitute not only homes, but differential experiences of selves, households, and citizenship. This type of consumption is based on the awareness of new "needs" – needs for housing space, but also needs for autonomy and for social and political affirmation. What these highlight, in turn, is the new central role consumption has come to play in shaping selves and relationships in the Galilee at the turn of this new century.

This, in turn, raises particular questions about the nature of consumption. Consumption may appear to us to be creative and freeing since, through it, new meanings and selves are shaped – as I showed here, people develop new senses of selves and new homes. New, larger, comfortable houses on the landscape do index the power that ordinary people have successfully mustered in developing something of their own. On the other hand, as I also argued, consumption constrains people: state power works to orient people's choices and to give the landscape a particular shape; changing social norms also constrain people to muster more resources; and while the consumption of some resources is conspicuously displayed to highlight people's capacity to act, the consumption of other resources, such as a woman's labor, need to remain inconspicuously hidden. Consumption has thus shown itself here to be a highly ambiguous medium. What, then, have we learned about it here?

Consumption, in the end, is about power. My study of home-making among Palestinian citizens of Israel has highlighted the fact that power operates from the bottom up as well as from the top down. But much more importantly, it has demonstrated how power now works through consumption to shape people anew. In the process are constituted "needs" for larger homes, for "love," for "privacy," for autonomous selves. In turn, these needs transform the way in which people imagine, evaluate, and quantify consumable resources – money, social relations, labor, and other things that can be put to use in the production of the objects of their desires. In that sense, consumption has become an area in which power works itself out as it reshapes people:

> In fact, it is already one of the prime effects of power that certain bodies, certain gestures, certain discourses, certain desires, come to be constituted as individuals . . . The individual which power has constituted is at the same time its vehicle. (Foucault 1980b: 98)

Consumption, seen through the production of homes, reveals these tensions of power as they are internalized and made manifest in Israel at the end of the twentieth century.

Acknowledgments

This chapter is based on ethnographic fieldwork conducted in the Galilee in 1989–1991 and 1999–2001. The earlier phase of fieldwork was funded by the MacArthur Council for Research on Conflict and International Cooperation at the University of Chicago, and by a Lady Davis doctoral fellowship. I thank John Comaroff, Nancy Munn, and Henya Rachmiel for careful comments on an earlier draft. Earlier versions of this chapter were presented at the International workshop on Consumption in the Middle East at Ben Gurion University of the Negev (2001) and at the International workshop on Gender and Consumption convened at Tel Aviv University (2001). I also thank participants of both workshops for their comments. Thanks also go to the people of Deir al-Asad, who hosted me during my research and answered endless questions, and especially to Sayideh and Hassan Othman and their family, who requested that I use their real names in this chapter. The responsibility for any errors is of course mine.

References

Anderson, B. (1991), *Imagined Communities*, rev edn, London: Verso.

Carmon, N. (1999), "Housing Policy in Israel: the First 50 Years," in D. Nachmias and G. Menahem (eds), *Public Policy in Israel*, Jerusalem: Israel Institute of Democracy.

Dadon, B. (2000), "Public Housing in Israel: A Proposal for Reform," *Policy Studies*, 46.

Falah, G. (1989), "Israeli Judaisation Policy in the Galilee," *Political Geography Quarterly*, 8: 229–53.

Firestone, Y. (1974), "Production and Trade in an Islamic Context: Sharika Contracts in the Transitional Economy of Southern Samaria 1853–1943 (I)," *International Journal of Middle East Studies*, 6: 185–209.

—— (1975), "Production and Trade in an Islamic Context: Sharika Contracts in the Transitional Economy of Southern Samaria, 1853–1943 (II)," *International Journal of Middle East Studies*, 6: 308–25.

Forte, T. (2000), *On Making a Village: Land, Transactions and Histories in a Palestinian Town in the Galilee*, Ph.D. dissertation, University of Chicago.

—— (2002), "Shopping in Jenin: Making Women, Homes and Political Persons in the Galilee," *City and Society*, 13(2).

Foucault, M. (1980a), "The Study of Geography," in *Power/Knowledge*, New York: Pantheon.

—— (1980b), "Two lectures," in *Power/Knowledge*, New York: Pantheon.

Gottdiener, M. (1994), *The Social Production of Urban Space*, 2nd edn, Austin: University of Texas Press.

Graeber, D. (2002), *Toward an Anthropological Theory of Value*, New York: Palgrave.

Jiryis, S. (1976), *The Arabs in Israel*, trans. I. Bushnaq, New York: Monthly Review Press.

Kallus, R. and Law-Yone, H. (2000), "National Home/Personal Home: the Role of Public Housing in the Shaping of Space," *Theory and Criticism*, 16 (Hebrew).

Kimmerling, B. (1983), *Zionism and Territory: The Socio-territorial Dimensions of Zionist Politics*, Berkeley: Institute of International Studies, University of California.

Lefebvre, H. (1991), *The Production of Space*, Oxford: Blackwell.

Lewin-Epstein, N. and M. Semyonov (2000), "Migration, Ethnicity and Inequality: Homeownership in Israel," *Social Problems*, 47(3): 425–44.

Lustick, I. (1980), *Arabs in the Jewish State: Israel's Control of a National Minority*, Austin: University of Texas Press.

Saporta, I. and Yonah, Y. (2000), "Land and Housing Policies in Israel," *Theory and Criticism*, 16 (Hebrew).

Scott, J. (1998), *Seeing Like a State*, New Haven and London: Yale University Press.

Shenhav, Y. (2000), "What Do Palestinians and Jews-from-Arab-Lands Have in Common? Nationalism and Ethnicity Examined through the Compensation Question," *Hagar: International Social Science Review*, 1(1): 71–110.

Werczberger, E. (2000), "Petty Landlords in Israel's Private Rental Sector," paper prepared for the ENHR Conference, June 26–30, Gaevle, Sweden.

Yiftachel, O. (1991), *The Influence of Israel's Land Use Politics in the Galilee on Arab Struggle for Land Control*, Haifa: Technion-Israel Institute of Technology.

Yiftachel, O. and Kedar, A. (2000), "Landed Power: 'The Making of the Israeli Land Regime'," *Theory and Criticism*, 16 (Hebrew).

Zureik, E. (1979), *The Palestinians in Israel: A Study in Internal Colonialism*, London: Routledge & Kegan Paul.

–9–

Consuming the Holy Spirit in the Holy Land: Evangelical Churches, Labor Migrants and the Jewish State

Rebeca Raijman and *Adriana Kemp*

> Zionism was and remains a national movement with the goal of establishing the State of Israel. We are Zionists. We love everything about the Jewish people. Our powerful desire for a church visa stems precisely from the desire to help the Jews. Otherwise, why should we be here? We are here to serve the Jewish people. Take my life but do not kill them. That is a divine imperative . . . common sense finds it hard to swallow this. Therefore, you have to be born again. (Dina, the pastor's wife, ER Baptist church, Tel, Aviv, February 8, 2001)

Popular versions of Protestantism[1] made their way to the Holy Land at the end of the twentieth century. Indeed, Evangelical Churches are relative "latecomers" to the Land of Jesus and have arrived in Israel as a consequence of international labor migration during the last decade. Dina's explanation of her presence in Israel – and her efforts to get a visa that will legalize her status – are an illustration of the dynamics of the localization of global processes through the creation of transnational religious spaces. She and her Church illustrate the well-known fact that migrants migrate with their religions: beliefs, practices, and institutions (Greeley 1972; Smith 1978; Warner 1993, 1998). These often provide the only alternative spaces for the production of a "sense of belonging" within the experiential context of uprootedness, displacement, and marginality. However, a less obvious implication of Dina's plea is that religious spaces may operate not only as an arena for the constitution of new identities in the face of discrimination and exclusion. They may also become a channel for advancing claims on inclusion and belonging within the host society.

Writing on the dislocations between place and culture that constitute the essence of globalization, anthropologist Arjun Appadurai argues for the creation of new "scapes" that challenge the equation between identity and national space (1990). According to Appadurai, the flow of people, capital, commodities, and symbols associated with globalization yields to the reformulation of familiar boundaries and power balances traditionally linked to the "nation-state." These dynamics have not bypassed the religious field. On the contrary, as our chapter shows, the economic processes that set the stage for the migration of labor in a globalized scale may become an inextricable part of the cultural processes whereby religious beliefs, rituals, and symbols are produced, disseminated, and consumed.[2] Our main question is, what are the new "sacriscapes" that emerge from the flow of labor migrants and their religions into the political space of an ethnonational state?

In this chapter we trace the creation of Evangelical Churches by and for Latin-American migrant workers within the context of the Jewish state.[3] First, we relate to the social significance of religious practices and beliefs, both as particular forms of production and consumption, for migrants' individual and collective identity in the host society. Specifically, we focus on the construction of identity via the articulation of symbols, rituals, and religious practices, in "protected" spaces such as immigrant Churches in Israel. We also stress the role of immigrant Churches in satisfying the needs for social status, prestige, and power, and recognition within the immigrant community.

Second, we focus on the process of translating Christian Zionist theology into the context of the Jewish state and its articulation as a discourse of belonging elaborated by migrant believers. In other words, we delve into the modes through which the theological position of Christian Zionism is translated into a sociological position of Christian migrants in a Jewish state.[4]

The chapter consists of three main sections. The first section describes the context of non-Jewish labor migration in Israel in general, and of the migrant workers from Latin America in particular, in order to understand the emergence of Evangelical Churches.[5] The second part focuses on the social significance of the Evangelical Churches in relation to labor migrants living in conditions of extreme marginalization and on the processes of identity formation they ensued. The third part presents the ways through which non-Jewish observant migrants interpret their structural position within the Jewish state rendering their religious beliefs into a claim for social inclusion.

Labor Migration in Israel

Labor migration from overseas countries is a relatively new phenomenon in Israel. It started in the early 1990s, when the government authorized the recruitment of a large number of labor migrants to replace Palestinian workers from the occupied territories (Bartram 1998). The deterioration of the political and security situation generated by the first Palestinian uprising –*Intifadah* – (which began at the end of 1987) brought about a severe labor shortage in the construction and agriculture sectors, in which Palestinian workers had been concentrated since the early 1970s (Semyonov and Lewin-Epstein 1987).[6] However, it was not until the Israeli government decided to seal the border with the occupied territories, at the beginning of 1993, that the large-scale recruitment of overseas workers began, primarily from Rumania (construction sector), Thailand (agriculture), and the Philippines (geriatric care, nursing, and domestic services).

The recruitment of overseas workers was consistent with the interests of both the state and the employers, as it was considered a temporary, low-cost solution to a temporary problem.[7] The result was that in the 1990s the ground was prepared for the transformation of overseas labor migration from a negligible phenomenon – as it had been until then – into an institutionalized process. As in other countries, the official recruitment of labor migration brought about an influx of undocumented migrants. Non-Jewish undocumented foreign workers arrive in Israel from almost every corner of the world – though mainly from East Europe, South Asia, Africa, and South America – and are employed primarily in the services sector. According to estimates of the Central Bureau of Statistics, by the end of the year 2000, there were some 240,000 overseas labor migrants in Israel, about 40 percent of whom have work permits, and together with Palestinian daily commuters they make up to 12.0 percent of the total labor force in Israel (Ministry of Labor and Welfare 2001).

The pattern of formal labor recruitment in Israel has placed these migrants in a peculiar situation. Because work permits are granted to employers and not to employees, documented labor migrants become a de facto "captive labor force," with all the flagrant violations of individual and civil liberties this entails. The official recruitment of workers is conducted through manpower agencies and employers, to whom the permits are allocated. By this means the state is supposedly not a party to the employment of the workers and therefore ostensibly bears no responsibility for their living conditions and conditions of employment (Raijman and Kemp 2002).

In contrast to their documented counterparts, undocumented migrant workers arrive haphazardly. They enter the country on a tourist visa valid for up to ninety days, which forbids them to work, and become undocumented by overstaying it. This method is not the only path to illegality. A very widespread way for a worker to become undocumented is to leave the employer to whom he/she is "attached" through the "bondage" system.[8]

Since the end of 1995, Israel's declared policy toward migrant workers has been to reduce their number drastically, a policy aimed particularly at those without papers, the "illegals." The overall target laid down by the Minister of Labor was to reduce the proportion of migrant workers to just 1 percent of the labor force. The deportation policy emerged as a patchwork affair and entailed the violation of basic human rights. Many migrants were deported when they tried to demand their rights from their employers or from the National Insurance Institute (social security); hundreds were held in detention for lengthy periods in harsh conditions and without being brought to trial; families fell apart after the father was apprehended, often before the eyes of the children. Under the cloak of the arrest and deportation policy, many migrants were brutalized by the police and by inspectors of the Ministry of Labor and Welfare (see for example Marmari 2000; Abrahami 2000).

With the Police arresting undocumented migrants in the workplace, in salsa clubs, in the streets, and most frequently in their own homes, illegality became the daily nightmare of every migrant. Suddenly home and street turned into dangerous places. Fearing arrest and deportation, migrants tried to avoid even the most casual encounter with the police. By contrast, Catholic Churches and the newly created Evangelical migrant Churches remain, so far, one of the few "protected" social spaces for labor migrants. The concept of the Church as a "protected space" is not without foundation: in contrast to other public places where migrants meet, the Churches have seldom been harassed by the state authorities, even if these are aware of their existence. Within this specific context we should comprehend the unique role played by Evangelical Churches for undocumented Latino migrants in Israel.

As in most Western European countries, migrant workers in Israel are considered an import of temporary workers and not prospective citizens. They are deemed outsiders in the cultural, social, and political spheres (Baldwin-Edwards and Schain 1994; Schnapper 1994; Weiner 1996). The exclusionary practices of the Israeli nation-state toward migrant workers are salient in particular with regard to undocumented migrants. The fact that they are undocumented makes them "invisible" in the eyes of state apparatuses in regard to social, political, and civil rights. The lack of legal status and work permits seems to be one, albeit not the only one, of the main catalysts for the development of informal patterns of organization in an unfriendly environment.[9] Paradoxically, the lack of state regimentation of working and living conditions among undocumented migrant workers leaves room for the emergence of new ethnic communities as a strategy for survival in a new society. During the last decade three ethnic communities have developed in Israel among migrant workers: Black African, Latin American, and Filipino. The great majority of African and Latino migrants are undocumented and the Filipino community displays a mixed pattern.[10] In the following section, we present a brief overview of the Latino labor migrant community in Israel, the focus of our chapter.

The Emerging Latino Migrant Community in Israel

A socio-economic profile of migrant workers from Latin America and of their emerging community will set the background for an understanding of the role of evangelical Churches in the everyday lives of Latin American migrant workers (see Table 9.1).[11]

Table 9.1 Socio-Demographic Characteristics of Latino Migrant Workers

	Percent and means (standard deviations)		
	Total	*Males*	*Females*
Age	33.7	32.7	34.3
	(8.9)	(7.9)	(8.2)
Country of Origin			
Argentina	1.3	3.0	–
Bolivia	5.2	9.1	2.3
Brazil	1.3	–	2.3
Chile	6.5	6.1	6.8
Colombia	39.0	33.3	43.1
Ecuador	32.4	42.5	25.0
Mexico	1.3	–	2.3
Peru	10.4	3.0	15.9
Uruguay	1.3	3.0	–
Venezuela	1.3	–	2.3
Year of Arrival			
% 1989–1992	15.5	21.1	11.4
% 1993–1995	39.0	42.5	36.4
% 1996–1998	45.5	36.4	52.2
Patterns of Migration			
Family migration	1.3	3.0	–
Family migration – stages (both parents)	16.9	18.3	15.9
Family migration – stages (single parent)	6.5	3.0	9.1
Both spouses – leaving children	9.1	6.1	11.4
Single parent – leaving children	15.6	3.0	25.0
One spouse – leaving spouse + children	11.7	15.3	9.1
Independent migration	39.0	51.6	29.5
Legal Status in Israel			
With work permit	10.4	18.2	4.5
Occupation in Country of Origin			
Professional and Technical	14.5	18.8	11.4
Clerks and Sales	34.2	31.2	36.3
Services – Craft	51.3	50.0	52.3
Education			
Years of formal education	11.8	12.9	11.0
	(3.4)	(3.6)	(3.1)
% holding academic degree	17.8	22.6	14.3
Income in Country of Origin ($)	325.8	415.0	256.3
	(228.0)	(240.1)	(195.5)
Occupation in Israel			
Domestic Work	75.0	41.0	100.0
Construction	8.0	19.0	–
Light Industry	9.0	22.0	–
Services	8.0	18.0	–
N	**77**	**33**	**44**

The Latin American community of migrant workers in Israel originates from all parts of the South American continent. Mostly young people (average age 34), they began arriving in Israel after 1993. Over half of the migrant men were single coming independently to Israel, compared with only a third of the migrant women in this category. Particularly interesting is the fact that a high percentage of women migrated alone, leaving their children in the home country in the care of husbands, parents, or other family members (25 percent). Likewise, many of the male workers left wives and children behind (15 percent); or both parents migrated to Israel and left the children with relatives in their countries of origin. Both male and female migrants send money to their kin who care for their children. In any case, the existence of a variety of family models, including families with children,[12] suggests the potential emergence of a community with different needs from those of migrants who were recruited formally by employers and arrived alone. The great majority of Latin American migrants has neither residence nor work permits. Most of our respondents lived in south Tel Aviv, in the vicinity of the central bus station, which in recent years has become an immigrant enclave.

Migrants' educational level and the occupational cost they pay because of their self-displacement is also essential for understanding the character and needs of the Latino community in Israel. Latino migrant workers displayed relatively high levels of human capital acquired in their countries of origin (about 12 years of study on average, with some 17 percent holding an academic degree). About half of the Latin American migrant workers held white-collar positions before moving to Israel (15 percent were employed in high-status occupations). Women worked mainly as secretaries and clerks, with only a small percentage employed in cleaning jobs. In Israel, nearly all of them work in personal services (the majority of the women and about half the men work cleaning homes and are dubbed "*nikayoneros*" – from the Hebrew word for cleaning).

Several recurrent themes illustrate the driving force behind the decision to migrate to Israel: the opportunity to save large amounts of money in a considerably short period of time; a strong desire for economic independence and a preference for self-employment or business ownership upon returning to their home country; an urge to secure a better future and education for their children, especially higher education; the determination to help their households and relatives pay family debts and, last but not least, the aspiration to buy a house or a plot of land. Although most of the migrants plan to return back home in order to enjoy from the money earned through migration, many times the endemic socioeconomic and political problems in their countries of origin makes them postpone their return.

The Latino migrants' willingness to pay the price of occupational downward mobility is due to the large salary differentials that exist between Israel and their home countries. Back home, the average monthly salary earned by migrants was \$326 (with women earning only about 60 percent of what the men made). These low wage levels – as compared to an expected average wage of between $1,000 and $1,500 a month for cleaning homes (based on payment of $7 an hour and in accordance with the number of hours worked) – account for people's readiness to pay the cost, not only in type of employment, but also the social and emotional price entailed in migration, this including the disruption of family life and the cost of "being illegal" and living at the margins of Israeli society.

However, economic inducements alone do not account for the creation of this new migration track which did not even exist ten years ago, connecting remote towns in the coffee-producer area in Colombia or farming villages in the Andes with the Shapira neighborhood in south Tel Aviv. As the "Holy Land," Israel is a magnet for adherents of various religions who want to visit the places sacred to them, including tens of thousands of Christians of all denominations who come on pilgrimage every year (Shoval 2000; Rinschede 1992; Shachar and Shoval 1999). The advent of the new millennium and the concomitant expectation of the Second Coming only heightened Israel's attractiveness for Christians who were regarded by Israeli authorities also as potential migrants.[18] The religious factor played a large part in the choice of Israel as a destination by Latin American migrants: a third of them cited religion as their main reason for migrating, and many of them arrived in Israel as part of a pilgrimage tour as a means of securing their entrance to the country. As will be seen, religious activity and its institutional venues, the Churches, act as a major catalyst for the migrants to organize themselves into communities. In fact, the migrants' Churches shape an open space, perhaps the only one, in which otherwise "invisible" migrants acquire a public presence of their own.[14]

Evangelical Churches in Israel

It is difficult to estimate accurately the number of Evangelical Churches that exist in Israel, since they are mostly the initiative of migrants who are residing and working in the country without a permit and are therefore outside the authorities' sphere of supervision.

Our field work within the Latino migrants' community in Israel shows that there are currently nearly ten Latin American Evangelical Churches operating in south Tel Aviv, all of them established by religious entrepreneurial migrants upon arrival.[15] The Churches vary in size, activity, and denomination – whether Pentecostal, Baptist, Assembly of God, Adventist, or groups organized by Messianic Jews – but all are evangelical. In fact, as Freston (1998) points out, the shifting boundaries between religions and denominations makes popular Protestantism in general, and Pentecostalism in particular, a true typological challenge, which merits study in its own right. The fluidity of the boundaries between Churches and denominations is very pronounced in the Evangelical Churches we are studying.[16] They have more than a thousand congregants, about half of them participating regularly, the rest occasional passersby. Arguably, then, about 7 percent of the Latino migrant workers are active to one degree or another in evangelical Churches.[17] This figure is comparable to the membership rate in Evangelical Churches in Latin America , where a "genuine Protestant revolution" has been under way since the 1960s (Freston 1998: 337; Martin 1990; Corten and Marshall-Fratani 2001).[18]

The Churches' existence is hardly a secret. Some of them are registered as autonomous associations or as the "subsidiary" of a recognized Church in Israel.[19] Although the Churches do not go out of their way to declare their presence, they are far from being underground organizations. Anyone who happens to walk by during a service hears the soulful chanting that emanates from their open windows. The Churches' public nature stands in blatant contrast to the desperate attempts by undocumented migrants to disguise their presence in public arenas and thus avoid attracting the attention of the authorities. The "extraterritorial" status of the migrants' Churches confirms the important, if somewhat neglected, fact that the status quo between state and religious institutions in Israel is not confined solely to Jews. It applies to Christian Churches too, including those of "illegal" migrants. It is precisely due to the state-religion status quo that migrant Churches can provide, albeit for brief and fragmented moments, a safe haven, in both the physical and the spiritual sense, for people who are excluded from every type of public "visibility" in Israel.[20]

Migrants' Churches: Individual and Collective Identity

The Church profile that emerges from the fieldwork we carried out over the past three years is not significantly different from that prevalent in the anthropological and sociological literature (Leon 1998: 163–194; Freston 1998; Martin 1995; Mayrargue, 2001). These are community-oriented Churches. Acting as magnets for recently arrived migrants, in most cases they effectively establish a congregation *ex nihilo* from an amorphous and fairly heterogeneous mass of new arrivals. The Churches' congregational character is reflected in two ways: first, in their involvement in diverse and comprehensive spheres of activity that make them resemble "total institutions;" and second, in their declared effort to deal with the day-to-day problems of the migrants and be of relevance to them, while purporting to hold the key to "solving" such problems.

The constitution of the Churches as a "total institution" is reflected in the recurrent invocation – both by the pastors and the congregation members – of metaphors borrowed from another closed institution: the family. The pastor is known as the community's "father" or "mother." The next layer consists of the deacons, the Church's "elder sons," who have specific positions (treasurers, organizers of prayer groups, maintenance officials, instructors of children, providers of guidance to young couples, and so forth). Then there are the believers, who address one another as "brother" or "sister."[21]

The depiction of the world of the Church as a "family" also has a distinct instrumental aspect: it is meant to strengthen the participants' commitment, particularly with respect to filling positions that are required for the Church's maintenance. The expectation that the Church's activity will be funded by the members of the congregation, and the sanctions imposed on those who are laggards in this respect, further reflect the "family spirit." The Evangelical Churches that we surveyed are financed largely by means of the "tithe" – a tenth of the donor's income – which is given to the Church once a month, and by other donations that are made weekly by the members of the congregation. Once every two weeks, food items are collected for a "family package" (*canasta familiar*) to assist the neediest members of the "Church family."

The meaning of the Church as an alternative family is of special significance in the case of labor migrants who are detached from kin networks and family support in the host society. It provides them with a new sense of belonging which helps them to cope with an alien, exploitative, and often flagrantly hostile climate. In other words, despite their extreme marginality and absolute exclusion, labor migrants develop diverse modes of dealing with reality and confer on it their own particular meaning. Religious practices are one example of this.

How does the Church address the migrants' day-to-day life and seek to make itself relevant to them? Latino migrants in Israel repeatedly refer to the Church as a "shelter" from the vicissitudes of everyday life. Anita,[22] a migrant from Colombia who is a regular worshipper at the CC Church, explains that she was drawn to the Church as "compensation" for the threatening and alienating surroundings of the area where she lives, near the old Central Bus Station: "There are a lot of drunk migrants from Poland, Romania, Portugal, and Russia. It's frightening," she says, adding, "The CC is like my family in Israel." For Maria, who like many other migrant women left her children back in her home country so that they could have a "better future," the Church constitutes "a form of self-help. It gives me the strength to go on."

The Church ritual acts as collective therapy and catharsis for the believers. The liturgical practice is highly physical and sensual: the prayers are accompanied by singing and dancing, the worshippers often enter a state of ecstasy leading to physical collapse. Marta, who is an assistant to the female pastor at CC, refers to the ritual in reflexive terms of "theotherapy." However, the ritual practice also has a saliently disciplinary aspect. Apart from its indirect didactic dimension (to "see and be seen"), it makes a direct appeal to the believer and commands him/her to accept God into his/her body and soul. The believer's response to the Church's interpellation takes the form of theosomatic physical reactions, such as trance, glosolalia, and falling down. Carmen, the charismatic pastor of KHZ, explains to her congregation that the collapse of worshippers after entering into a trance is due to their acceptance of the holy spirit. "The word *kavod* [honor]," she says, using Hebrew terms, "means *kaved*, [heavy], such is the glory of all-powerful God. Therefore, the body of those who respect and accept God falls and collapses."

The Church's socio-therapeutic role is of particular importance for undocumented migrants who are daily persecuted by the authorities. As one of them concisely reflected on his daily experience: "I know when I'm leaving home, I never know if I'm coming back." The Churches' psychosocial role is emphasized by the sociology of religion and migration literature (Hurh and Kim, 1990; Taylor and Chatters 1988; Leon 1998; Patillo-McCoy 1998). According to these studies, the migrants' attraction to religion should be seen in the context of the psychosocial strategies people resort to in attempting to cope with macrosociological changes. Turning to the Churches is portrayed as part of the attempt by status- and power-deprived groups "to restore their lost honor" and as an alternative structure of opportunity in which participation affords status and strength in the community hierarchy (Frazier 1963: 43, quoted in Min 1992: 1374). This is especially so with regard to the Church leaders and those who hold key positions in the community's religious life, most of whom are in Israel without residence and work permits, but it is also valid in large measure for the ordinary members of the congregation, whose participation in the Church gives them a sense of belonging and comradeship.

The Churches' "compensatory" role finds clear expression in the believers' devoted response to their exacting demands. One to three times a week, adherents are required to attend a range of activities, each of which lasts an average of about three hours, usually in the evening or late at night; and strong social control is exercised on the congregation to take part in underwriting the Church's operation by paying a "tithe" and making "donations." Given the fact that these are hard-up people who do intensive physical labor for an average of ten hours a day five or six days a week and who conduct their lives in the "underground," their participation in Church practice is far from self-evident.

While constructed as a "shelter" or "protected space" for undocumented and persecuted migrants, Churches are not altogether insensitive to events in the outside world. On the contrary, the outside world against which the Church is supposed to protect the migrants penetrates the Church space in the form of the pastoral sermons and the migrants' prayers. The evangelical liturgy is a central element for understanding how the Church "speaks" to the migrants and allows them to bring their day-to-day life into the religious arena. Apart from the sermon delivered by the Church leader, the evangelical ritual creates a broad platform for the believers' active participation by means of group prayers or petitions, and testimonials.

Petitions, which are prayers on specific subjects that are submitted to the pastor by the believers, generally make public the everyday problems encountered by the migrants: difficulties at work, disputes with the employer or the landlord, worries about the children, and anxieties about deportation and police violence. Such a prayer comes from Lorna, an active participant in the CC Church that asks God to make her "invisible in the eyes of the police." Every month the pastor chooses a limited number of petitions for which the congregation is asked to pray. If there is a large number of petitions, the pastor divides the congregation into smaller task groups, which divide the work of prayer among them. In the LLM Church, for example, the "opening" petitions of May 1999 dealt with giving thanks to God; liberating the souls of the Christians in the world; and blessing the Jewish people in Israel and praying for their protection from wars and enemies.[23]

Another liturgical practice through which the mundane outside world penetrates the Church space is the testimonials. These are delivered by the Church leaders or by members of the congregation who are called to the pulpit. As the word suggests, they are "testimony" of the Lord's appearance in the individual's day-to-day life. However, an equally important goal is to bring migrants to the Church and persuade them that their participation is "worthwhile." As a member of the ER congregation put it, "Everything we ask from God comes to pass. I asked Him to let me get to the Promised Land, and so it was. In work, too, I asked and I received. About wages, I asked, I received. God is present in the *ba'albayit* [using the Hebrew word for landlord], in work, in everything that happens to us. The more we earn, the larger the tithe. Those who uphold the word of the Lord, He compensates them doubly. God is the Lord of money, and the money is for spreading His word in Israel, the land of the Gospel" (interview with Juan Pablo, KH).

The believers' remarks reflect their perception that participation in religious life produces immediate results, visible mainly in the economic sphere. This approach, which is not foreign to Latin American migrants, is based on the importation of the "theology of prosperity," which developed as a distinctive element in South American Evangelicalism (Oro and Seman 2000; Mayrargue 2001). According to this theology, "God is the gold and the silver. He is the key to the gates of the Promised Land. He helps us in the spiritual world and in the material economic world" (interview with Pedro, ER Church).

If religious faith and practice confer meaning on the day-to-day life of people that find themselves uprooted, culturally, geographically, and socio-economically, the Church acts as their concrete physical anchor. The precarious life conditions of the immigrants would even more intensify the need for such emotional support and help-giving functions of the Church (Hurh and Kim 1990). Churches take on a new meaning for the migrants, different from that ascribed to them in the home country. Whereas back home the Church is one of many social spaces in which people can participate, in a migration situation it is one of the few legitimate venues at which undocumented migrant workers can take part and obtain some sort of public acknowledgment and visibility. Thus the Church provides a platform for social interaction that is so diverse as to encompass simultaneously the activities of a spiritual center, bank, school, employment bureau, and community center (Patillo-McCoy 1998). Consequently, it is not surprising that people who shunned religious affiliation in the past turn to the Church and in some cases become active in it, in the wake of their migration.[24]

The constitution of the Church as a "protected space" and its increasing appeal to previously non-observing people, reflects in more than one way the structural position of undocumented labor migrants whose access to the public sphere is limited almost exclusively to those social spaces they have created by themselves. These spaces of "cultural autonomy" provide the micro-social arena for the development of distinct identities that lie outside the range of direct supervision of dominant groups. In this sense, the Church space corresponds to the sociological definition of the term "free space," as it appears in the literature on social movements. As Evans and Boyte put it: "Particular sorts of public places in the community [. . .] are the environments in which people are able to learn a new self-respect, a deeper and more assertive group identity, public skills, and values of cooperation and civic virtue" (1986: 17, quoted in Polletta 1999: 3). In other words, migrant Churches as "free space" are an institutional expression for the "weapon of the weak" and reflect the fact that the authorities' methods of control are not one-directional and all-embracing (see Scott 1985).

However, the establishment of a "protected space" has another aspect, which is not taken into account by those who emphasize its empowering capabilities: an empowering space is not necessarily a space of resistance. It can provide a platform for raising claims for inclusion within the dominant group which are not in conflict with hegemonic definitions of membership and belonging. As Lehmann poignantly points out, "strategies devised for coping with an inegalitarian and exclusionary structure – such as the creation of free spaces – are not necessarily equatable with subversion or a challenge to the existing reality" (Lehmann 1996: 1–22).

Christian Zionists in a Jewish State: Claiming Legitimacy through Religion

> Shake off the dust and bless this house! That is the message I convey to the members of the congregation. How wonderful it would be if the government were to take notice that we, the Christians, love Israel. That we are your only friends. If we only had a visa, we could convey to the whole world a message of love for Israel. (Dina, pastor of ER Church)

Although Christian Zionism is an important principle in evangelicalism, it becomes a crucial one for labor migrants in Israel. Religion becomes a way of legitimizing their presence in a Jewish state and a means by which migrants' claims for inclusion in the host country are channeled.

Our main argument in this section is that with their Christian belief in the Return to Zion as a prologue to the advent of the messiah, and their concomitant identification with the Jewish people's right to the Land of Israel, evangelical migrant workers are challenging the basic assumption according to which only a Jew can be a Zionist. How is the theological position of Christian Zionism translated into a sociological claim for inclusion that seeks to overcome the marginality of non-Jewish migrants into a Jewish state?

When asked to define the main goal of his Church, the pastor of the ER Church declared ardently that "its purpose is to encourage Christians in the world to pray for the people of Israel, to connect with the tradition of Israel and to become acquainted with the reality in the Land of Israel." In fact, he imparted to us not only his personal belief but the main tenets of Evangelicalism, which are based on Christian love for the Jewish people and the Land of Israel, where Jesus was born and buried.[25]

The desire to work for Israel as Christians was a recurrent motif in all our meetings with Church leaders. It is also a recurring element in the collective prayers and petitions of the Church members in which their desire to support the Jewish state and to help solve the conflict in the Middle-East is overtly articulated as the migrants' *raison d'être* in the Holy Land.

Evangelicals consider themselves bound by the Old and the New Testament, believing that Jesus was the messiah but also being committed to the Jewish tradition and heritage. They define themselves as Christian-Jews. The blurring of the differences between evangelical Christianity and Judaism is given expression both in religious practice and in the believers' narratives of identity. The Church setting is permeated with a mixture of symbols drawn from Judaism and Christianity. Hanging next to one another above the main podium of the ER Church are a Star of David, a menorah, and a crucifix. There are usually readings from both the Old and the New Testament during the service, in an effort to examine how the prophecies of the earlier book are fulfilled in the later one.

Religious boundaries are also constantly blurred in the celebration of religious holidays. Evangelists celebrate Jewish and Christian holidays alternately. In the KHZ Church the pastors and some of the worshippers wore a *kippa* (head covering) and draped a *talit* (prayer shawl) over their shoulders during the ceremonies. Jewish songs are often sung during Cult (a favorite is "*Hinei ma tov umana'im*" – "how good and pleasant it is" for brethren to sit together), in the original Hebrew, if possible. If the congregation is unfamiliar with the Hebrew text, the words are projected in transliteration on a large screen.

The fact that a *collage* of Jewish-Christian practices takes place in Israel adds a surplus value to them. Apart from the "informative" aspect borne by syncretic practices, the significance of Christian-Judaism in Israel is not circumscribed to theology but rather derives from the congregants' situation as undocumented migrants facing arrest and deportation. On the one hand, the dissolving of the boundaries enables the migrants to express their identification with Judaism and with the fate of the Jewish people over the centuries as part of their Christian faith; while on the other hand, it enables them to justify their presence in Israel as a kind of "right of return," to which they are entitled by their common heritage with Judaism. This logic is manifested in the way many members of the LLM Church defined their identity: they claimed to be descendants of the Spanish *marranos* (Jews who formally converted to Christianity under pressure of the Inquisition but secretly continued to observe their religion). Their migration to Israel is then legitimized on the grounds that they are Jews whose Judaism was disavowed and are now reclaiming it.

The translation of theological beliefs into a quest for belonging is not detached from the ambivalent attitude of Evangelicalism toward Jews and Judaism. Church leaders emphasized time and again that the Church thrust is not to judaize Christians but rather to christianize Jews.[26] This is more clearly expressed in the missionary activities geared by the Churches to convert Jews which did not spare the authors of this article either.

"The paradox," the pastor of ER Church explained to us, "is that the people of Israel does not recognize the revelation of its own Bible because it does not recognize him [Jesus] as the messiah." Evangelicals feel that they bear responsibility for healing the Jewish people, purging it of evil, and leading it out of darkness. That responsibility looms far higher in Israel due to their belief that the building of the Third Temple and the war of Gog and Magog will usher in the return of Jesus and the conversion of the Jews. Hence their benediction: "Let us pray for light on Israel. O Lord, God of Israel, we ask for peace, God of Abraham, Isaac, and Jacob, God of Israel, illuminate our hearts with the light of Jesus."

Similarly, the lighting of the first candle of the Hanukkah festival was interpreted as symbolizing Jesus Christ's presence in the Land of Israel: "The Jewish people today exists in darkness, and it is up to us, as believers, to serve it as a light and illuminate the points of darkness. For that, we need prodigious spiritual powers. Spiritual power brings light." In the pursuit of that goal, the most prominent members of the Church, those with international reputations, are enlisted.[27]

The ambivalence toward Judaism and the quest to save Jews from themselves is not novel as a theological stance. However, it gains an instrumental value for Christian labor migrants in Israel. As the leader of the ER Church expressed it, "We [the heads of the Evangelical Churches] have a special mission in Israel . . . We want Jews to come to our Church and see that we identify with the Jewish people and are not troublemakers."

While the above-mentioned examples reflect the Evangelicals' attitude toward Judaism, the Churches' performative repertoire is replete with examples of identification with the State of Israel and their support for Zionism. One example is the Israeli Independence Day celebrations that were held in the KHZ and ER Churches. In both cases a grandiose event was held, which included dancing with Israelis and community singing. Similar celebrations are not held in the Churches to mark the independence days of the members' home countries. The organizers of the Independence Day festivities in the Churches say that they are an expression of the Churches' solidarity with Israel. Their presence in Israel, they explain, imbues the evangelical principle of "love of Zion" with a unique meaning; not only does it enable the believers to return to the Jewish roots of Christianity – which would not be possible to the same degree in Latin America – it also "reinforces" their belief that they will become better "Ambassadors of Zion" in their home countries in Latin America.

Their identification with the fate of the Jewish people is apparent from remarks made by Dina, the wife of the pastor of the ER Church. In 1999 she devoted herself to sending press clippings and photographs about Israeli soldiers who were killed in Lebanon to Churches in Latin America. It is essential to familiarize people with the Israeli reality in order to create identification and closeness with the Jewish people in Israel, she explained. These "spiritual consignments" are part of what Levitt calls "social remittances" in which migrant communities are involved. Through them, migrants create a border-crossing network of ideas, practices, identities, and social capital, which blur the boundary between home country and country of destination (1998: 76–7). Social remittances are carried by migrants on their trips back and forth between the two countries or, alternatively, are disseminated by means of technological devices such as the Internet, letters, telephone calls, and video cassettes, which evangelical migrants are very adept in using. On Dina's last visit to her home country, Chile, she spent much of her time lecturing on Israel in various public forums, including evangelical media.

The translation of the Christian Zionist theology into a sociological claim for inclusion made by Christian migrants in Israel carries political implications which, in the local context, cannot be ignored. If evangelical theology seeks to "update" Jewish symbolism and intertwine it within the semiotic world of Evangelicalism, the Israeli context in which Christian migrant workers articulate their beliefs – the context of the Israeli–Palestinian national conflict – "localizes" the pro-Jewish theology and instills it with a political significance which is not neutral regarding the national conflict. This was made manifest in January 2000, when Israeli right-wing groups held a mass rally for a "united Jerusalem" outside the Old City's Jaffa Gate, in the presence of the mayor, Ehud Olmert. The demonstration was organized by an association called "One Jerusalem," most of whose founders are from the United States and some of whom are engaged in Christian fundamentalist activity.

Prior to the demonstration, supporters were urged to sign a petition "to save Jerusalem" and "preserve it under the sovereignty of the State of Israel." We received the petition via e-mail from one of the leaders of the Latin American Churches, and they also disseminated it within their communities and among their acquaintances.

About a month later, shortly after the elections for Prime Minister, we interviewed one of the Church heads who told us in no uncertain terms of his preference for the right-wing candidate, Ariel Sharon. "Our position regarding Jerusalem is the position of the Tanach [the "Old Testament"]. It is God's will that Jerusalem be and remain united," he asserted, referring us to Zechariah 12:2. "The Evangelicals are in favor of Israel, while the Catholic Church is in favor of [Palestinian leader Yasser] Arafat," said Pedro, from the ER Church. According to the pastor, his support for Sharon also reflects the opinion and wish of millions of people around the world, who pray for a united Jerusalem.[28]

The "Zionist" solidarity displayed by evangelical migrants is buttressed by Evangelicalism's theological attitude toward "Islam." The collective prayers, which are a type of communal narrative articulated within the Church space itself, often disclose a hostile approach to "Islam" and "Arabs," with no clear distinction always being drawn between the two. "Arabs" and "Islam" are invoked as stereotypical concepts that are synonymous with "terrorism" and are the embodiment of "the Other" in Judeo-Christian civilization. The attitude toward Muslims elicits a theological explanation – "the existence of the Arab nation stems from Abraham's mistrust of God" – and reflects an unequivocal hierarchical differentiation between a "true" religion such as Evangelicalism and a sect, since Islam, in this view, "is a sect and not a way of life."

The negative stereotyping of Arabs is rarely based on personal acquaintance. There are very few contexts in which migrants meet Israelis, still less members of Israel's Arab population. The only direct contact that the representatives of the migrants' Churches have with Arabs is in meetings with Protestant pastors who are Arabs, at clerical events or in conferences held in Jordan and Egypt, where Evangelicalism has grown in recent years as a result of missionary activity.

Christian Zionist theology thus becomes not only a basis that legitimizes the presence of undocumented migrant workers in Israel; it also legitimizes a particular type of religious nationalism whereby migrant workers find themselves taking a stance on contested ostensibly "local" issues such as the Israeli–Palestinian conflict, the right to the Land, the return to Zion, and the status of non-Jews in Israel. Evangelist migrant workers and their Churches may be calling into question the foundations of Israel as a Jewish immigration state and society, though they pose certainly no challenge to its Zionist character. The migration of Evangelicalism to the Holy Land in the late 1990s thus serves as a clear instantiation of the "glocalization" (Barber 1995) processes underway in the late modernity whereby new hyphenations are being produced and articulated. The mixture between religious and national identity introduced by non-Jewish Zionists in Israel during the last decade is a case in point.

Conclusion

What are the new "sacriscapes" that emerge from the flow of labor migrants and their religions into the political space of an ethnonational state?

This article adduces two main arguments concerning the nature of collective spaces opened by and for disenfranchised migrant workers and the nature of the challenges they pose to the nation-state in the global era. Our first argument is that Evangelical Churches in Israel become the only public space where undocumented migrants living in conditions of extreme marginality acquire a public presence of some sort, within the limits of the emergent migrant community. Thus religious spaces and the production and consumption of new symbols and rituals allow for new configurations of social and cultural group identity for otherwise excluded non-Jewish migrants. Indeed, much of the attraction that Evangelical Churches hold for Christian migrants workers in Israel, as well as the socio-therapeutic function they fulfill, lie precisely in their ability to exploit the "status quo" that exists between them and the state. According to it, Christian Churches are posited as "islands" that are protected from the supervision of the authorities. They become "protected" or "free" from the state's scrutiny thanks in no small measure to their ability to take advantage of existing institutional arrangements with the authorities, which oblige the state to protect other religions, or at least not to interfere with them.[29]

Do they therefore serve as an arena of contestation and resistance? Our contention is that the connection between "protected spaces" and "spaces of resistance" is an empirical rather than a conceptual question. Its elucidation thus necessitates a dual examination: first, of the role played by migrant Churches in the creation of new collective identities, and second, the modes through which migrants translate their theological beliefs into a sociological claim for inclusion and membership.

This duality is particularly interesting in the case of Evangelical Churches established by migrants in Israel: as migrants' Churches, they seek to serve a community of believers who come to the Church in the hope of finding compensation for loss of self-respect and social status, and a physical and spiritual shelter from the persecution of the authorities. The Church setting opens a new space for participation as well as for the articulation of a collective identity for uprooted migrants. Within the Church bounds they cease to be "aliens" or "illegal" and reaffirm their belonging to a larger and inclusive family of Christianity.

At the same time, by invoking a pro-Zionist form of Christianity, evangelical migrants are justifying not only their presence as "foreigners" in the Jewish state but also claiming to be included in it as members of the Israeli society. Indeed, Christian Zionism as deployed by migrants in Israel acquires a unique significance. Whereas abroad, Christianity is used to legitimize pro-Zionist attitudes and perceptions, in Israel Zionism is adduced to legitimize the Christian presence in a Jewish state. Thus, the discursive practices of Evangelical migrants in the Holy Land offer an original reading of the "law of return": who is entitled to return to Zion and on what grounds? In this sense, evangelical migrant workers' bring into the local *sacriscape* a new prototype of "national-religion," one fraught with challenge but which seemingly, and for the foreseeable future, is not subverting the hegemonic definitions of Israel as a Zionist state.

Acknowledgments

This research was supported by the Israeli Science Foundation found by The Israel Academy of Sciences and Humanities. The authors wish to thank Tamara Barsky, Alejandro Paz, and Valentin Nabel for their efficient research assistance. We are also grateful to Carl Schneider for his careful reading and helpful comments.

References

Abrahami, I. (2000), "Strangers to the Law", *Ha'ir*, 20(7): 22–3.

Appadurai, A. (1990), "Disjuncture and Difference in the Global Cultural Economy," *Public Culture*, 2(2): 1–24.

Baldwin-Edwards, M. and Schain, M. A. (1994), "The Politics of Immigration: Introduction," in M. Baldwin-Edwards and M. Schain (eds), *The Politics of Immigration in Western Europe*, Essex: Frank Cass.

Barber, B. (1995), *Jihad Versus MacWorld: How Globalism and Tribalism are Changing the World*, New York: Times Books.

Bartram, D. (1998), "Foreign Workers in Israel: History and Theory," *International Migration Review*, 32(2): 303–25.

Corten, A. and Marshall-Fratani, R. (2001), "Introduction," in A. Corten and R. Marshall-Fratani (eds), *Between Babel and Pentecost: Transnational Pentecostalism in Africa and Latin America*, Bloomington and Indianapolis: Indiana University Press.

Escobar, J. S. (1997), "Religion and Social Change at the Grass Roots in Latin America," *Annals, AAPSS*, 554: 81–103.

Evans, S. and Boyte, H. C. (1986), *Free Spaces: The Sources of Democratic Change in America*, New York: Harper and Row.

Frazier, E. F. (1963), *The Negro Church in America*, New York: Schocken.

Freston, P. (1998), "Pentecostalism in Latin America: Characteristics and Controversies," *Social Compass*, 45(3): 335–58.

Gifford, P. (2001), "The Complex Governance of Some Elements of African Pentecostal Theology," in A. Corten and R. Marshall-Fratani (eds), *Between Babel and Pentecost. Transnational Pentecostalism in Africa and Latin America*, Bloomington and Indianapolis: Indiana University Press.

Greeley, A. (1972), *The Denominational Society: A Sociological Approach to Religion*, Glenview, IL.: Scott, Foresman and Company.

Hopkins, D. L., Lorentzen, A., Mendieta, E., and Batstone, D. (eds) (2001), *Religions/Globalizations: Theories and Cases*, Durham and London: Duke University Press.

Hurh, W. M. and Kim, K. C. (1990), "Religious Participation of Korean Immigrants in The United States," *Journal of the Scientific Study of Religion*, 19: 19–34.

Kemp, A., Raijman, R., Resnik, J., and Schammah-Geser, S. (2000), "Contesting the Limits of Political Participation: Latinos and Black African Migrant Workers in Israel," *Ethnic and Racial Studies*, 23(1): 94–120.

Lampe, A. (1998), "The Popular use of the Charismatic Movements in Curazao," *Social Compass*, 45(3): 429–36.

Lehmann, D. (1996), *Struggle for the Spirit: Religious Transformation and Popular Culture in Brazil and Latin America*, Cambridge: Polity.

Leon, L. (1998), "Born Again in East L.A.: The Congregation as Border Space," in R. S. Warner and J. G. Wittner (eds), *Gatherings in Diaspora: Religious Communities and the New Immigration*, Philadelphia: Temple University Press.

Levitt, P. (1998), "Local-Level Global Religion: The Case of U.S.-Dominican Migration," *Journal for the Scientific Study of Religion*, 37(1): 74–89.

Marmari, H. (2000), "A Stop to the Deportation Policy," *Ha'aretz*,14(1): B-1.

Marshall-Fratani, R. (2001), "Mediating the Global and Local in Nigerian Pentecostalism," in Corten, A. and Marshall-Fratani, R. (eds), *Between Babel and Pentecost: Transnational Pentecostalism in Africa and Latin America*, Bloomington and Indianapolis: Indiana University Press.

Martin, B. (1995), "New Mutations of the Protestant Ethic among Latin American Pentecostals," *Religion*, 25: 101–17.

Martin, D. (1990), *Tongues of Fire: The Explosion of Protestantism in Latin America*, Oxford: Blackwell.

Mayrargue, C. (2001), "The Expansion of Pentecostalism in Benin: Individual Rationales and Transnational Dynamics," in A. Corten and R. Marshall-Fratani (eds), *Between Babel and Pentecost. Transnational Pentecostalism in Africa and Latin America*, Bloomington and Indianapolis: Indiana University Press.

Min, P. G. (1992), "The Structure and Social Functions of Korean Immigrant Churches in the United States," *International Migration Review*, 26(4): 1370–94.

Ministry of Labor and Welfare (2001), *Report of the Special Committee on Foreign Workers Employment in Israel* (Hebrew).

Oro, A. P. and Seman, P. (2000), "Pentecostalism in the Southern Cone Countries: Overview and Perspectives," *International Sociology*, 15(4): 605–28.

Patillo-McCoy, M. (1998), "Church Culture as a Strategy of Action in the Black Community," *American Sociological Review*, 63: 767–84.

Polletta, F. (1999), "'Free Spaces' in Collective Action," *Theory and Society*, 28: 1–38.

Raijman, R. and Kemp, A. (2002), "State and Non-State Actors: A Multi-layered Analysis of Labor Migration Policy in Israel," in D. Korn (ed.), *Perspectives and Practices of Public Policy: The Case of Israel*, Lanham: Lexington.

Raijman, R., Kemp, A., Schammah-Gesser, S. and Resnik, J. (2001), *Searching for a Better Future: Latino Labor Migration to Israel*, Discussion Paper 105, Tel-Aviv University: Golda Meir Institute for Social Research and Labor.

Rinschede, G. (1992), "Forms of Religious Tourism," *Annals of Tourism Research*, 19(1): 51–67.

Schammah, S., Raijman, R., Kemp, A. and Reznik, J. (2000), "'Making it' in Israel?: Non-Jewish Latino Undocumented Migrant Workers in the Holy Land," *Estudios Interdisciplinarios de America Latina y el Caribe*, 11(2): 113–36.

Schnapper, D. (1994), "The Debate on Immigration and the Crisis of National Identity," in M. Baldwin-Edwards and M. Schain (eds), *The Politics of Immigration in Western Europe*, Essex: Frank Cass.

Scott, J. C. (1985), *Weapons of the Weak – Everyday Forms of Peasant Resistance*, New Haven and London: Yale University Press.

Semyonov, M. and Lewin-Epstein, N. (1987), *Hewers of Wood and Drawers of Water: Noncitizen Arabs in the Israeli Labor Market*, New York: ILR Press.

Shachar, A. and Shoval, N. (1999), "Tourism in Jerusalem: A Place to Pray," in R. Judd and S.S. Fainstein (eds), *The Tourist City*, New Haven: Yale University Press.

Shoval, N. (2000), "Commodification and Theming of the Sacred: Changing Patterns of Tourist Consumption in the 'Holy Land'," in M. Gottdiener (ed.), *New Forms of Consumption: Consumers, Culture, and Commodification*, Lanham, MD: Rowman, Littlefield.

Sigmund, P. E. (1999), "Introduction," in P. E. Sigmund (ed.), *Religious Freedom and Evangelization in Latin America: The Challenge of Religious Pluralism*, Maryknoll, NY: Orbis.

Smith, T. L. (1978), "Religion and Ethnicity in America," *American Historical Review*, 83: 1155–85.

Taylor, R. J. and Chatters, L. M. (1988), "Church Members as a Source of Informal Social Support," *Review of Religious Research*, 30(2): 193–203.

Warner, R. S. (1993), "Work in Progress: Toward a New Paradigm for the Sociological Study of Religion in the United States," *American Journal of Sociology*, 98(5): 1044–93.

—— (1998), "Immigration and Religious Communities in the United States," in R. S. Warner and J. G. Wittner (eds), *Gatherings in Diaspora: Religious Communities and the New Immigration*, Philadelphia: Temple University Press.

Weiner, M. (1996), "Determinants of Immigrant Integration: An International Comparative Analysis," in N. Carmon (ed.), *Immigration and Integration in Post-Industrial Societies: Theoretical Analysis and Policy Related Research*, London: Macmillan.

Weisberg, J. (1992), "Daily Commuting Guest Workers: Employment in Israel of Arab Workers from the Administered Territories: 1970–1986," *Israeli Social Science Research*, 7: 67–85.

Afterword

Daniel Miller

There are two major contributions that make this a particularly important volume. The first is the way it helps us rethink our sense of what Israel is and the second the way it helps us rethink our sense of what consumption is. I want to concentrate on the second of these but in brief I also feel the first is particularly important for a non-Israeli readership such as myself. I am well aware that at the present time Israel has become increasingly reduced to a rhetoric of politics upon which everyone is expected to have a stance. In itself I have no desire to detract from this. The politics of Israel is important to all of us and all of us may feel that we should indeed take a stance upon it, and that not just the opinions but also the actions of the outside world are becoming increasingly important and necessary. But however positive we may feel about this stance-taking, there are clear negative consequences. As a result Israelis and Palestinian Israelis both can become reduced to rhetorical figures that stand for the political positions that we want to take with regard to them. They become homogenized within a politicized landscape and become in essence tools useful as demonstrations of what outsiders want to stand for. What becomes lost is any sense that there exists life other than within this political field, or indeed that the politics has ramifications and is often lived out not just in obvious and overt acts of violence but in more subtle permeations of everyday life. Indeed we tend to forget that people even have everyday life, that they need to work, sleep, eat, be educated, go to films, get married, and so forth. Furthermore we become only interested in a simplified version of Israel that fits within our own increasingly polarized agenda of needing to be on the right side. The actual dynamism and diversity of the society becomes lost. So particular groups such as the immigrants from Russia or the laborers from Latin America only surface if we hear that they have developed as new political parties.

All of which makes this a very timely book indeed. It forces all its readers to engage at a much more grounded level with people's lives. The focus on consumption necessarily forces us to address these mundane and everyday issues of how people live their lives, how they get by on a day-to-day level as individuals, households, families, and groups. Furthermore the editors have been extremely successful at presenting a wide spectrum of such lives. So that what previously was Israel, now becomes the distinctions of the ultra-orthodox and the secular, the Russian immigrants and the kibbutz, the older inhabitants as Palestinian Israelis and the newest migrant laborers. Even the unmarked dominant population becomes split apart as the central wealthier suburbs look very different from those who feel themselves as the periphery of Beersheva. In short, this book succeeds first of all as a work of education that informs the outside world of the diversity and complexity of contemporary Israel in a highly effective manner. Not using the typical parameters of ethnicity, gender, and class as sociological categories, but rather seeing such polarities only where they do and often surprisingly when they do not merge in relation to this everyday world of consumption.

My own primary concern, however, is with something different. It is to consider this volume as an exercise that helps us return to a fundamental question as to what actually consumption is. Because I think that this volume produces some important answers to this question which turn out to be very different from the often glib assertions of people who think they already know what consumption is. There is a rhetoric about modern consumerism, that has clearly never engaged with this kind of ethnographically based scholarly encounter with consumption as an actual practice. Having said this, I find one other thing that emerges clearly from this volume: whatever consumption is, it cannot merely be reduced to that everyday practice. Modern consumption includes both that rhetorical, what we increasingly call discursive, level of that which we attribute to it in discourse, and also that which people actually seem to be doing. Often the most interesting observations lie in the discrepancy that becomes evident between these two things. I want therefore to summarize both the discourse of consumption and then its practice, before considering this discrepancy.

The Attribution to Consumption

So the first contribution of this volume lies in the way it makes clear that, for many people, consumption is important, largely because of what they can attribute to it. Furthermore this attribution is almost never neutral. It is a very strange mixture of the negative and positive. Almost all the moral debate surrounding consumption is negative, and yet it still manages to capture something people aspire to in practice. At one level this is to my mind a fundamental property of consumption. The very word "consumption" means to use up, to remove something from the world because it has been consumed. Its opposite is "production" which means to add something to the world and to create. With this being so, I have argued in various publications that both what we call consumer societies but equally non-industrial societies studied by anthropologists tend to have a discourse about production as a fundamental good and consumption as one of the forms in which we understand the nature of evil.

In the chapters of this volume most of the evil attributed to consumption comes in its form as a threat to some valued aspect of prior society. It is seen as intrinsically more individualistic, more competitive, and thereby a means by which people escape from or neglect important social relationships that previously made up family and community. This idea of the threat from consumption seems common to the wide spectrum of peoples represented here. The affluent suburbanites studied by Birenbaum-Carmeli are as worried about the threat to family values as are the Palestinian Israelis studied by Sa'ar, though the latter constructs this more in terms of the traditions of gender relations. The kibbutz studied by Grossman blames consumers in the form of tourists for their loss of authenticity as much as Russian migrants studied by Bernstein and Carmeli worry about their loss of communal values. In the latter case even the fact that they don't have to struggle any more to find the appropriate consumer items seems from the hindsight of nostalgia a kind of loss.

This is one area where, despite extreme differences, the communities are united. On the one hand the secular and socialist movements such as the kibbutz did not merely produce, but constructed a whole ideology around the essence of production as the self-creation of society (in the socialist sense). The kibbutz movement which for a long time stood for the essential and special nature of Israeli society was, with its communal ownership and collectivism, almost a pre-emptive strike against this imagined destructive impact of consumption. So not surprisingly Grossman shows them as regarding consumption, particularly their consumption by tourists, as central to the breakdown of both their ideology and their system. But the religious groups that have risen to prominence at the same time as the kibbutz has declined, and that seem to be taking their place as standing for Israel in the international arena, are equally adamant about the destructive nature of consumption which many rabbis fulminate against as the evil of modernity. So El-Or and Neria find no difficulty in assuming that were the ultraorthodox to actually embrace the forms of consumption that they seek to view while in the malls, it would be destructive to their way of life.

The other element in this discourse is that there is indeed something called Consumption which has a particular form and against which their actual consumption practice may differ. Even the volume editors assume that Israeli consumption is unique, with the implication that there is somewhere where it isn't, i.e. where this purer form of "real" consumption or the consumer society exists. In general this tends to be associated with the USA as is made abundantly clear by Markowitz and Uriely. The importance of seeing this as discourse is also evident from their chapter, where the authors note that the construction of consumption in Beersheva is not actually much like that which they recognize from the USA itself, but more that which manages to represent what the discourse of consumption implies such US shopping malls might be like. One important aspect of this is the assumption that the USA is the land of choice and that this is what consumption brings. There is also the sense that consumption could almost transcend the very diversity which is the basis for the volume's organization. It is not that the Palestinian Israelis studied by Sa'ar and Forte would by virtue of becoming part of the consumer society be politically reconciled. Indeed as Forte notes the state uses consumption in various ways against them. It is rather that consumption appears in this discourse to have an almost apolitical resonance that makes people more like each other in their daily lives and concerns because they all become more like "the consumer society" as an abstracted state of being. Notwithstanding its relationship to destruction and evil there is also a sense that it is part of the inevitability of being modern, and not to be part of it is to be left out, either by choice as in the case of the ultraorthodox or because of oppression as felt by some Palestinian Israelis.

The Attributes of Consumption

I always teach my course on consumption by assuming that the "normative" consumer society is Norway. I do this because it is a country that is just as affluent as the USA but is remarkably different in respect both to values and lifestyles. The point thereby made is that consumption has no intrinsic normativity. There is no reason to think that the USA is closer to some given quality of consumption than Norway or anywhere else. Israeli consumption is unique simply because all consumer societies are unique. Many of the things we assume to be associated with consumption are actually particular to the USA and existed in that society prior to mass consumption as documented by De Toqueville. The reason we tend not to see this is that we focus upon the discourse of what is attributed to consumption rather than on what it actually looks like as a practice. One of the major contributions of this volume, however, is that it provides an excellent opportunity to examine consumption as a practice. What is it that people do and what does it seem to do to them?

If we take the range of discussions in this volume as an excellent resource to answer this question precisely because they are so diverse and particular, we come to some very surprising answers. First, so far from looking like some vanguard of modernity, we might start to see consumption as a highly conservative activity. In a wide range of cases we find that the first concern of groups when they become more affluent is simply to be able to achieve goals that were clearly constructed in prior times. The Russian immigrants have always wanted to be able to afford to put on a proper Zastolie meal for their compatriots. In the past this was very difficult to do well, but now they are able with some frequency to create precisely that sense of having eaten and drunk far too much that satisfies the promise of this event. The Palestinian Israelis studied by Forte understand the house as a process rather than a thing, that should objectify the development of relationships in the extended family. Notwithstanding the pressures of the state to limit their access to land and property, they find ways to use traditional forms of value such as the capacity of jewelry and the construction of buildings to develop this relationship to possessions. At the same time Sa'ar shows ways in which they move with some fluidity between the possibilities of different forms of supply for consumer goods both in the occupied territories and within Israel itself. Women in this community may use mobile phones but, as the whole of Israel is discovering, mobile phones have much more to do with cementing and developing relationships than with separating from them.

The ultraorthodox find many ways to encompass consumption to make it an expression of both what they are and what they are not. They can identify "kosher shoes" and other goods that become both acceptable to them and often in turn an expression of them. But at the same time they can do something they are very good at, which is to explore and debate the boundaries between acceptable and unacceptable aspects of each of these new commodities. This concern with boundaries may be one of the reasons that their relationship to the mall is so voyeuristic. Migrant laborers take to the consumption of highly conservative religious traditions that they might have rejected in their own homeland, that make their relationship to Israel based more on discourses of messiahs and the Holy Land rather than on their actual experience of oppression and isolation. One reason for this conservatism is that we sometimes forget that the desire for wealth has rarely been a discovery of the advent of mass consumption. This desire may be just as strong in peasant societies or indeed emanating from any of poverty. So for many, consumption is the achievement of an ancient dream and the dreams that were forged over centuries of difficulty and constraint. Many of these desires are pretty mundane, and I would say this is a little neglected in this volume. The sense of being able to achieve a regular supply of food, of a wardrobe of clothing, a substantial house, a shopping area protected from the weather, and so forth. These mundane desires which are experienced as the escape from poverty are, I suspect, rather more present on the lips of informants than in the writings of anthropologists.

It is not just the conservatism of consumption as a practice that is striking, it is also how far the practice of consumption differs from that which is usually attributed to it. Birenbaum-Carmeli's subject of study is probably the most affluent of all the consumer groups portrayed in this volume, and the one that most systematically refutes these generalizations. What she shows is the use of consumption to create a whole series of social relationships, including ones of neighborhood, ones of collective responsibility, and ones remarkably close in certain respects to the socialist aspirations for equality and sameness as against competition and individualism. But similar points are found throughout this volume. Sa'ar writes with a kind of surprise that the consumption is not unidirectional and it is quite hard to generalize about the way it impacts upon gender and family life among Palestinian Israelis; but in general both her chapter and that of Forte show consumption as a vehicle for the development rather than the destruction of extended family relations. The ultraorthodox studied by El-Or and Neria are among the poorer sections of the community, but it is striking that the main transformation of Israeli society that has taken place with the growth of affluence and consumption is actually the rise in numbers and importance of this same ultraorthodox community with their extreme antipathy to individualism and secular competition. They may well compete and often fragment, but this is over religious orthodoxy, not possession of goods. We might think this an exception and yet we see similar things happening with a remarkably different group, the recent migrant labor from Latin America and Africa, who also seem to respond to consumption by developing their own highly evangelical Christianity in parallel to the Jewish communities.

One might think that the transformation in the kibbutz is the one case that does at least concur with the discourse of consumption. But I suspect the decline in the kibbutz regime has much more to do with the decline in the previous fetishistic relationship to an ideology of production than to a fetishism of consumption. It forms part of a much wider decline in socialist experiments with possibilities of a new society, rather than falling a victim to any necessary features of a consumer society. Indeed there is a more profound question arising from this instance. There is a claim in various parts of this volume that consumption leads people to an emphasis upon their own concerns based around a new sense of choice, and to ignore larger concerns such as the plights of the Palestinian Israelis. But actually this could be reversed. The great moment in the discovery of choice as part of the post-enlightenment transformation in the concept of the self was the Zionism that led to the emergence of the kibbutz, the idea that individuals could of their own free will choose to repudiate the place of their birth and associated traditions and choose to forge a new land with a new ideology. There is no sense of a radical construction of the self around consumption as profound as that found in the history of the kibbutz. Furthermore, most historians seem to feel that the emphasis upon production and self-construction in early Zionism paid no more regard to the situation of the Palestinian Israelis than we find in contemporary consumer-led society. If anything the relationship to production was more absorbed and blinded to the larger picture. Discussions in this volume may focus upon the desire to associate oneself with the modern as part of the impact of consumerism, but actually I am not sure that even the BIG mall is as driven by this desire to be and look modern as was the passion for modernity expressed in these socialist and Zionist movements of a century ago. Consumption may as the editors note feel like a route by which people form part of a new cosmopolitanism that at one level will unite the world. But this was precisely the feeling and aspiration of socialism, as is evident in any of the writings of the time of its formation.

There is much in this volume that does not speak to the extension of choice, which is why Forte wants to concentrate on the way power is realized through new forms of authority and constraint. But equally the people who live near and use the older parts of Beersheva did not choose to be designated as old. It was an effect of constructing an ideal of the modern, the new, in the shopping mall BIG. In the same way people do not choose to live as old Jerusalem or old Jaffa, they find that the desire to express modernity through emblems of consumption simply impose a new identity on those who are not part of this modernity. It is also not straightforward to characterize the movement to evangelical Christianity among new migrants as simply one of choice, given the terrible and isolated conditions they find themselves in and the need to find some kind of collective solace and support.

So overall this volume consists of a series of case studies in which the practice of consumption as described by ethnography appears remarkably different from the discourse of consumption as described by ethnography. How on earth can we reconcile this extraordinary disparity? Well actually much of the explanation lies precisely in this relationship. If we look deeper into these case studies we may imagine that much of the practice is itself formulated in order not to accord with the discourse. We may imagine that the people studied by Birenbaum-Carmeli are well aware of what are constantly discussed perils of modern consumption. But they have a clear moral agenda for themselves which is determined not to make this happen and which leads them to transform consumption into something quite opposite from these supposed effects. Again we can see why the ultraorthodox are so interested in observing that which their religion depends upon taking a clear-cut stand in contrast to. The Palestinian Israelis are also quite clear about what they don't want to happen to their society, and redouble their efforts to make consumption conform to their values as in a very different way do the Russians and the new non-Jewish immigrants.

This to my mind is a very important conclusion and one well illustrated by this range of discussions. Consumption isn't and never was that which is claimed by the discourse upon consumption. It certainly has the capacity to create what the discourse claims, that is, an individualistic, competitive, materialistic society. It also has the capacity to be a highly conservative means by which people reinforce and retrench a wide spectrum of distinct values based around their ideals of family, community, and citizenship. Neither is a given, but often in modern societies it is the very existence of the discourse, and the fear and sense of threat that this gives rise to that is the main factor in ensuring that its expectations are not actually realized by the very practice of consumption.

It is possible to reach this conclusion only because of the quality of the chapters contained in this volume. The authors are well aware of the discourse of consumption and its power, but as the editors note they insist upon taking this as part of their data, not as separate from it. Overall what comes across is the integrity of their collective ethnography, such that we have a confidence in our ability to see what is actually going on the ground as part of the everyday lives of these peoples.

Their considerable achievement is to have succeeded in creating a sense of immediacy and experience that encompasses such a wide spectrum of groups and to show such a clear-eyed view of the contemporary in a country that is so often sacrificed to its past.

Notes

Chapter 2

1. It is tempting to argue that this global/local split is a spatial replacement for an earlier temporal modern/traditional dichotomy, and that "glocal" now substitutes for "modernizing." It may well be, however, that time and space are only conflated, and each represents, rather than substitutes for, the other.
2. We should note too that this sense of freedom might also be related to the absence of security checks at BIG's main entrance. Every automobile entering an enclosed mall in Israel, including Beersheva's Kenyon ha-Negev, is subject to close scrutiny.
3. It should be noted that the cost of cars and their maintenance in Israel is approximately 30 percent higher than in the United States.

Chapter 3

1. The *Intifada* is the popular uprising of the Arabs in the Occupied Territories against the Israeli occupation. It started in 1987 and lasted for several years.
2. Most of the Tel Aviv Arab population resides in Jaffa, a historically Palestinian part of the city.
3. Oriental Jews are the ones whose origins are in Asia or Africa; Ashkenazi Jews originate in Europe and America.
4. The ensuing figures are based on my neighborhood survey of 1990.
5. This datum is typical of all the Jewish population in the country, see Levi, Levinson and Katz 1993.
6. The respective national figures are less than 60 percent and 25 percent, CBS, Israel's Annual statistical review 1990, table 22.1).
7. Left- and right-wing are used here in the hawkish and dovish sense of the terms commonly used in Israeli politics.
8. Within the Jewish population of Israel, left wing supporters tended to be more educated, wealthy Ashkenazis, while right wing supporters were generally less educated, poorer Oriental Jews (Ben-Rafael and Sharot 1991; Yiftachel 1997).

9. Such movements were popular in Israel in the 1950s and 1960s when the country was predominately run by socialist parties.
10. Israel's best selling newspaper (*Yedioth Aharonoth*) wrote in 23.7.89: "The rent in [another shopping center] is 50$ per sq. m. and is one of the highest around. There are, however, more expensive places. In RAG, shopkeepers are charged 65$ per sq.m." Product prices were quite routinely reported in weekly citywide comparisons, which often showed RAG's stores to be the most expensive ones.
11. This was a relatively low status municipality official.
12. According to the Jewish tradition, bread mustn't be consumed during Passover. Secular Israelis, however, often do not observe this rule and purchase large quantities before the holiday. Bread shortage is therefore a recurrent event on these particular days.
13. It is within this framework that one can understand the dismay caused by an article in a widely read national newspaper, which depicted prices in the RAG center as moderate. One frustrated resident dismissed the depiction as false while another laughed it off as a "wishful thinking," thus restoring the local image of wealth and sophistication.
14. Members of the committee were strict in promoting only consensual issues that raised no intra-neighborhood disagreement whatsoever. An exemplary case of a rejected initiative was the idea to campaign for a bus route throughout the neighborhood. The offer was rejected on the grounds of potential opposition on the part of residents living along the future route.
15. This issue was dealt with on a neighbourhood scale, as it was perceived as threatening the whole neighborhood by decreasing the value of local property (see Birenbaum-Carmeli 2000: 30–2).
16. On the tracing of these traits to the founding ideologies of Judaism, Zionism, and socialism see Shapira 1977.
17. Such disputes, which were anyway rare, have been carried out beyond the neighborhood's limits, e.g., when some school parents initiated the integration of a privately funded curriculum into the regular studies, some parents who could not afford to participate were severely condemned. This school was, however, located outside the neighborhood, although its initiators were all RAG residents (Birenbaum-Carmeli 1999).
18. These original public-housing residents registered for subsidized housing and were randomly cast lots that granted them the right to purchase a unit in one particular project rather than another.
19. The war metaphor prevailed all neighborhood activities.
20. Interestingly, following the criticism and media attention that this depiction drew RAG's residents – apparently wishing to rehabilitate their social position in the general Israeli arena – donated an armored ambulance to West Bank settlers (June 17, 2001, *Yedioth Aharonoth*; June 21, 2001, *Ha'aretz*).

21. Before the outbreak of the *Al Aqsa Intifada*.
22. This was primarily a result of collective expansion projects that the public-housing owners initiated (Birenbaum-Carmeli 1998). These projects, some of which had started in the previous decade, included all the buildings' residents and resulted in immaculate stylized facades that rendered RAG more homogeneous also in physical appearance.
23. The success may also be related to the economic slowdown, though the designer items sold for the price of their ordinary un-used equivalents.

Chapter 4

1. The Kibbutz general assembly, Gvanim Archive: June 16, 1960.
2. The Kibbutz general assembly, Gvanim Archive: June 17, 1961.
3. Gvanim Archive: November 28, 1962.
4. *The Kibbutz Newsletter*, Gvanim Archive: February 21, 1964.
5. *The Kibbutz Newsletter*, Gvanim Archive: March 21, 1969.
6. *The Kibbutz Newsletter*, Gvanim Archive: June 21, 1969.
7. "Model Hitparnessut" document, 1997, Gvanim Archive: 1997.
8. The Kibbutz general assembly, Gvanim Archive: December 9, 1996.
9. The Kibbutz general assembly, Gvanim Archive: 15.02.1998.

Chapter 5

1. The ultraorthodox Jews call themselves *Haredim*. The terms are used interchangeably here.
2. These numbers are based on the inclusion of the eastern (Palestinian) part of Jerusalem as an integral part of the city.
3. A major part of this area is satellite towns and villages around Jerusalem, which were annexed to the city for political reasons (4 dunams = 1 acre).
4. "The *haredi* space in Jerusalem is undergoing a process of growth and expansion on the one hand, and insularity and segregation on the other. The growth and the expansion are in demography and territory, while the insularity and segregation are primarily socio-cultural. These processes are leading Jerusalem's *haredi* population into a state of acute ghettoization" (Shilhav 1993).

5. There were times (mainly in the period 1967–1980) when Jews used to shop in the old city of Jerusalem. Due to the political situation they have ceased to do so. Arabs shopped in the Jewish city until the October 2000 *Intifada*.
6. As large as Jerusalem is, it has one main entrance from the west, known as "the entrance to Jerusalem."
7. The central bus station has temporarily moved for renovations.
8. Glatt Kosher is a stricter level of kashrut than the one acceptable to most orthodox Jews.
9. Jews who come from Asia, North Africa, and several parts of Eastern Europe belong to the Sephardic communities, as opposed to the Ashkenazic communities. The nonreligious discourse calls them *Mizrachim* – those who came from the Orient, the East. Religious people prefer the term *Sephardim*.
10. In Israel, like in Jewish communities elsewhere, some people decide to become religious. These *Hozrim Bitshova* undergo a procedure that takes time and varies from individual to individual. The man in this case may have progressed faster than his wife and is already wearing the long side locks, while his wife is dressed modestly with long sleeves and a long skirt but does not yet cover her hair.
11. A nickname for orthodox people, *dosim* is the Ashkenazic pronunciation of the Hebrew word *datiim* meaning religious ones.
12. Jews are required to pray three times a day, the time dictated by the location of the sun in the sky.
13. *Mitnagdim* ("opposers" in Hebrew), or Lithuanians, is the name for the ultraorthodox community that stood against the Hassidic movement in Europe in the mid-eighteenth century. This group is more lax than the Hassidim in some performances of modern life. *Mizrahi* ultraorthodox men are usually dressed like *Mitnagdim*, while their women have a special style of dress, covering their hair with hats and kerchiefs instead of wigs.
14. Yiddish is spoken mainly among the Hassidim (but not solely). Because it became a sign of strictness and resistance to the Zionist Hebrew, people who speak Yiddish tend to be more conservative than other ultraorthodox.
15. The National Orthodox community aims to combine orthodoxy and modern life style.
16. Immediately shifting to the subject of army service is no surprise. I (Eran) presented myself as a student learning about the leisure habits of the *Haredim*. He, a National Orthodox of *Mizrahi* origin, locates my interest in the context of the ongoing debate in Israeli society about the unequal participation of *Haredim* in national burdens like work, taxes, and military service. The best way to legitimize a community in nationalistic Israel is to say "they serve in the army" (men of course).
17. Pashkevills are posters printed by and for the ultraorthodox communities. They are the alternative communication channel for all sorts of information:

calls for political demonstrations, preaching modesty, condemning a certain individual, advertising a kosher show for small children on the holidays.

18. This applies also to nearby Rivlin and Hillel street cafés, which are more "Tel Aviv-like." They are frequented by Israelis in their twenties who come to eat, hang out, and later at night go to the clubs.
19. Summer is high season for tourism in Israel. In ordinary times organized groups of Jewish teenagers come for several weeks. On their "free evening" in Jerusalem they end up strolling the Ben-Yehuda pedestrian strip, the *midrachov*.
20. The Breslow Hassidic group are disciples of Rabbi Nahman from Ukraine. Rabbi Nahman had no successor and his sect is undergoing a revival lately, due to its appeal to *Hozrim Betshova* and the "new-age" style of worshipping developed by the sect.
21. Belongs to the Hassidic sect of Karlin. Moishe was born and raised in the USA as modern orthodox and decided to come to Israel to strengthen his religiosity. He married an Israeli ultraorthodox woman and has 10 children. Moishe works for the Israeli Government as an advisor on religious matters concerning immigrants from the former USSR, and manages to draw and maintain his own borders and connections with secular friends. Moishe insisted on being our guide on Malchi Israel Street, a tour that lasted four hours and ended with candle-lighting and a Hanukkah meal at his large apartment nearby.
22. Some people light the candles at sunset; others like Moishe do it when the stars come out.
23. *Kikar Hashabbat* is not the official name of the circle. It was given by the local ultraorthodox who hold their gatherings and demonstrations there. One held there to preserve Sabbath rules in the area prevented trucks carrying dairy products from passing through.
24. Stuffed fish and chopped liver are traditional Eastern European Jewish dishes served on Sabbath and holidays.
25. The civilian activities of ultraorthodox people are quite limited, since they do not join most organizations and create their own communal ones. *Hatzole* (help) and *Zak"A* are ultraorthodox organizations manned solely by volunteers who provide urgent medical care, and collect body parts following terror attacks and road accidents. The volunteers attend courses given by the police and the Israeli counterpart of the Red Cross, and their devoted work is greatly appreciated by Israeli society.
26. This is an important fact, since most ultraorthodox people do not own cars.
27. This pejorative, which derives from the negative nickname *Blacks,* is used although they usually come to the park wearing the white shirt without the black jacket and sometimes the shirt is worn outside the black pants. This dress is probably attributable to the recreational activity, the hot August weather, and the more relaxed *Haimish* (at home) feeling in this open public space.

28. The courts were the only place I saw kids cursing *Haredim* who stared at them, and teasing them about their sexual conservatism. It was an exception but served to further mark the courts as a secular-dominated zone.
29. One dog-owner I spoke with told me that during those weeks she has many run-ins with the *Haredim* who are not used to dogs, are afraid of them, but tend to tease them.
30. Before the last *Intifada* there were also Arab soccer groups, who would begin their practice with a Muslim prayer.
31. He was invited by his friend G. Sholem, and could not make up his mind. Other friends who had fled the Nazis to the USA also invited him and he was trying to make his way across the ocean, a journey he failed to complete.
32. The wealthy people in the community spend the summer abroad in better climates, others might spend a week in the city of Safed in the Galilee mountains. More and more hotels in Israel serve Glatt Kosher food and are adapting themselves to their new customers with, for example, separate pool hours for men and women.
33. A triangle shaped by three pedestrian mall streets.
34. The manager of Center One said that parents are alarmed to hear that their sons go there.
35. Once in a while a poster will be hung in the ultraorthodox zone calling on the people not to eat at those food stands where genders mix and people eat standing and exposed. The Talmud says that the one who eats outdoors resembles a dog.
36. "Symbolic" because the media are symbolic of secular values, of those who show and talk the forbidden. Fashion stores display immodesty, another symbolic site the ultraorthodox community negotiates for.

Chapter 7

1. The chapter draws on material collected during two periods of anthropological fieldwork, 1993/94 and 1997–1999, which I conducted in the urban communities of Haifa and Jaffa respectively. During and between these two concentrated expeditions I also maintained active social relations with people in a variety of rural communities inside Israel, and some of the stories I present here derive from these acquaintanceships. Notwithstanding some important differences between urban and rural populations, my arguments in this chapter with respect to consumerism refer to Muslim and Christian Palestinians nationwide, excluding Bedouins and Druzes.

2. According to Eshet (1996), about 80 percent of the shopping malls in Israel were inaugurated during the late 1980s and the 1990s.
3. Between 1980 and 1998 the gross domestic product in Israel more than tripled (S. Swirski and E. Conur, 2000 Report).
4. In his work on popular culture and consumerism in a Cairene quarter, Zayed (1987) describes a similar spread of consumption over a variety of markets and what he calls "domains of interaction."
5. See for example Weaver (2001) on the case of the Mexico-US border region; Berdahl (1999) on residents in the former border region between East and West Germany; and Wilson (1995) on cross-border shopping in Northern Ireland.
6. In Western societies too, consumption has been discursively linked to women, and through them to eroticism and sexual morality (Roberts 1998).
7. See Cohen 1998 and McGovern 1998 on the construction of consumption as a vehicle of democratization – creating equal opportunities in the marketplace – in post-Depression USA.
8. For example, the average income per Israeli-Palestinian household falls in the fourth decile and the income of most families is lower than that (Kraus and Yonay 2000; Swirski and Conur 2000). In 1999, the average income of Palestinian families was 60 per cent that of Jewish families. This resulted from a combination of large size of families, low wages of those employed, high rates of unemployment, and low rates of women's labor-force participation. (Israel 2000). Further, when sources other than employment, such as real estate, capital, and pension, were taken into account, the income gap between Israeli Jews and Palestinians was more glaring still.
9. In 1994, the year the interview was conducted, a gross household income of NIS 10,000 fell in the eighth decile (Israel 1996), which was and remains well above the class location of most Israeli-Palestinian households. As to Mūsa's self-employment, in the early 1990s, the vast majority of Israeli-Palestinian men were wage-earners rather than self-employed (Lewin-Epstein and Semyonov 1993).
10. Notably, Egypt is also an important market of Arabic books, and Israeli Palestinians may go there especially for that purpose.
11. In 1967, when Israel occupied the West Bank and Gaza Strip from Jordan and Egypt, it practically abolished the old borders, allowing Israeli citizens to move freely back and forth across its recognized international border with the newly occupied territories (known as "The Green Line"). Non-citizen Palestinians also could enter Israel, although their movement was much more limited. Palestinians who were Israeli citizens were allowed to move between the various territories much more freely than non-citizens, albeit with periodical control and arrests by Israeli authorities.

12. Palestinians from the PA also buy goods from and in Israel (see for example Balas 2000), but their consumption is beyond the scope of this chapter.
13. To date I know of no consistent study of the informal sector among Israeli Palestinians. My ethnographic observations indicate that this is a growing and important component of the Israeli-Palestinian economy, and I agree with Semsek (1987) that it bears great significance for consumerism.
14. I do not include here consumption through the Internet and purchases made on trips to non-Middle Eastern countries because I have no systematic data about such practices. My impression is that while these are certainly relevant markets for some local Palestinians, they constitute relatively a very small portion of their overall consumerism.
15. A popular word that people use in this context is "poor" (*faqir*). In the vernacular, beside material poverty this word signifies humbleness, disempowerment, and naiveté, and connotes clear paternalism.
16. On the link between consumption and collective images of modernity, see for example Featherstone (1987) and Abu-Lughod (1995).
17. For example, for over a decade sociologists writing about the identity of Israeli Palestinians have been debating whether they are undergoing "Israelization" or "Palestinization" (Rekhess 1989; Rosenhak 1998; Rouhana 1989; Smooha 1989). Conversely, the material presented here shows that despite their essentialist construction in national rhetoric, these identities are not necessarily mutually exclusive.

Chapter 8

1. The remarks in this first section derive from a larger research project I am currently pursuing on the cultural constitution of the Israeli real-estate market.
2. I am concerned here with the relationship between land control, real estate, and citizenship. I note that the state constitutes differently its territorial presence and control within the territories it occupied after 1967. Palestinians in the occupied territories, who are not citizens of Israel, have proven even more vulnerable to land takeover by Jewish institutions.
3. For a suggestive analysis of property and its legitimization through the legal system, see Rose 1994. Her treatment of the relation between property and its justification through foundation narratives in American law helped me to draw connections between foundation narratives, territorial control, and real estate in Israel.

4. The latest example of this has been the establishment of middle-class communities in small settlements on both sides of the 1967 border; these were intended to attract suburbanites and at the same time to consolidate the state's claims to border settlements during the most recent peace negotiations.
5. This policy has not been entirely successful, however, and public housing in peripheral settlements tends to be readily available.
6. Rent controls and taxes on rental income were instituted by British Mandate authorities at a time of heavy Jewish immigration, and were retained after the foundation of the state. While various reasons were given in retrospect for preferring mortgage rather than rent subsidies, there is no explicit articulation of this policy. This pattern was manifest in the 1950s when "abandoned" property was offered for rent and within very few years for sale to its tenants; it was also expected that renters in peripheral towns would eventually purchase their apartments from the state (Carmon 1999). Such a policy has contributed to linking citizens' financial investment to the state projects of land control and settlement.
7. According to Almagor (cited in Dadon), the cost of land constitutes 33 percent of an average Israeli apartment. Note also that the land is not technically sold, but leased for 49 or 99 years, after which ownership reverts to state land institutions. Here again is another mechanism through which the state maintains nominal control over land.
8. For discussions of these experiences, see Sa'ar in Chapter 7 and Markowitz and Uriely in Chapter 2 in this volume, and Forte 2002.
9. People in Deir al-Asad mostly use the word "balad" (village/country) when referring to the place where they live. According to the Israeli administration, Deir al-Asad is defined as a village. I decided to use the word "town" here to reflect the fact that Deir al-Asad had over 7000 inhabitants in the 1990s, the size of many small towns all over the world. My intention is also to avoid categorizing villagers in terms with orientalist connotations.
10. For recent exceptions and the waves they have raised, see Yiftachel and Kedar 2000.
11. In the framework of the 1950s land survey, which was started in "Arab areas," land administrators instituted over 800 lawsuits in Deir al-Asad alone against inhabitants who were required to prove the legitimacy of their ownership.
12. This and the following analysis was inspired by Graeber 2002.
13. Implicit in this argument is a departure from Bourdieu's static notion of social capital. Neither persons, nor their relationships, nor the ways in which these are expressed, are constant; rather, they are reshaped through particular actions over time. What is being accumulated is the capacity to redefine these rather than a palpable, quantifiable commodity (see Graeber 2002).

14. While distinction is definitely displayed here through conspicuous spending, it is also drawn by the masking of specific resources, in this case that contributed by women. This pattern of inconspicuous consumption reinforces the continuity of certain social norms.
15. This pattern is currently found in many different forms. Thus for example a wealthy man whose daughter married into a family of lesser means bought her very fancy gold for the wedding, which she displayed as if it came from her future husband rather than from her father. This was meant to enhance the status of the family into which she was marrying, and to give her leverage within it at the same time.
16. For a political economic description of partnership contracts in the late nineteenth and early twentieth century, see Firestone (1974; 1975). For a description of the cultural and social meanings and practices involved, see Forte (2000).
17. A major expense at that time is the dowry a boy's parents have to give to the girl's. Others are wedding expenses, and the costs of setting up a new household.
18. This didn't prevent Hassan and his older brother Mohammad from building homes together in the 1970s, each contributing his own savings and earnings. Currently they share electricity bills, because having one bill rather than two comes out cheaper for both.

Chapter 9

1. The use of the term "popular Protestantism" describes a broad range of religious practices with different degrees of institutionalization and diverse theological emphases, which are differentiated from the historical currents of Protestantism (Escobar 1997: 100; Sigmund 1999).
2. For a thorough discussion on the multifaceted relation between religions and globalizations, see Hopkins et al. 2001.
3. This chapter is part of a more extensive research project on "The Emergence of New Ethnic Communities in Israel: Migrant Workers from Latin America and Africa," funded by the Israel National Academy of Sciences. Within the framework of this study, we are examining the development of institutional sites by undocumented migrant workers, including Churches established by the migrants themselves. Africans and Filipinos also established impressive networks of Evangelical Churches, which are scattered around Israel from Nahariya in the north to Herzliya, Tel Aviv, and Jerusalem in the center, and Eilat in the far south. This chapter does not deal with these Churches.

4. Israel is a country of immigration inhabited by Jews from practically every country in the world. Unlike other receiving societies, Israel is committed to the successful absorption of its (Jewish) immigrants and actively encourages immigration of Jews but discourages non-Jewish immigration. The Israeli Law of Nationality, which came into effect in 1952, complemented the Law of Return of 1950. The latter law, based on the *jus sanguinis* principle, confers onto Jews, and only Jews, everywhere the right of immigration, while the former gave them, virtually automatically, Israeli nationality. Thus, Israel can be viewed as an immigrant-settler society based on an ethno-nationalist structure, defined both ideologically and institutionally.
5. This chapter does not deal with established Christian Churches that existed in Israel before the arrival of the migrant workers. Although they too serve migrants, they exist independently of them.
6. By 1987, Palestinian workers from the West Bank and Gaza comprised about 7 percent of the labor force. They concentrated in construction, agriculture and services (Weisberg 1992).
7. For a detailed analysis of the political configuration that led to the decision on the massive recruitment of foreign workers, see Bartram 1998: 310–16.
8. Those in the latter category are dubbed "runners" in the local employers' jargon.
9. While the state permits provide a formal infrastructure of incorporation into the labor market, the workplace conditions resemble a kind of "total institution," so to speak, which leaves little or almost no margin for migrant associational initiatives. Legally recruited workers come alone without families. They live and work in the same place, thus transforming the way specific jobs are performed. For example, construction workers live on the construction sites, agricultural workers live in agricultural sites, and nursing workers live in the patient homes.
10. It should be noted that Filipino migrants are formally recruited through agencies to work as care-workers for the disabled and elderly.
11. Data was collected through in-depth interviews with 80 migrant workers from Latin American countries.
12. Fifty percent of these children are between the ages of six and twelve and attended primary schools at the time of the interview. Approximately 30 percent were younger than six and attended private kindergartens run by other Latino migrant women. Another 20 percent comprised children aged between 12 and 18 who attended secondary schools.
13. See Ronen Bergman, "They'll come, they'll pray and they'll go back home," *Ha'aretz*, Oct. 27, 1999; Nina Pinto, "Police fear mass suicide and attack on Temple Mount," *Ha'aretz*, Oct. 26, 1999, A-3; Lily Galili, "End of the millennium: Police operating against Christian cults with great zeal," *Ha'aretz*, Oct.

26, 1999, A-3; Lily Galili, "Apocalypse 2000 doesn't generate only Christian cults; Americans looking for Jewish cults too," *Ha'aretz*, Nov. 7, 1999; Nina Pinto, "Two Christian groups deported from Israel," *Ha'aretz*, Nov. 7, 1999.

14. It should be noted that Churches are an extremely important institutional site of migrant workers. At the same time, they are not the only site at which migrants spend their leisure time and organize their community. The Latin American community has two additional sites of meeting and organization: soccer clubs and dance clubs. These sites provide an opportunity to listen to music and eat food that evokes the home country. Their primary function lies in organizing events of a community and entertainment character (for a detailed description of the Latino migrant community, see Kemp et al. 2000; Schammah et al. 2000; Raijman et al. 2001).
15. Fieldwork for the present study was conducted in several Evangelical Churches in the neighborhoods of South Tel-Aviv, during 1998–2001. The ethnographic research included participant observation in the whole range of activities held within the congregations (holidays, rituals, special prayer groups, outings, home visits, and the like), and interviews with religious leaders and active members of Churches.
16. Thus, for example, some of the Churches started out as Baptist congregations but over time came to be identified with Messianic Jews.
17. It is difficult to estimate accurately the number of migrant workers from Latin America in Israel, as the great majority are in the country illegally. In 1996 the Ministry of the Interior estimated that they numbered about 15,000, from all parts of South America. Data of the Central Bureau of Statistics (CBS) show that between November 1995 and December 1996 the number of migrants from Latin America in Israel without a permit increased by 43 percent – a highly significant increase, by any standard (CBS, July 30, 1998, Press Communiqué 159).
18. According to Freston (1998), about 10 percent of the population of Latin America is declaredly affiliated with Evangelical Churches. In Brazil, for example, Protestants constitute 13 percent of the population, of whom 62 percent belong to Pentecostal Churches, making the Pentecostal Church in Brazil the second largest in the world (1998: 1). Lampe (1998: 430) cites a Pentecostal "boom" that has been under way in the Caribbean since the 1970s, which has quadrupled the number of adherents there.
19. For example, the Baptist Churches established by migrants were accorded official status after being recognized by the established Baptist Church in Israel. To obtain such recognition, a new Church must undergo a tough admission test administered by the recognized Church.
20. According to Abrahami, "there was a kind of unstated agreement between the Israeli police and community leaders: The police do not enter houses of

worship." However, this agreement was violated last June 2001 when the police came to an African Church and arrested the pastor who was staying in Israel without a permit (*Ha'aretz*, June 20, 2001). So far, this is the only case reported with regard to police raids in churches, thus confirming the rule that Churches are still considered "protected spaces."

21. The family is not only an organizational metaphor, it is also a primary object for the Churches' activities. They hold seminars and workshops for young couples on subjects related to "family" and "family life," such as living as a couple, the family from the biblical perspective, introducing children into the world of the ritual, and the like. Church-organized extracurricular activity (welcoming the Sabbath twice each month on Friday evenings, outings around the country, special seminar days, and more) also emphasized the value of family life and communality.
22. We use pseudonyms to designate the names of the migrants and the Churches.
23. The list of petitions becomes significantly longer ahead of a Friday-night vigil, totaling up to 31, one for each day of the month. In this case, the opening petition, for which the whole congregation prays together, dealt with overcoming terrorists' plans to attack Israel and with the salvation of Jews in Israel and throughout the world. This was followed by a prayer for the end of the conflict in Yugoslavia. Other petitions addressed more personal requests: the pregnancy of one of the congregation's members, the cancer of another, the success of a visit to Holland and Sweden of "Brother" Lopez; and there were also community requests, such as a prayer for those who were in prison, for the children of the migrants in Israel, and for the establishment of a clinic in Guinea by the mother Church. Our research team was also the subject of a monthly petition, in the VDLA Church.
24. This phenomenon has also been noted by Corten and Marshall-Fratani (2001).
25. Gifford has defined the Christian Zionist theology as follows: "God works through two agents on earth: the Church and Israel . . . Since God will accomplish his end-time purposes through Israel, and Israel is a pre-requisite of Christ's return, Israel must be defended by every means possible. This leads to unquestioning support, on supposedly biblical grounds, for everything the modern Israeli government wants or attempts" (Gifford 2001: 74). Therefore, being against Israel is being against God and his will.
26. This appears to be a controversial position that differentiates between Messianic Jews and Evangelical Churches.
27. In an event held in the Shalom Hotel in Jerusalem two years ago, to mark the visit to Israel of the leader of the international LLM Church from Venezuela, the guest's main (and lengthy) sermon was devoted to the movement's love for the Jews. The movement's major task in Israel, he said, was to develop an approach to non-believing Jews in order to apprise them of the similarity

between the evangelical religious doctrine and what they perceive to be the foundations of the Jewish doctrine.

28. While we cannot offer an empirical generalization, the support for the Israeli right-wing position by Evangelical migrants is not accidental. This support was given further credence on several occasions. For instance, during conversations with Palestinian Israeli citizens who are active in Baptist Churches openly expressed enthusiastic support for Sharon and for any candidate who would ensure the integrity of Jerusalem under Jewish rule. And Christian migrant women from the Philippines, who are active members of one of the largest Pentecostal Churches active in Israel, told us about intensive collective prayers that were held for "one and united Jerusalem" in the run-up to the elections.
29. That this unwritten "status quo" exists is shown incontrovertibly by the fact that no case is shown in which the authorities tried to interfere with the Churches as such or with their activity. According to the response to a written questionnaire that was submitted to the head of the department of Christian affairs in the Ministry for Religious Affairs, the ministry is not aware of the existence of the Evangelical Churches. This is quite peculiar, but suggests one of two possibilities: a lack of interest in the subject or an unwillingness to admit an interest in the subject. Both possibilities corroborate our thesis of the existence of a "status quo" in religion/state, which is not limited to the Jewish religion alone (Marshall-Fratani 2001).

Index